# MIRACLES

Center Point
Large Print

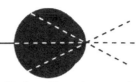

**This Large Print Book carries the
Seal of Approval of N.A.V.H.**

# MIRACLES

---

## WHAT THEY ARE,
## WHY THEY HAPPEN,
## AND HOW THEY CAN
## CHANGE YOUR LIFE

---

## ERIC METAXAS

CENTER POINT LARGE PRINT
THORNDIKE, MAINE

The text of this Large Print edition is unabridged.
In other aspects, this book may vary
from the original edition.
Printed in the United States of America on permanent paper.
Set in 16-point Times New Roman type.

ISBN: 978-1-62899-474-2

Library of Congress Cataloging-in-Publication Data

Metaxas, Eric.
 Miracles : what they are, why they happen, and how they can change your life / Eric Metaxas. — Large Print edition.
 pages cm
 Summary: "A measured and wide-ranging exploration of the phenomenon of miracles from serious discussion of the compatibility between faith and science to astonishing but well-documented stories of actual miracles"—Provided by publisher.
 ISBN 978-1-62899-474-2 (library binding : alk. paper)
 1. Miracles. I. Title.
 BT97.3.M48 2015
 231.7′3—dc23
                                                      2014046537

For Ed Tuttle—

and with best wishes
to practically everybody else I know.

# CONTENTS

Miracles are not in contradiction to nature. They are only in contradiction with what we know of nature.

—SAINT AUGUSTINE

But my belief that miracles have happened in human history is not a mystical belief at all; I believe in them upon human evidences as I do in the discovery of America. Upon this point there is a simple logical fact that only requires to be stated and cleared up. Somehow or other an extraordinary idea has arisen that the disbelievers in miracles consider them coldly and fairly, while believers in miracles accept them only in connection with some dogma. The fact is quite the other way. The believers in miracles accept them (rightly or wrongly) because they have evidence for them. The disbelievers in miracles deny them (rightly or wrongly) because they have a doctrine against them. The open, obvious, democratic thing is to believe an old apple-woman when she bears testimony to a miracle, just as you believe an old apple-woman when she bears testimony to a murder. . . .

If it comes to human testimony there is a choking cataract of human testimony in favor of the super-natural. If you reject it, you can only mean one of two things. You reject the peasant's story about the ghost either because the man is a peasant or because the story is a ghost story. That is, you either deny the main principle of democracy, or you affirm the main principle of materialism—the abstract impossibility of miracle. You have a perfect right to do so; but in that case you are the dogmatist. It is we Christians who accept all actual evidence—it is you rationalists who refuse actual evidence being constrained to do so by your creed. But I am not constrained by any creed in the matter, and looking impartially into certain miracles of medieval and modern times, I have come to the conclusion that they occurred. All argument against these plain facts is always argu-ment in a circle. If I say, "Medieval documents attest certain miracles as much as they attest certain battles," they answer, "But medievals were superstitious"; if I want to know in what they were superstitious, the only ultimate answer is that they believed in the miracles. If I say, "A peasant saw a ghost," I am told, "But peasants are so credulous." If I ask, "Why credulous?" the only answer is—that they see ghosts. Iceland is impossible because only stupid sailors have seen it; and the sailors are only stupid because they say they have seen Iceland.

—G. K. CHESTERTON, FROM *ORTHODOXY*

# INTRODUCTION

Most readers will consider this volume a departure from my previous oeuvre, and from my recent biographies it is certainly a departure. In fact, the subjects of those books, William Wilberforce and Dietrich Bonhoeffer, do not seem to have had any experiences that could be described as miraculous, at least not in the sense of that word as it is used in this book. Their deeply inspiring lives—their extraordinary actions and accomplishments—were manifestly fueled by their passionate faith in the God of the Bible, yet we have no record of that God speaking to them or revealing himself to them in any ways that would qualify for mention in a book like this. So perhaps we should let their exemplary lives stand as evidence that one can have a world-changing and even saintly life of faith without miraculous experiences. This is a helpful counter-point to the thinking that these experiences are the ne plus ultra of the Christian faith. On the other hand, let this book and the accounts herein stand as a helpful counterpoint to those who believe such stories impossible.

In considering what form this book should take, I felt a large part of it should be miracle stories themselves, since they are perhaps the best evidence we can have for miracles. (Some readers may wish to skip directly to those stories and read the first part of this book second, a choice I would cheerfully countenance.) I decided to limit the book only to the stories of people I knew personally. This naturally limits the scope of what stories I could include, but the advantage is that I wouldn't have to wonder about the character and credibility of the people telling these stories. It also underscores how tremendously prevalent such stories are. I did not scour the known world for these tales but only asked people I knew well enough to trust their accounts. There are many friends and acquaintances I did not ask because it became clear to me that had I asked every friend for stories like these, I would have had far too much material for this book and might never have finished it. But the wealth of the miracle stories I was able to find within a fairly close circle of friends makes one wonder how many other stories are out there among my friends, and yours.

I vetted these stories and all their details as carefully as possible. It was vital to me to get as much specificity as I could, and anything that did not seem clearly to be a miracle, I simply did not include. I often asked questions to get clarification on things. Many times the person telling the story was assuming something that— unless I teased it out and made it explicit—would have felt like a hole, whether in the logic of the story or in the artistic shape of it, or both. I asked questions I thought the reader would ask and tried to answer them in the course of telling the story.

I heard some stories that very likely were miracles but that might have been natural coincidences. The slightest question in my mind whether something was genuinely miraculous eliminated it from consideration. But all in all, listening to people tell these stories of God's direct intervention in their lives was tremendously affecting. It is humbling and exhilarating and it can be simultaneously enlightening and stupefying, because the idea that the God of the universe would humble himself to touch the lives of any of us is, in the end, far beyond our full comprehension.

To those who might think these stories merely subjective accounts and not objective evidence, it must be said that history comprises the subjective accounts of human beings; and from these subjective accounts we arrive at an "objective" truth—which is itself still somehow and to some extent subjective. There can never be a question whether such things are subjective; the only real question can be whether those subjective accounts are reliable. Answers to that question are themselves subjective, depending on the point of view and presumptions of the person making that judgment. This is not to say that there is no such thing as objective truth, or to lead us into a swamp of relativism. On the contrary, it is to say that we must do the hard work of sifting what information we have, of carefully considering the witnesses, as it were. This is what every jury must do when it decides a case in law, and it is what every person must do in deciding what to make of any story. Here we stand. We can do no other. To shrink from that task is to shrink from life itself.

# PART ONE

---

# THE QUESTION
# OF MIRACLES

# 1

## BELIEVING IN MIRACLES

If the whole universe has no meaning, we should never have found out that it has no meaning: just as, if there were no light in the universe and therefore no creatures with eyes, we should never know it was dark. Dark would be without meaning.

—C. S. LEWIS

In a 2013 article in *The New Yorker* about faith and belief, Adam Gopnik wrote the following: "We know that . . . in the billions of years of the universe's existence, there is no evidence of a single miraculous intercession [*sic*] with the laws of nature."

I thought this was an extraordinary statement. To anyone who has experienced the miraculous or who knows people who have experienced it, or who is familiar with the literature of miraculous accounts, it's difficult to imagine being so confidently dismissive of something that seems at the very least to be entirely possible, and at best to be entirely certain. As someone who lives in Manhattan and who is familiar with the world in which such writers live, I'm afraid I'm not all that surprised. Nonetheless, it's extraordinary. In the article, Gopnik continues: "We need not imagine that there's no Heaven; we know that there is none, and we will search for angels forever in vain."

Of course, the reason the writer makes these statements has to do with his presupposition that this world is all there is. That way of seeing the world dismisses outright any possibility of anything beyond the material world of time and space. It can be summed up in the words of the late Carl Sagan, who glumly intoned, "The Cosmos is all there is and all there ever will be." He tried to put some hopeful English on this bleak equation by observing that we were made "of the same material as the stars," as if being composed of the same elements as distant balls of burning gas could be a poetic consolation to us. Of course the word "stars" carries with it the connotation of magic and wish-fulfillment, but why trade on that when one is saying that there is nothing beyond the material world, and therefore such things as magic and miracles and wishes do not exist and should be abandoned? And if we are not more than aggregates of the elements on the periodic table, why should we want that poetic consolation? Isn't playing to that desire a contradiction of the main point? Is Dr. Sagan trying to have it both ways and therefore hedging his bet? Or is he simply catering to a television audience by fudging the paralyzing bleakness of what he is saying?

If someone insisting on that strictly materialistic worldview encounters a miracle, or something purporting to be such a thing, he must, by definition, deny that it can be a true miracle. If he insists that the only "evidence" of a miracle he could ever accept must be "naturalistic" evidence, then there obviously can never be any such evidence. It is a tautology, a self-defeating koan, along the lines of "Could God make a rock so big that even he couldn't move it?" Can one take it seriously?

The second part of this book contains a host of stories that are, if not some kind of evidence for miracles, then what? What does the reader make of them? Are they honestly believed hallucinations? Mere coincidences? Are they lies? Or might they really be miracles?

The stories in this book represent the tiniest fraction of all such stories. For a more academic treatment of the topic of miracles, and for many more accounts than we have here, one should look through Craig S. Keener's magisterial, authoritative, and extremely thorough two-volume work, *Miracles*. Anyone wanting a scholarly 1,200-page and definitive rebuttal of Mr. Sagan's aphorism could start there.

So imagine that there was compelling evidence—

some might even say proof—that a supreme being was trying to communicate with humans. Imagine that such evidence was abundant but essentially ignored or dismissed by the news media and by the academic institutions of the Western world. Would that constitute a conspiracy? Some would say that it would. The author of this book would not. But wouldn't it be scandalous nonetheless? If you're wondering where that evidence is, this book means to present some of it for the reader's consideration.

Whether one believes in miracles or the miraculous has mostly to do with the presuppositions one brings to the subject. What presuppositions do we have in asking whether there might be something beyond the natural world? All of us have presuppositions about the nature of things, about whether something can be beyond what we experience with our five senses. Sometimes our presuppositions are the result of our education, but they are just as often determined by, or at least partly the result of, our upbringing and the culture in which we were raised.

When I was growing up, no one I knew talked about miracles much, if at all. The church we went to every Sunday in New York City—in Corona, Queens—was not a place where priests discussed miracles. Miracles were something that happened a long time ago, if they ever had really happened. But if they had happened back then, why they didn't *still* happen was not something anyone ever questioned or spoke about either. It was just a sort of sad truth that everyone acknowledged in how they behaved, in how they didn't talk about the possibilities of miracles. Our not talking about it was part of the larger sadness, but that sadness was just part of the way things were, as far as we all knew.

I remember being in Sunday school class at age five or six and coloring a scene from the Bible. I don't remember the specifics of it, but I think it pictured a bearded patriarch and an angel. I do remember longing for what people had in those remote, long-ago days: a real connection with God and angels, with the world of miracles and magic. What was keeping us from having that too? I had no idea, but I felt that something inside me was made for that connection with the world beyond this one, for a connection with something more real and more true and more alive than anything I was experiencing or being told about in church. I knew that if I so longed for that world, there must be a reason I longed for it. Why would I long for something that didn't exist? Where did that longing come from? It was such a deep and innate longing that it seemed to come from a place more real and true and alive than the place I was currently living in, as though my longing was part of my true nature, before it had become broken off, as though it was a vestige of who I really was and would be again someday. It was as though I was a prince exiled from another kingdom and whenever I saw hints of that other kingdom, I hoped to find the way back.

Some people would say that this longing is just a vestige of childhood and nothing else. It is what makes us long for Santa Claus, but then we grow up and move into the world of reality and see those things for what they are. We face the grim reality of being alone in the universe, a universe with no meaning, and we must finally grow up and bravely face that universe and that lack of meaning. We must face the fact that this world of matter—of atoms and molecules and things we could detect with our five senses—is all there is and all there ever was or ever will be. We must come to terms with the idea that our lives only have the meaning that we give them, that our desire for meaning itself is meaningless. But who can bear such thoughts? Unless they are true. And if they are true, what is truth? Can there be such a thing as truth if the world is devoid of meaning?

What is it in us that rebels against this lie of life without meaning—and not only a lie but a monstrous lie that stands against everything we somehow know to be true and good and beautiful? Why do we sometimes feel that we are exiles from someplace glorious? What is this innate feeling that we have shared across cultures, centuries, and continents? We can spend our lives denying it, but our very bones and atoms cry out that this denial of meaning is a lie, that everything in us not only longs for that other world and for meaning, but also needs that other world and needs meaning more than food or water or air. It is what we were made for and we will not rest until we find it again.

Until I was an adult who had found faith and this world of meaning, I knew very little about C. S. Lewis. He was the Oxford don who turned from atheism to belief in God because late one night in 1930 he was walking along a wooded path behind Magdalen College with his friend J. R. R. Tolkien. This was years before Tolkien wrote *The Lord of the Rings* and long before Lewis wrote his famous Chronicles of Narnia. They were just young men who had survived the grim horrors of World War I, who had seen the ghastly hell and death of the trenches and the gas warfare, and who were now brilliant young professors at Oxford University. But as they walked and talked along that path, long past midnight, Tolkien had the grounding of a deep belief in something else, and Lewis did not. Tolkien felt that this world was not all there is, but Lewis felt that it was, that the sad horrors of the war they had both survived told them this, that this ugly world was all there is and ever would be and we must face this, although it made us sad to think of it. But surely Lewis—or Jack, as his friends called him—sometimes also wondered why, if it were true, it would make us sad. If it were true, why would something in us want it *not* to be true? What was that something in us, and how did it get there? What was the meaning of the fact that we should desire something else? What was the meaning of our desire for meaning?

Lewis and Tolkien both knew and loved mythology and the myths of ancient cultures. They knew the old stories of the Greeks and the Romans, and they knew and loved the stories of the Norse gods. In his autobiographical memoir, *Surprised by Joy*, Lewis recalled how his heart had been pierced when he had read those lines from the Norse Ballads of Henry Wadsworth Longfellow: "I heard a voice cry, 'Balder the beautiful is dead, is dead!'" Why had this so pierced his heart? Why should this nineteenth-century poem about a fictional character move him so? What was the meaning of that? But after the death of his mother and the pains of life and the horrors of the war he had at least halfway pushed aside such feelings and had come to embrace the sad belief that we could not go back, and all of these stories were just stories. Beautiful stories, but just stories.

But Tolkien had another idea, although for him it was no longer just an idea. He knew that all of these ancient and beautiful stories were echoes of something larger and truer. They were signs that the human race knew of another world that had once existed and would exist again and even now existed in another realm, outside time. He knew the myths of the gods who died in a sacrificial way but who would rise again and live, but he did not know them as unconnected to the world of reality and history. For him they were echoes of a larger reality that had at one time burst through into history, but only once. So that night on the dark wooded path with his friend Jack he asked the question that would change Jack's life. He asked Jack to consider whether it was possible that one time this myth had coincided with history—whether one time eternity might have broken through into time. Tolkien suggested that it had, that the myth of the god who had died and come to life was an echo of a greater story—of perhaps the greatest story that ever was told—and that one time in history this eternal story had bloomed into reality, had broken through into history and time as a crocus breaks through the snow. And it had changed everything forever and ever, had brought spring into winter, had brought eternity itself into time. Lewis had never considered *that*. But Tolkien pressed him to consider it and so now he would consider it, and it would haunt him. What if this were true and had happened? And if it had happened, how could we know?

What if all the myths and fairy tales were pointing to something that was not only true but also truer than anything we knew in this world, to a realm that was truer and more real? What if this world of materiality and corporeality were only the "shadowlands," and what if we were meant for another place that was more real and more true? What if our hearts' longing for that other place was what led mankind over the years to make a place in our world for myths and religions and fairy tales—and what if the God who had created us and loved us had found a way to break through into our world and to offer us his hand, to say, *If you take my hand I can take you back to where you once lived and to where you really belong, because your heart knows that you do*? Would you take his hand and let him take you there? Would you believe the miracle of his breaking through into this world? Might you believe in the possibility of miracles just enough to believe that that one miracle had happened, once? Because if you believe in just that one miracle it will open up the world of miracles itself, will lead you back into a world where those miracles themselves point to the larger truth, point to the place where they came from and are signposts to that place, signs for us *here* to know that there is a place *there*—and the signs do not just point to that place and tell us that it's true, but somehow they show us how to get back there, if we can see them for what they are, if we can see the signs and read the signs and dare to follow them.

We must think about these things. We must wonder about them and about our lives and about life in general. It is healthy to wonder. We have a deep need for wondering. "Wonder" is of course the root of the word "wonderful," so we must wonder generally and we must wonder specifically. What if we could accept that our childhood love of Santa Claus was indeed fantasy but not *merely* fantasy? What if we could accept that although Santa Claus didn't really exist as Socrates existed, our desire for him to exist pointed to something that did exist, pointed to something that Socrates himself had longed for? What if those who simply believed in anything were only half-wrong, because their desire to believe pointed to something that *was* true, not just in the world itself but inside them?

And what if those who knew Santa Claus didn't really exist were themselves only half-wrong, because their rejection of that kind of sloppy, childish belief pointed to a desire to only believe in what was real, what was *really* real and not *just* a myth or a childhood story, a desire to believe in things that are as true as the facts in history books and as real as the atoms and molecules we learned about in science books? What if the half-truth of the desire for something beyond us could meet up with the half-truth of the desire for only what is really real and true, which we can know and see and touch in this world too? What if those two halves could touch and become the one true truth we were both looking for?

This is a book about that.

# 2

--- ❖ ---

## WHAT IS A MIRACLE?

There is no standard definition for miracle to which we may all turn. In fact, what is and isn't a miracle is extremely subjective. Nonetheless a discussion of what miracles are—and are not—is well worth having.[1]

*Webster's* dictionary defines a miracle as "an extraordinary event manifesting divine intervention in human affairs." More colorfully and memorably, C. S. Lewis once explained that a miracle is something unique that breaks a pattern so expected and established we hardly consider the possibility that it could be broken. "If for thousands of years," he said, "a woman can become pregnant only by sexual intercourse with a man, then if she were to become

---

1. The Catholic definition of "official" miracles, which involves a complex and rigorous assessment of the potential miracle by experts both scientific and theological, is not the definition we will be dealing with in this book, although it is safe to assume that any miracles "officially" recognized by the Vatican under that definition would indeed be considered miracles under the wider definition we are using here.

pregnant without a man, it would be a miracle."

Though we probably weren't expecting ribaldry from Lewis, his observation gets our attention. The skeptic and philosopher David Hume spoke famously against miracles but defined them as "a transgression of a law of nature by a particular volition of the Deity, or by the interposition of some invisible agent."

We may essentially concur with Hume on this definition, which is probably as close to a standard definition as we will be able to settle on. But I would further simply say that it is when something outside time and space enters time and space, whether just to wink at us or poke at us briefly, or to come in and dwell among us for three decades.

## CAN A RATIONAL PERSON BELIEVE IN MIRACLES?

No sooner does the subject of miracles arise than someone must ask whether anyone can today really believe in such things. But consider the following. Science today teaches that the universe came into being via the Big Bang, approximately fourteen billion years ago. According to this generally accepted theory, all matter in the known universe—more than one hundred billion galaxies, each of which contains hundreds of billions of stars and many more planets—exploded out of something smaller than the period at the end of this sentence.

But who was behind all of that? Many people would say that God was, although people's definitions of God and how he created the universe will certainly vary. That a creator was behind it all might be shocking to say in some circles, but for most people on the planet, it is essentially taken for granted. But if we believe that God created the universe out of nothing—ex nihilo, to use the famous Latin phrase—how can we possibly quibble over smaller miracles like turning water into wine or giving sight to a man born blind? Believing that God could create the universe but could not perform any infinitely smaller miracle is illogical. It is very much like saying, "Oh, yes, I certainly believe that Tolstoy could write *War and Peace*, and did, but I could never believe he'd be able to move a comma in the manuscript. That would be too much." If God actually created this universe—somehow—can we not believe he would be able to do almost anything else? It seems we would have to.

So if, like most people, we can agree with the first words of the Bible, "In the beginning, God created the heavens and the earth," why wouldn't we agree with the innumerable instances in the Bible that follow of his miraculous intervention? If God could speak the universe into existence, could he not afterward speak *into* that existence?

31

## EXAMINING MIRACLES CRITICALLY

If believing in the possibility of miracles is logical, or at least certainly not illogical, that does not mean we should believe in anything claiming to be a miracle. On the contrary, we should examine miracles with the greatest critical rigor possible.

Mark Twain said that if you dissect a joke, you kill it, just as you must kill a frog before dissecting it. Of course there's some truth to this. As a sometime humorist, I well know how this can work with jokes. If you must explain why something is funny, you will almost certainly kill the humor. There are many who say the same thing about faith and miracles. They are in love with the idea of believing, with the ineffable magic of it, and don't think any of it should be examined too closely. For these people, exactly *what* one believes in matters less than belief itself, and they don't want to get too close to the details of it, lest they eff the ineffable and the fairy dust be blown away. But true belief is really not like frogs and jokes at all. We must examine what we believe. We must blow away the fairy dust. Though there is great mystery involved, it's not *all* mystery. Exactly *what* we believe is vitally important. Do we believe in something that's really true? Or are we afraid to find out? We have to separate the fake miracles from the real ones, or we do the real ones a grave injustice and do the truth itself an injustice too.

It is vital that we not have a "Disney" theology that only says "Believe!"—one that is *merely* about childlike wonder—because if we aren't careful with what we believe in, we will end up believing in anything. To believe in anything is to potentially believe in nonsense, some of it downright harmful. It's one thing for children to believe in Santa Claus and the Tooth Fairy, but at some point we need to grow up and be able to deal with the fact that some things are actually not real. If an adult really believes in Santa Claus or in the Tooth Fairy, we know that something is wrong. We wouldn't humor such a person, but we might consider having him committed. At some juncture, we must gird our loins and make these distinctions between what is real and what is imaginary. It's vitally important.

So when we talk about miracles, we talk about things that, to some extent, must be criticized and understood, otherwise we are merely being so open-minded that we are simply gullible. It's one thing to be innocent and another thing to be naive or willfully ignorant. By critically examining things like the phenomenon of life on Earth (see chapter 4) or the existence of the universe (see chapter 5) or the resurrection of Jesus (see chapter 8) or the healing of my friend Paul's marriage (see chapter 11), we help determine if these things really are miraculous, or aren't. If it turns out that through our critical examination we discover that they are actually *not* miraculous, that's all to the good. We don't want to get excited about nothing, and we don't want to believe in anything. We want to know what is actually miraculous and what is not actually miraculous. True faith is not a leap in the dark; it's a leap into the light.[2] We shouldn't be afraid of the facts. If God is God, he is the God of reality and facts and science and history.

So the facts matter. They aren't beside the point. If something turns out to seem genuinely miraculous, then we are free to enjoy it, to rejoice in it, and to celebrate the true wonder of it. We don't need to hedge our bets. When we finally know something to be true and real, we can really leap and shout with abandon, because we've determined that the thing we are leaping and shouting about is worth leaping and shouting about. If it turns out that the thing we believed in or wanted to believe in is not true and real, we may experience a momentary letdown, but in the end we will be in a far better place than if we had blindly clung to something that was really just wish-fulfillment or a feel-good invention or a flight of fancy.

---

2. I first said this publicly in an "I Am Second" video. It is viewable at www.iamsecond.com.

We are therefore not talking about the mushy idea that lurks behind such pop-cultural clichés as "Miracles happen!" or "Believe!" Those sloppy and vague concepts only add to the confusion about miracles. They add to the thoughtless and uncritical view of these things, so that everything wonderful is thought to be a miracle, when everything wonderful is actually *not* a miracle, in the sense that we mean. We need to be brave enough to dissect a frog now and then, to see what's inside. In the case of real miracles, they are never in danger of disappearing just because we look at them. If they are real miracles and are from God, they can stand being poked at and examined. So soapy bromides like "Miracles happen!" and "Believe!" which we see carved on artificial rocks sold in places like SkyMall catalogs, are the sworn enemies of a rigorous examination of miracles. Serious questions are to be tolerated and encouraged, but thoughtless gullibility on the one hand, and flippant, dismissive cynicism on the other, are not.

## WHAT IS THE MEANING BEHIND MIRACLES?

When I was nine, my class at Beaver Brook Elementary School in Danbury, Connecticut, visited what we called the "Nature Center," which was really just a small piece of riverbank on the Still River. One day as we studied plants, our teacher explained to us that there was no hard-and-fast definition or category of "weeds." One person's weed is another person's nonweed. If there is a dandelion in your lawn, you'd probably call it a weed, but if you eat dandelion greens in your salad, you might not. He explained that the whole idea of weeds was essentially subjective. I was shocked when I learned this. Surely everyone could agree on what was a weed and what was not. But I was wrong.

One man's miracle is another man's eye-rolling *What's the big deal?* weird coincidence. So when we are talking about miracles, one thing we *can* say objectively is that context matters—and who is experiencing the miracle matters. If God is behind a miracle, and we can agree that that is ultimately what makes a miracle a miracle, then a large part of his performing the miracle has to do with communicating with the people who are observing or experiencing the miracle. So we can ask, if a miracle happens in the woods and there's no one around to see it, is it a miracle? To put it yet another way, why would God perform a miracle if no one realized he had done it? How can we ever conceive of a miracle apart from it being a communication from God to one or more people, at the very least to let them know he exists and cares about them? If a miracle happens in the woods and there's no one around to see it, it's actually *not* a miracle.

The Greek word for miracle is *"simaios,"* which means "sign." Miracles are signs, and like all signs, they are never about themselves; they're about whatever they are pointing toward. Miracles point to something *beyond* themselves. But to what? To God himself. That's the point of miracles—to point us beyond our world to another world. They are clues that that other world is not in our imaginations but is actually out there, wherever "out there" actually is. Peggy Noonan once wrote that she thought miracles existed "in part as gifts and in part as clues that there is something beyond the flat world we see." If miracles exist at all, they exist not for their own sake but for us, to point us toward something beyond. To someone beyond.

As far as this goes, we could say that everything that exists is a miracle, albeit a miracle of creation and not a miracle of overt divine intervention in the sense that the parting of the Red Sea is a miracle (I will explain this difference in chapters 4 and 5). In fact, everything that exists is not just a miracle of God's creation but also a miracle of God's sustaining, because things could appear and then vanish. But they don't. They are here and they remain here, in one form or another, either as energy or matter. So we can ask why something was created, but we can and should also ask, *Why does it keep on existing?*

It is a curious fact that human beings are rarely

satisfied that things just *are*. The very existence of the universe prompts us to ask why. Why does the universe exist? And why do we want to know why it exists? For some reason, human beings long to see the meaning behind things. So just as what we call miracles point to something outside themselves—which is to say God—the miracle of the very existence of things does precisely the same. Things point beyond themselves. For example, a lion isn't just a lion; it is an image of royalty and courage and ferocity. Human beings, who are created in the image of God, cannot be satisfied with just the thing itself. We somehow long to know what things *mean*. Once human beings come into the picture, the question of meaning enters the picture. We cannot help it. It's in our nature, which is a nature that mirrors God's own nature.

Therefore not just those things we would clearly recognize as miracles but every single thing in creation ultimately points beyond itself to the creator, who is by definition outside temporal and material existence and outside his own creation. Everything has meaning! It's in the nature of things. *De Rerum Natura*.[3] This is the absolute opposite of the nihilistic view of the

3. For a spectacular treatment of this subject, pick up Thomas Howard's glorious book *Chance or the Dance?* It's one of the finest books I've ever read.

universe that there is no such thing as actual meaning, because meaning is just something that humans artificially impose on other things. According to this nihilistic and materialistic worldview, nothing means anything. Everything just *is*.

The essential meaning of miracles, then, is to point us to the God behind the miracles. In the New Testament we see that Jesus performed miracles precisely to prove that he was who he said he was. And in the Old Testament, God performed signs and wonders to attest to who he was. People have their faith strengthened and deepened by miracles, and many people actually come to faith through miracles. My own conversion to faith is an example of this, as I relate later in this book, and my faith has been dramatically strengthened by miracles that I have experienced personally, as well as by miracles that have happened to people I've known and whose judgment I've trusted.

## DO MIRACLES STILL HAPPEN?

There is a popular idea in our culture that even if miracles might have happened at some point in the past, in our modern, scientific world, they are simply no longer possible. But if miracles cannot happen now, how exactly is it that they could have happened in some distant past? Has the fundamental reality of the universe somehow changed, and when did that happen? If we believe miracles cannot happen today but happened to our distant ancestors, what we really seem to be saying is not that miracles happened back then but, rather, that all those people back then were naive enough to believe they happened. It is to say that miracles never happened, but gullible people thought they did. Perhaps we find the idea charming and think ourselves generous for having it. But that is a tremendously patronizing view of other human beings. Shouldn't we give the people in the past the same respect and dignity we would like people to give us? Can we not admit that if miracles ever really did happen in the past, they can still happen today? And if they cannot happen today, can't we be honest and admit that they never happened in the past either? We cannot logically have it both ways.

But this leads to another important question: Why do we sometimes have such a patronizing attitude toward people of previous eras? Do we really think they didn't have the sense to know the difference between what normally happens and what normally does *not* happen? Do we think that just because they didn't have telescopes and microscopes that they wouldn't have the human sense to know whether something really happened or didn't? Shouldn't wise people of any era want to know the difference between an unhinged hallucination and an actual vision, strange and inexplicable as the latter might be? We are wrong to have the idea that we from our superior position can pat these distant naifs on the head and allow them to cling to their fantasies, just as we allow our five-year-old to believe in the Easter Bunny.

We should be clear that whenever we talk about actual miracles occurring—whether today or in the biblical past—we are talking about things that are very, very far out of the ordinary in any era of history and are therefore attention-getting in any era. That's because it seems to be precisely God's intention to get our attention when he does something miraculous. He doesn't want to manipulate us in our ignorance into believing something that actually did not happen. If he is the God of reality, he wants to do just the opposite, to startle us.

Certainly one of the most dramatic examples of this is in the resurrection of Jesus, which we shall treat at length in a subsequent chapter. But for our purposes here, let's simply state that two thousand years ago, Jesus's rising from the dead was considered as impossible and staggering as such a thing would be considered today. People in the first century did not rise from the grave any more than they do now, in the twenty-first century. If someone is restored to warm, breathing life from literal, stone-cold death, it is equally outrageous and unbelievable in any century. On the other hand, if someone rises from the dead in a fairy-tale world where unicorns fly and horses talk, it has no meaning and no impact and is no "miracle" at all. But what happened when Jesus rose from the dead in Jerusalem twenty centuries ago was about as meaningful and impactful as anything could be. It was so shocking and incomprehensible that no one would have believed it unless there had been literally hundreds of eyewitnesses, not to his actual resurrection, of course, but to his having been resurrected. But even with hundreds of eyewitnesses, there were many who simply could not believe it and refused to believe it, which is perfectly understandable. But the point of it, as we see when we read the New Testament Gospel accounts was precisely to end discussion of who Jesus was, to be a thing so extremely and frighteningly out of the ordinary that many who were skeptics would at last believe.

The parting of the Red Sea is another example of how atypical and staggering such things were at the time they occurred. God very much meant it to be so. If the Red Sea parted every few years it would have meant nothing when it parted 3,500 years ago so that the Israelites could escape the approaching Egyptian soldiers. We could then regard its parting just in time for the Israelites to escape Pharaoh's army as a happy coincidence of timing. But since the Red Sea never parts of its own accord—it is many hundreds of feet deep where the Israelites would have crossed—we may conclude that God was intentionally doing something inexplicably and toweringly attention-getting. That was plainly the point of it. It is not in any way presented in the pages of Exodus as something that might be taken for granted. It was meant to be taken—and *was* taken—as epochal, as a hinge in the history of the world.

The point of this, and most other miracles, is that no one would ever forget it. So how can something have not been dramatically out of the ordinary when we see that it was meant to forever change the way the Israelites perceived God and themselves? In fact, it was the ultimate mnemonic device. Whenever the Israelites would doubt God after that event, whenever they doubted that he had chosen them and made them his own people in an unprecedented way, whenever they doubted that he had a plan for them and a path for them and a future for them, they only needed to remember what he had done back there when the army of Pharaoh was bearing down upon them to annihilate them forever. They would remember that it had really happened, that God is not just real but that he is *that* real, so real that he sometimes intervenes in dramatic ways.

Though it's less remembered by Gentiles, God

similarly parted the waters of the Jordan River just before the Israelites went into the Promised Land. Immediately after it happened, they built a memorial of stones precisely so that they would not forget that this outrageous event actually happened. It hasn't happened since and isn't expected to happen again. To mark them forever, the Jewish people have put these events into their calendars, and, of course, they mark the parting of the Red Sea and the Exodus with annual celebrations of Passover.

But since logic dictates that God could have saved the Israelites from Pharaoh's army in an infinity of ways, and in ways infinitely subtler than parting the Red Sea, it is obvious that he didn't part the Red Sea to save the Israelites as much as he parted the Red Sea to communicate himself to the Israelites. This itself tells us much about the God behind miracles. If he could do what needs doing in other ways, why does he do what he does the way he does it? It is to speak to us about himself.

It's therefore appropriate to conclude that a miracle is something that really only happens *in context*. The parting of the Red Sea is a miracle precisely because the Israelites *perceived* it as a miracle—as an outrageous and otherwise inexplicable event that God made happen, which was precisely God's intention. If it was merely a freak of nature, something that happened to happen, it would not be a miracle. If it happened forty thousand years before the Israelites existed, it wouldn't be a miracle. What makes it a miracle is that God performed it specifically to make himself known, to communicate with human beings. When God pokes into our world through the miraculous, he is communicating with us, otherwise we cannot appropriately use the term "miraculous" to describe an event.

# 3

---

## MIRACLES AND SCIENCE

To force a naturalistic paradigm on
everything has the effect of closing down
science, rather than opening it up.
—JOHN LENNOX

Before we delve into the personal evidence for
miracles and miracle stories themselves, I
thought we should first address the big picture—
and the big questions that surround this subject.
So in the next three chapters we will be talking
about the compatibility of science and the
miraculous, and about how science is more and
more giving us evidence for the very miraculous-
ness of our own existence. These are heady but
supremely fascinating subjects.

The idea that science is somehow at odds
with faith and miracles is false. It's actually not
only false but also demonstrably illogical. Still,
it's a resilient old canard, one that peskily refuses
to crawl off and expire. So let's do our part in
trying to dispatch it from this world as we are
able.[4]

There are many leading scientists who unapologetically believe in God and miracles, who see no conflict between a life simultaneously dedicated both to faith and scientific inquiry. This alone should be dispositive. For example, Francis Collins, who appeared on the cover of *Time* for his work heading the Human Genome Project, and who is now the director of the National Institutes of Health—and who for his fame as a scientist was on President Obama's 2008 transition team—is a Christian who has been quite public about his faith. Indeed, in his book *The Science of God*, he explains how it was science itself that led him to embrace his Christian faith. Another top scientist, Cambridge's Sir John Polkinghorne, after being recognized as one of the top quantum physicists of the twentieth century—and being elected to the Royal Society—was ordained as an Anglican priest and now regularly writes and speaks on the compatibility of science and faith.[5] And, finally, Dr. William D. Phillips, who won the Nobel Prize in physics in 1997, has spoken widely about how his dedication to science and

4. Much of what we say in this chapter can be found in Dr. John Lennox's excellent book *Gunning for God: Why the New Atheists are Missing the Target*, which we heartily recommend to anyone wishing more on this and other worthy subjects.
5. We have twice now had him as our guest at Socrates in the City, where he spoke on "Belief in God in an Age of Science" and "Can a Scientist Pray?"

God are not merely compatible but conjoined and logically inextricable from one another. The list of contemporary men and women of science who believe in the God of the Bible and in miracles is virtually endless.

We are only surprised by this—if we are—because our culture has so forcefully promoted the idea that faith and science are at odds, but the ironic and virtually unknown reality is that modern science itself was essentially invented by people of Christian faith.[6] That's because they believed in a God who had created a universe of staggeringly magnificent order, one that could be understood rationally, and one that it was therefore worth trying to understand. Many of them believed their scientific work was a way of glorifying God, because it revealed the spectacular order and manifold genius of God's creation. Isaac Newton himself was a serious Christian, and Galileo, who because of his battles with the Catholic Church is often thought of as a scientist at odds with Christian faith, was in fact a committed Christian. To add just two from the many others we might name, John Clerk Maxwell and Michael Faraday were both men of deep Christian faith, whose breadth of scientific genius can hardly be overstated, and

_____

6. For a full treatment of this subject, see *The Soul of Science* by Nancy Pearcey and Charles Thaxton.

whose faith explicitly underpinned their zeal to understand the laws governing the universe.

Today we take the idea that the universe can be understood rationally for granted, as though it were a given. But the idea ought to startle us. Though we hardly consider it, the comprehensibility of the universe through scientific inquiry is a radical notion, one that points directly to God as the creator. No less than Albert Einstein acknowledged it and declared it for the ages:

> Science can only be created by those who are thoroughly imbued with the aspiration towards truth and understanding. This source of feeling, however, springs from religion. To this there also belongs the faith in the possibility that the regulations valid for the world of existence are rational, that is, comprehensible to reason. I cannot imagine a scientist without that profound faith.

He also said the following: "Science without religion is lame; religion without science is blind."

Though Einstein did not believe in the personal God of the Bible, this greatest of modern scientists clearly beheld with awe the towering surprise at the heart of all scientific inquiry—that it is at all possible. That somehow the universe can be rationally understood. The glorious gift of this was not lost on him. In another place, Einstein said this:

> Everyone who is seriously involved in the pursuit of science becomes convinced that a spirit is manifest in the laws of the Universe—a spirit vastly superior to that of man, and one in the face of which we with our modest powers must feel humble. In this way the pursuit of science leads to a religious feeling of a special sort, which is indeed quite different from the religiosity of someone more naive.

## THE LIMITS OF SCIENCE

Another reason science is not at odds with faith—or with the miraculous—is that the realm of the miraculous is by definition beyond the scope of science. Science is limited to describing the universe of matter and energy that came into being via the Big Bang. To speculate beyond that is to go beyond the realm of science, strictly speaking. But many atheistic scientists insist there is *never* any reason to speculate beyond the universe of matter and energy, because there *is* nothing beyond that. They insist that the universe is all that is. The problem is that they cannot by any means prove this scientifically, so for them to make this claim at all is itself "unscientific." Ironically, in doing so, such scientists are themselves reaching beyond the world of science.

As John Lennox has said, "Rationality is bigger than science." The world of *scientific* inquiry does not encompass all *rational* inquiry. This is a tremendously important point. So yes, science has limits. It can describe the universe of matter and energy, but it cannot *account* for that universe. Ludwig Wittgenstein said, "The great delusion of modernity is that the laws of science explain the universe for us. The laws of nature *describe* the universe . . . but they *explain* nothing."[7]

So on the larger issue of how the universe came to explode into being in the Big Bang, and on the issue of where all of that matter and energy suddenly came from, science must remain silent. It can go all the way back, fourteen billion years, to the Big Bang, but there it must stop. It can tell us what *is,* but it cannot tell us *why* it is or where "what is" came from. Science cannot speak to these "bigger" questions. Einstein himself said, "You can speak of the ethical foundations of science, but you cannot speak of the scientific foundations of ethics." For example, science can tell us what is possible for us to do in terms of scientific research on stem cells or on cloning,

---

7. Author's italics.

but it cannot tell us if that research would be ethical or unethical. For such questions we must venture beyond the borders of science.

The name for that border, actually, is what is called a "singularity." As we will explain in chapter 5, the fundamental laws governing all the matter in the universe were set in place a fraction of a fraction of a second after the Big Bang. Science simply cannot look into a realm "before" such laws existed. It cannot tell us why those laws were put in place at that precise time, nor whether those laws were predetermined in some way or by someone. But here is what science *can* tell us: that fourteen billion years ago all matter and energy in our universe came into existence. But there is a problem with this. The First Law of Thermodynamics says that energy and matter cannot be created or destroyed. If this is true, how is it possible that all the energy and matter in our universe were created in the Big Bang? According to all that we know from science, that is impossible. Yet science knows that it happened.

There is no disagreement that energy and matter from outside a "closed system" can be put *into* that closed system. But isn't that precisely what a miracle is—the injection of something from *outside* this world of time and space *into* this world of time and space? Why can that not happen again? And again and again and again? If it happened once, in the Big Bang, how can we possibly insist that it can never happen again? On what basis can science make such a claim?

Of course, once the energy and matter have come into the closed system of this universe, that energy and matter are subject to the laws of this universe. C. S. Lewis grappled with this in his typically brilliant way:

> If God annihilates or deflects or creates a unit of matter, He has created a new situation at that point. Immediately nature domiciles this new situation, makes it at home in her realm, adapts all other events to it. It finds itself conforming to all the laws. If God creates a miraculous spermatozoon in the body of a virgin, it does not proceed to break any laws. The laws at once take over. Nature is ready. Pregnancy follows, according to all the normal laws, and nine months later a child is born.

So just as in the creation of the universe, here too in the miracle of the virgin birth, something came from "outside the system." Once that matter and/or energy entered, it was bound by the rules within the system—it had to follow the laws of our universe. But how did it come in? And why did it come in? And where is the world "outside" this world of matter and time? Science cannot tell us. But surely we can ask and can use reason to try and answer these questions. Surely rational human beings *should* ask such questions and do their rational best to find what answers they can.

Isn't the miracle of the virgin birth like the creation of the universe in the Big Bang? If God could insert the entire universe from "outside" the system, why couldn't he insert a sperm cell into the otherwise "closed system"? The head of a sperm cell is approximately five millionths of a meter by three millionths of a meter. If the entire universe erupted into being through a rent in the fabric between being and nonbeing, why couldn't something as small as a sperm cell do the same? If we can accept a single singularity of the Big Bang, on what basis can we reasonably claim no other such singularities are possible? If God is "outside the system" and can reach "inside the system" to create the universe, can't he reach inside the system at other times, to do what we would call miracles?

John Lennox reiterates this idea, that miracles signal a transfer from outside our closed system into our closed system, and once the transfer has been made, the "inside" laws take over. "What Christians are claiming about the Resurrection of Jesus," he says, "is not that he rose by some natural processes; that would violate the laws of nature. No. Christians claim that Jesus rose because God injected enormous power and energy from outside the system. Now, unless you have evidence that the system is totally closed, you cannot argue against the possibility of miracles."

There is the rub. How can scientists argue against the possibility of miracles unless they have real scientific evidence proving that the system is totally closed? Doesn't all that we are coming to know from the new world of quantum physics make the case that it is totally closed less and less plausible?

## WHAT IF SCIENCE ITSELF POINTS BEYOND SCIENCE?

So what if everything we learn from science points us toward the idea that information came in from outside the system, from a world beyond the realm of science? What if science points us beyond science?

For example, many scientists in examining the staggering order of the universe have come to the conclusion that it did not come into being randomly but instead must have been designed by some kind of intelligence—by a designer. What if the scientific evidence for "design" is overwhelming? Hard-line scientific naturalists and atheists say we must never be open to this possibility and must dismiss it out of hand. But why?

It is perfectly logical to consider the idea that the appearance of intelligence must signal actual intelligence. If we find the ten-foot-tall letters *H-E-L-P* dug into the sand on a deserted island, who among us could believe those marks perhaps had been formed by the natural, nonrational forces of water and wind? Something inside us recognizes that it is not random, that there is an intelligence behind it, and we must rationally be open to this possibility.

John Lennox agrees. "I want to be free to follow the evidence where it leads," he says. "That is, to my mind, the true Socratic spirit of science. To force a naturalistic paradigm on everything has the effect of closing down science, rather than opening it up." But fear of provoking the ire of hard-line scientistic ideologues has kept many more open-minded scientists from speaking their minds, much less publishing on the subject. But there have been encouraging signs.

Just ten years ago, probably the most prominent atheist of the twentieth century, Antony Flew, concluded that a God must have designed the universe. It was shocking news and made international headlines. Flew came to believe that the extraordinarily complex genetic code in DNA simply could not be accounted for naturalistically. It didn't make logical sense to him that it had happened merely by chance, via random mutations. It is a remarkable thing that Flew had the humility and intellectual honesty to do a public about-face on all he had stood for and taught for five decades.

If someone says that it is "antiscience" to speculate as Antony Flew and John Lennox and more and more are doing, it is like a baker insisting that everything in the world outside his bakery is "antibaking." He may feel that way, but it's a bizarre claim. Rational thought that extends beyond the strict confines of science is not "antiscience" at all. One must wonder why some scientists would try to exclude all rational inquiry that is not strictly scientific. That act of exclusion is, of course, itself unscientific. With no scientific evidence that the system of this universe is completely closed, they nonetheless insist that it is. The only honest thing to say from the point of view of science is that we cannot know, that that extremely important question is simply beyond the scope of science to answer.

There are many important things beyond the scope of science. Asking why the universe exists or asking what is the meaning of life—or simply loving our children—are beyond that scope, but profoundly worthy activities nonetheless. When did scientists come to play the sour role of sneering at anything beyond the sphere of their chosen field?

Certainly many of the scientists who insist there is nothing beyond science and nothing beyond the universe of matter and energy—and who further insist that speculation that there might be something is "antiscience" and "irrational" must know there is no scientific or rational basis for such claims. We must assume that they are simply ideologically uncomfortable with such speculations and wish to do all they can to put an end to them. But we must call this tactic what it is: a bluff. And let us call this bluff. Let us say that ironically this is not science and let us say that very ironically it is itself "antiscience."

We must assume that if one devotes one's life to discovering what can be known, one may be naturally uncomfortable with the humbling idea of saying *We don't know* or *We cannot know*. One may be not only uncomfortable but even somehow fearful of Mystery and threatened by her. But it is a kind of secular fundamentalism and Pharisaism that gives in to these feelings, that bristles and bridles and blushes at anything that threatens the sacrosanct inviolability of their closed system. So in their harrumphing declarations they would banish Mystery herself, with mud and rocks sealing her in a cave and hoping she never escapes. But Mystery, though hidden, is part of all truth, and the truth, of course, will out.

# CAN WE PROVE THAT
# A MIRACLE HAPPENED?

Convincing reasonable people that something happened and "proving" that something happened are not the same thing. If we are talking about a miracle like the resurrection of Jesus, we cannot "prove" that it happened any more than a prosecutor can "prove" that someone committed a crime. The prosecutor can convince a jury and that jury might even agree unanimously on a verdict, but that's not quite "proof" in the purest sense of the word. Ultimately, whether something can be "proved" or not is a little bit besides the point. In a court of law we talk about things like "reasonable doubt." We condemn people to death or set them free based on conclusions that are not, strictly speaking, "proved," but for which we nevertheless have enough evidence to make firm conclusions and to deliver final verdicts. Examining miracles is usually something like that.

With regard to medical "miracles," it's certainly possible to prove that something "happened." One can show before and after X-rays and/or photographs; one can get testimony from doctors. But we cannot prove that what happened was necessarily a miracle. Just because something happened (e.g., a tumor vanished overnight or perhaps even before someone's eyes) does not mean that we can prove what happened was miraculous, that God was behind it. These are separate issues. So just because something miraculous-seeming happened does not necessarily make it miraculous. It's more honest to say that we don't know how something happened. Many doctors have attested to extraordinary events but cannot make the leap to say that God was behind what occurred.

In a Veritas Forum held at Harvard University in 2012, John Lennox said the following:

> [N]ormally, when we think of science, we think of inductive methods. We do an experiment 100 times. We get the same result and we expect that to happen the 101st time. Well, you can't repeat a resurrection to see if it happened or not and what wc therefore have to employ are the methods of forensic science.

Setting up a classic scientific experiment with falsifiable results is simply not always possible every time we wish to decide whether a miracle happened. But we can certainly decide whether one happened with the evidence obtained from other methods, just as we would do in a court of law.

# THE GOD OF THE GAPS

In the nineteenth century, the evangelist and scientist Henry Drummond coined the term "God of the gaps." It is the idea that whatever one cannot explain or understand, one attributes to "God." But this is essentially a negative definition of God, and of course as science progresses, our need for this "God of the gaps" diminishes. In his famous *Letters and Papers from Prison*, the German theologian Dietrich Bonhoeffer wrote:

> . . . how wrong it is to use God as a stop-gap for the incompleteness of our knowledge. If in fact the frontiers of knowledge are being pushed further and further back (and that is bound to be the case), then God is being pushed back with them, and is therefore continually in retreat. We are to find God in what we know, not in what we don't know.

Since Bonhoeffer wrote those words in 1943, this positive view of God has been increasingly affirmed. As scientific knowledge increases, we have more evidence, not less, pointing to a creator. For example, as recently as March 2014, astronomers announced the discovery of what they believed to be primordial gravitational waves, further solidifying the case for the Big Bang. Surely to anyone ideologically wedded to a materialistic worldview, this must all be confusing and disturbing.

The science of archaeology has similarly uncovered more and more evidence for the historicity of the Bible. For example, for centuries, the world knew nothing of the Hittites apart from the references to them in the Old Testament, but in the early twentieth century, archaeologist Hugo Winckler discovered thousands of tablets inscribed with Akkadian cuneiform. This and other discoveries proved beyond any doubt that the Hittite empire had indeed existed, just as the Bible said. Similarly, in 1994 a broken stele was discovered at Tel Dan in Northern Israel, bearing an inscription referring to the "House of David." Until that time, there was no reference to the royal house of David outside of the Old Testament, and many had thought it was simply mythic.

In the nineteenth century, Darwin postulated that the gaps in the fossil record would slowly be filled as more and more fossils were uncovered. He had hoped to show the streamlined unbroken and steady development from one species to the next. But just the opposite has happened. Instead of finding fossils to fill in the gaps between other fossils, scientists have uncovered more and more of the same kinds of fossils. We have found more examples of the species we have already discovered, and no clear and incontrovertible links between them.

But all of these things are nothing when compared to the evidence that points to the idea that our universe could never merely have happened, that it had to have been intended because it has such an overwhelming appearance of design. The more science uncovers about the conditions necessary for life to exist, and the conditions necessary for the universe to exist, the more science points to a creator. We will plunge into the fascinating details of this in the next two chapters. As the self-proclaimed agnostic and famous physicist Robert Jastrow has put it, "For the scientist who has lived by faith in the power of reason, the story ends like a bad dream. He has scaled the mountains of ignorance; he is about to conquer the highest peak; as he pulls himself over the final rock, he is greeted by a band of theologians who have been sitting there for centuries."

John Lennox gives us the following conclusion: "The more we get to know about our universe, the more the hypothesis that there is a creator God, who destined the universe for a purpose, gains in credibility as the best explanation of why we are here."

# 4

---◆◈◆---

## IS LIFE A MIRACLE?

Miracles, in the sense of phenomena we cannot explain, surround us on every hand: Life itself is the miracle of miracles.

—GAUTAMA BUDDHA

If Spring came but once in a century, instead of once a year, or burst forth with the sound of an earthquake, and not in silence, what wonder and expectation there would be in all hearts to behold the miraculous change!

—HENRY WADSWORTH LONGFELLOW

People are often heard to exclaim that *Life is a miracle!* It's difficult to know what that means, because it can mean many things. Generally speaking, it seems calculated to provoke us to wonder at the amazing things all around us, that we might appreciate them and delight in them. Along these lines, Ralph Waldo Emerson said that "the invariable mark of wisdom is to see the miraculous in the common." And George Bernard Shaw said, "If we could see the miracle of a single flower clearly, our whole life would change."

Still, the idea that "life" is a miracle is quite different from what most of us think of when we think of miracles. Typically, most of us think of more instant and dramatic things, as when a blind man receives his sight, or a tumor disappears overnight, or a dead man rises from the grave. For some good reasons, the sentiment that "life is a miracle" can sound like a Hallmark cliché. But what if it's not? What if life—the simple existence of life on Earth—was as much a miracle as any of these other impossible, dramatic, breathtaking things? What if the existence of life on Earth was demonstrably more outrageous and more astounding than the virgin birth?

## LIFE ON PLANET EARTH

It's exceedingly rare that we should pause to consider the idea of our existence on planet Earth. We tend to take it entirely for granted, and this is hardly surprising, just as fish take water for granted and the birds and bees air.

We know that our planet supports life, and some of us even know that, to the best of our knowledge, no other planet in the universe supports life. But do we know why that is? Why should this planet be perfectly suited to supporting life? As it happens, it shouldn't. But we shall come to that.

Many people, though, are of the opinion that

other planets must support life. We simply haven't found them yet. The idea is that there are so many planets in our incredibly vast universe, sheer odds must dictate that some of them must be able to support life. One often hears that to think otherwise—to think that our planet is the only planet in the unspeakably vast universe to support life—is to be hopelessly arrogant. However, this is neither logical nor true. Whether it is arrogant is another story. But based on what we know today, anyone who asserts that it is not true is doing so not out of scientific evidence but out of blind ideology.

To be fair, a half century ago, when this idea originated, it was completely logical. That's because, at the time, we had very limited knowledge concerning the parameters necessary for a planet to support life. In fact, when Carl Sagan and others declared this idea to great fanfare, we knew of only two conditions that needed to be fulfilled for a planet to support life. We believed that certain kinds of stars were necessary, and we knew that there needed to be a planet just the right distance from those stars. Given those two parameters, Sagan and his colleagues estimated that about 0.001 of all stars in the universe could have a planet that would support life, and given the vast numbers of planets and stars and galaxies, there would have been a spectacularly high number of planets that could support life. All we then needed to do was find that life, which we promptly tried to do with something called SETI, the Search for Extraterrestrial Intelligence.

But as the years have passed and our failure to find the merest hint of life has sunk in, scientists have discovered more and more conditions necessary for life to exist. They have themselves begun to understand why we haven't succeeded in finding a hint of extraterrestrial intelligence. The more that we have studied and measured the universe, the more we have seen that the conditions for life are far more stringent than previously thought. The number of variables necessary for life on a planet in the universe has exploded, while the number of possible planets that could conceivably support life has withered. The number shrank all the way down to zero years ago, and as the number of variables necessary to support life have con-tinued to grow, the number of planets that could support life has sunk further and further *below* zero. The odds *against* a planet supporting life have grown and grown, to unfathomable and dizzying heights of impossibility But the popular understanding of this situation has not come near to catching up with the science.

As of now, fifteen years into the twenty-first century, we know of so many conditions that are absolutely necessary for a planet to support life that not only is it extremely improbable that any other planets can support life, it's extremely improbable that *our* planet should support life. To speak statistically and logically, life of any kind should not exist and we shouldn't be here. Our existence is a statistical and scientific virtual impossibility. That may certainly sound far-fetched, but it's what the most advanced science now leads us to conclude: that the odds are stacked so dramatically against even a single planet in the universe possessing the proper environment to support life that the existence of this planet and life is an anomaly of an impossibly high order. Yet here we are, existing—and not merely existing but thinking about the idea that we exist. What are we to make of this?

Understanding some of the details will help, so let's examine a few of the parameters scientists have determined to be crucial for life. As we say, that number has leapt higher and higher with every year since 1966, when Carl Sagan made his calculations.

The sheer and increasing number of these conditions is staggering, but only a handful of them are easy for us laymen to fully comprehend, so we will limit ourselves to those.[8] What follows

---

8. For a fuller list of those variables and some non-layman-like explanations as to why they are vital to the existence of life, we recommend Hugh Ross's excellent books *The Fingerprint of God* and *The Creator and the Cosmos*.

here is therefore a tremendously abbreviated list—just a taste, really. But we should keep in mind that each of these conditions is crucial. If any *one* of them is not met, life of any kind cannot exist. But since each of these many, many variables lines up perfectly—as they must—some physicists have come to use the expression "fine-tuned universe." This is because—whatever one's ideology on the subject might be—it has the overwhelming appearance of having been "fine-tuned" to support life. By whom is, of course, another story.

The first variable we may touch upon is simply the size of our planet. Most of us have watched or read enough science fiction that we cannot imagine the size of a planet should make much difference, but from a science *non*fiction perspective, this is mistaken. That's because the size—or really, the mass—of a planet determines how much gravity it has, which determines much else. Though it may come as a surprise to us, if our planet were ever so slightly bigger or smaller, life here couldn't exist.

If Earth were slightly larger, it would of course have slightly more gravity, which has interesting implications. It's not just that a person who weighs 150 pounds would weigh more. It's that if Earth had just a little bit more gravity than it now has, methane and ammonia gas, which have molecular weights of sixteen and seventeen, respectively, would remain close to our surface. Since we cannot breathe methane or ammonia, which are toxic, we would die. More to the point, we would never have come into existence in the first place. If you're thinking we might have evolved to where we could breathe those gases, that's more science fiction than reality. Simply put, life cannot coexist with large amounts of methane and ammonia. But if Earth were just a bit larger, these deadly gases would not dissipate into the atmosphere but would stay right down here where we would have to inhale them.

On the other hand, if Earth were a tiny bit smaller and had a bit less gravity, water vapor, which has a molecular weight of eighteen, would *not* stay down here close to the planet's surface but would instead dissipate into the atmosphere. Obviously, without water we couldn't exist. As we've all heard, our bodies are 75 percent water. To think that the size of Earth must be almost exactly what it is or we wouldn't exist is sobering and, frankly, not so easy to believe. But it's a fact that we need a planet small enough to allow poisonous gases of molecular weights sixteen and seventeen to evaporate, and large enough so that water vapor, with its molecular weight of eighteen, will not evaporate.

Before going further, we should say a word on the unique properties of water. As we all learned in grade school, a gas is less dense than a liquid, which is less dense than a solid. As something moves from one state to the next, the molecules get closer together and it gets denser and, of course, heavier. But if this is true, why does ice float? Shouldn't it be denser than liquid water, and shouldn't it sink?

Water does indeed become more dense as it cools toward becoming solid (ice)—*until* it hits 39.2 degrees Fahrenheit, at which point it begins becoming *less* dense. So by the time it is actually solid, it is lighter than it is in its liquid state, and it floats. If water did not have this genuinely bizarre quirk, lakes would freeze from the bottom up, killing the fish and other freshwater life, which would have a subsequent deadly effect on other life-forms. The reason water has this vital property is that each water molecule possesses two hydrogen atoms that are connected to the oxygen atom in a V shape whose angle is about 104.5 degrees. Because of this obtuse angle, water solidifies into hexagonal structures that take up a lot of space and are therefore lighter than liquid water. Marveling at this is not inappropriate.

But there are still other properties of water that are dramatically anomalous and make life on Earth possible. Water's high boiling point is one, and its ability to dissolve a large number of chemical substances is another. Water also retains heat exceptionally well, allowing bodies of water on our planet to help stabilize and moderate temperatures. Once again, if water did not have *all* of these rare properties, life would be impossible.

Just as most of us don't think much about how strange a liquid water is, nor rejoice at the perfect size of our planet, who among us can be said to have given much thought to the speed at which our planet rotates? Every time we watch a sunrise or a sunset we see exactly how fast the planet is rotating, but what of it? If it went a bit slower or faster, would it make a significant difference? Wouldn't life have adapted accordingly? Science says no.

As we suspect the reader knows, our planet rotates once every twenty-four hours. We may all wish there were a few more hours in the day, but it seems that if that were the case and Earth rotated ever so slightly slower, the temperature swings between night and day would be inescapably deadly. If Earth's nighttime side were dark a few hours longer, the nighttime cold would get dramatically colder and the daytime heat would get dramatically hotter. As a result, life on this planet would simply have been impossible. If our planet rotated a bit more quickly and therefore gave us shorter days, it would produce impossibly high winds. Just how high, we cannot say. Winds on Jupiter are routinely one thousand miles per hour, so if Earth rotated slightly faster than it now does, we may conservatively imagine that it would produce winds sufficient to make impossible a stable environment conducive to life of any kind.

Another critical criterion for life on Earth is the presence of an extremely large planet in our solar system. We are thinking specifically of Jupiter, whose efforts on our behalf most of us have taken for granted. But without the Jovian giant where it is, comets and comet debris would strike us about a *thousand times* more frequently. Jupiter's diameter is more than eleven times that of Earth's; its surface area is 122 times the surface area of Earth, and one could fit 1,320 Earths in a sphere the size of Jupiter. For more perspective on Jupiter's jumbo dimensions, consider that it has about two and a half times the mass of all the other planets in our solar system combined.

What exactly does this have to do with comets avoiding us here on Earth? Since Jupiter is composed of gas, it's not nearly as dense as Earth, but it still has 318 times the mass of Earth, and therefore 318 times the gravity. So most of the comets that come anywhere near Jupiter are pulled toward it. It absorbs many of them into its gaseous depths without so much as a hiccup. But in most cases it actually just deflects them away from us and out of our solar system entirely.

# THE MIRACLE OF THE MOON

Jupiter's grand significance to life on Earth, however, must pale in comparison to the significance of our moon.

We may begin with the moon's size, which is the most insignificant—but nonetheless still tremendously significant—reason for its importance to life on Earth. The moon's considerable gravity gives our oceans their ebbing and flowing tides. If the moon were slightly bigger, it would cause our tides to be much more extreme, since a larger moon would of course exert that much more gravitational pull. With one-hundred-foot tides, there could be no coastal cities or towns or villages. If the moon were slightly smaller and had less gravitational pull, the tides would be insufficient to cleanse coastal seawater and replenish its nutrients. If the moon were any size other than the size it is, life as we know it wouldn't exist.

The size of the moon—and its distance from Earth—are also responsible for stabilizing Earth's rotational axis. If it were not stable or were not at its current optimal angle, we could not be here. Without Earth's tilt we would not have our seasons, and our temperatures would be much less stable. So if the moon weren't precisely the right size and distance from Earth, our rotational axis would have changed over the eons, making terrestrial life quite out of the question.

Perhaps the most dramatic of these considerations has to do with the way our moon was formed. Of all the things we will consider, this may be the most difficult to fathom. Most scientists have now concluded that the moon didn't form at the same time as Earth but about a quarter of a billion years later. There are other theories, but as of now most of them have fallen out of favor. As with much else in this chapter, the consensus around what happened has formed only recently, thanks to our increasing knowledge on this subject, and it's a consensus that continues to grow.

Here's what science tells us: Four and a quarter billion years ago, Earth was much smaller than it is now and was still in a molten state. It wasn't even really the Earth yet at all, so let's call it "Earth." Then, out of the infinite reaches of black space, traveling silently on a fixed trajectory for millions and millions (and millions and millions) of years and light-years, a planetary body *larger than Mars* homed in on "Earth" and hit it directly amidships. This unfathomably perfect collision of two bodies in the incalculable vastness of outer space made life—and therefore you and me— possible.

The roughly Mars-size mass that hit "Earth" was for the most part absorbed into "Earth," so that "Earth" went from being "Earth" to actually being Earth. Our size was, via this collision, dramatically increased to what it is today, to the size we have already said is vital to the existence of life. But the remaining chunks produced by this cataclysmic collision began orbiting Earth and eventually coalesced to form what we now know as the moon.

But another thing happened as a result of this collision, without which life could not exist: The head-on collision between these two objects was so *perfectly* aligned—and therefore so cataclysmic—that it blasted most of Earth's previous atmosphere into outer space, leaving us with the atmosphere we now have. The previous atmosphere of Earth was forty times as thick as our current atmosphere, so sunlight could not reach our surface. If this collision had not happened *precisely as it happened,* we would not exist. Our atmosphere and our size were absolutely incapable of supporting life before but perfectly capable of supporting life after.

The addition of the extra mass to our planet also increased Earth's iron content dramatically, allowing marine algae to flourish, which in turn allowed other marine life to flourish, which in turn allowed life on land to flourish. To say we wouldn't be here without this collision happening precisely as it did is an impossibly large under-statement.

But perhaps what is hardest to understand is that the current, perfect state of Earth is the result of a seemingly random collision 4.25 billion years ago. It is no exaggeration to say that in the infinitude of space, for two bodies to collide as they did is like two bullets being shot from guns on either side of the Grand Canyon and meeting so perfectly head-to-head in midair that they canceled out each other's momentum and dropped vertically together into the canyon below. For such a thing to occur is essentially an impossibility and yet somehow science tells us that this happened. It can hardly be understood sufficiently, but if this collision had been ever so slightly less than head-on, or if these hurtling giants had missed each other by a hairbreadth, we wouldn't be here.

Who could deny that to believe this collision happened randomly and "by accident" takes more faith than believing it was somehow "directed" to happen. This is not to say that the collision didn't happen randomly and accidentally, only that believing that it did is so extremely implausible that the alternative must be at least considered. The human mind longs for meaning and for answers to such extraordinary mysteries: Just how might something so outrageously precise have simply "happened"?

But if that astonishingly perfect collision hadn't happened precisely as it did, and if the size of Earth or the size of the moon were slightly different, or if the rotation of Earth were slightly faster or slightly slower, or if Jupiter weren't as big as it is and positioned exactly where it is, life here couldn't even be dimly possible, much less a reality.

And these are just a small handful of the parameters necessary for life to be possible.

As we said, in the 1960s, when Carl Sagan was trying to calculate how many planets in the universe might potentially support life, there were only two fine-tuned characteristics worth bothering with, which gave him the very hopeful result that about one in every ten thousand planets should support life. Given how many planets there were in the universe, it was clear there must be life out there in abundance. But by 2001 the number of fine-tuned characteristics necessary for life had leapt to 150, and when we do the calculations we discover that the odds of a planet supporting life are less than one in ten to the seventy-third power. That's a one followed by seventy-three zeroes. In the known universe, the number of planets is only about ten to the twenty-third power. According to these figures, the odds of any planet being able to support life are one in ten to the fiftieth power. To express this more visually and without concern for conserving zeroes, that is one in 100,000,000,000,000,000,000,000,000,000,000, 000,000,000,000,000,000. It doesn't make any sense at all that Earth should have beat those odds, but we did. Somehow.

This returns us to the further surprising subject of our moon. Since most of us typically don't think about the moons orbiting other planets in our solar system, we don't appreciate the particular strangeness of Earth's moon, which is radically different from the other moons in our star system. To begin with, Earth is the only planet in our solar system that has only one moon. We take this as a matter of course, as though seeing one moon in the sky were the only option. Mercury and Venus are, of course, moonless. Mars has two moons, both so tiny that they almost shouldn't be called moons. One (Phobos) has a diameter of fourteen miles—the length of Manhattan—while the other (Deimos), has a diameter of less than eight miles. The Brobdingnagian planet Jupiter has nine major moons (although astronomers keep finding new ones, putting the latest real number at fifty and counting), while Saturn has twelve major moons (as with Jupiter, astronomers have found many smaller ones, putting the most recent number at fifty-three and counting). Uranus has twenty-seven known moons, and Neptune has fourteen. These facts put our single moon in some context. In our solar system it's unique.

When comparing the size of moons to the planets they orbit, Earth's moon is also anomalous, being far and away the largest. There exist other moons larger than our moon, but they orbit planets like Jupiter and Saturn and Neptune, all dramatically larger than Earth. We've already mentioned the size of Jupiter, and Saturn has a diameter 9.5 times that of Earth's, 764 times the volume, and 83 times the surface area. Relative to the size of its planet, our moon is by far the largest moon in our solar system. The point of this is to say that all that the moon is responsible for, as we've said before, is that much more rare when compared to the other moons in our solar system.

We cannot leave the subject of the moon until we touch upon the almost unthinkably amazing subject of eclipses. Most of us haven't considered that for eclipses to occur as they do, the sun and moon must appear almost *precisely* the same size in the sky. As with so many things, we take eclipses for granted. They are just a part of the way things are. But when we know the details of the sizes and numbers of the moons throughout our solar system, the idea that the sun and our moon appear almost exactly the same size from our Earth-bound vantage point is essentially preposterous and bizarre. But it is this freakish fact that makes them cover each other so perfectly during a total eclipse. Though it has no bearing on the existence of life as far as we know, like all else we have examined, it gives such startling evidence of design—and therefore a designer—that we can hardly ignore it.

The details are as follows: The moon has a diameter of 2,159 miles. In order for a total eclipse to be possible, it must look the same size as the sun, whose diameter is 864,327 miles. If you divide 864,327 by 2,159, you get 400.337. In other words, the sun is almost exactly four hundred times the size of the moon. So in order for them to look the same size from Earth, the distance from Earth to the sun must be about four hundred times the distance from Earth to the moon. What are the odds that that should be the case? Nonetheless, the average distance of the sun from Earth is almost exactly 93,000,000 miles, and the average distance from the moon to Earth is roughly 238,857 miles. If you divide 93,000,000 by 238,857, you get . . . 389. That number is so close to four hundred that they really *do* look precisely the same size to us here on Earth. Can we avoid being taken aback by this? If we should be less startled than spooked, who could blame us? Can we avoid at least wondering whether it's all been somehow arranged?

Is there any escaping the conclusion that the existence of life on planet Earth, or of life of any kind anywhere, is an astonishing, incomprehensible miracle? Can we ever again really take our existence here for granted, knowing how superlatively precarious it is? If God made everything in the vast universe just as it is simply so that we could exist, we must begin to wonder why. What are we to him that he would do all this? Why would he make it all so extravagantly, even so unreasonably perfect? If it was all done just for us, the question arises: Who are we?

# 5

---·◆·---

## THE MIRACLE OF THE UNIVERSE

Why do we exist?

—ANONYMOUS

In chapter 4 we discussed the statistical impossibility of life on Earth. But what of the existence of the universe itself? Is it possible for us to gain some idea of what the odds might be that *it* should exist? Most of us probably take the existence of the universe for granted, which is understandable. But let's consider whether it's appropriate that we take its existence for granted.

Since the dawn of human consciousness, many people have asked, *Why do we exist?* But it is usually asked as a philosophical question, meaning *What is the meaning of our being here?* But *Why do we exist?* is as much a scientific question as a philosophical question. In other words, why does anything exist? Why is there *something* rather than nothing? Why is the universe here? If the question is considered carefully enough, it is inescapably dizzying.

Before we get much further, we have to explain

that we wouldn't be asking this question—certainly not in the same way—if we didn't believe that the universe had a beginning. For many cultures and in many eras, it was believed that the universe had always existed and therefore had no beginning. The ancient Greek philosophers held this view, and in the modern era, until the middle of the last century, most scientists held this view as well. Of course, the ancient Hebrews believed that God created the universe out of nothing, but almost no other culture held to the belief that the universe had come into existencc at a specific point.

The term that the scientists used for a universe that had always existed, and that had never been created, was the "Steady State model." But by the middle of the twentieth century, many scientists began to abandon this idea to conclude that the universe did have a beginning after all. It seemed that humble Moses, writing thirty-five centuries earlier, had gotten that right. This is itself a witheringly strong argument for the divine origin of the Bible, though that's a wider discussion for another time. Even as the evidence for the universe's beginning increased, some scientist still clung to the Steady State model—and some still do today—perhaps in part because the idea of a creation seemed to imply a creator, which is for some an unpalatable thought. But as the evidence continued to grow, more and more believed that the universe was created in what eventually came to be known as the "Big Bang," a term unintentionally coined by the physicist Sir Fred Hoyle in a 1949 BBC interview. According to this view, the whole universe arose—or actually exploded—out of nothing and has continued to explode, or expand, ever since. But it wasn't until 1964 that there was solid evidence to make this the generally accepted theory. That's the year the famous "background radiation" was accidentally discovered by Arno Penzias and Robert Woodrow Wilson. After this discovery, the scientific consensus formed that our universe came into being some billions of years ago. The latest estimate puts it at about fourteen billion years.

When we think of the Big Bang, we cannot be blamed for thinking of an explosion that is like other explosions, which tend to be messy and generally rather unpredictable. But the Big Bang—the primal ka-boom that created the hundreds of billions of galaxies, each containing hundreds of billions of stars and planets—was a dramatically different kind of explosion. It was an explosion that was so extremely and precisely controlled that we cannot really fathom it. Nothing human beings have ever been able to do can begin to approach the precision of it. And it is only because it was precisely as controlled as it was that the universe exists.

But the details of the precision are worth

considering. Indeed we must consider them if we wish to have some idea of the wild miracle of our existence.

We may begin with the simplest example of control: the speed of the explosion. We now know that if the speed of this universe-creating explosion had been ever so slightly different, the universe would not exist. If it had been the tiniest bit faster, for example, matter would have dispersed so efficiently that none of it would have clumped together to form galaxies. If that had happened, there would have been no stars or planets. But if the universe had expanded ever so slightly slower, it would have clumped together into an almost infinitely dense lump that contained all the matter in existence. Literally. And because of this big lump of everything, there would be nothing else. No galaxies or suns or planets. Of course life of any kind would not have been even remotely possible.

But to say that it was controlled or precisely calibrated can hardly begin to explain the degree of control involved. In fact, the speed at which the cosmos expanded out of that microdot in question was so outrageously perfectly calibrated that physicists say it constitutes the "most extreme fine-tuning yet discovered in physics." Astrophysicist Hugh Ross says an "analogy that does not even come close to describing the precarious nature of this cosmic balance [between too fast and too slow] would be a billion pencils all simultaneously positioned upright on their sharpened points on a smooth glass surface with no vertical supports."

There are many more examples of the universe's fine-tuning as it exploded out of the gate fourteen billion years ago. We'll only touch on a handful, again underscoring the idea that if any *one* of these were different by, in some cases, a fraction of a fraction of a fraction of a percent, the universe itself could not exist.

Some illustrations of the fine-tuning of our universe deal with the so-called four fundamental forces physicists talk about, and with which most laymen are unacquainted. These four forces are 1.) gravity, 2.) the electromagnetic force, 3.) the weak nuclear force, and 4.) the strong nuclear force. Most of us know what gravity is and does. The strong nuclear force holds the nucleus (meaning the protons and neutrons) of an atom together. The weak force deals with radioactive decay and neutrino reactions, among other things, and the electromagnetic force essentially holds atoms and molecules together. And if any of these forces were in the slightest degree different, our universe would not exist. But how were the values of these four fundamental forces determined, and how is it that they just happened to be precisely right for our universe to come into being?

Perhaps more impressive is that each of these crucially precise values was established once and for all within one-*millionth* of a second after the Big Bang. In other words, immediately. Trying to comprehend something happening before the first millionth of a second of the universe's existence is rather beyond our conceptual capacity. But it's a fact known to all those who study such things that by the time the universe was one-millionth of a second old, the values of these four forces were set, as it were, in cement. Nor have these forces deviated in the slightest in the fourteen billion years since. Given this track record, we can presume they'll be the same tomorrow. And as we have said, each of them has a value that, like the speed of the exploding universe, is so heart-stoppingly precisely calibrated that we can hardly take it in. If one of these four forces were ever so slightly different, our universe would not exist.

Let's consider the value of the strong nuclear force. As we've said, this governs how tightly protons and neutrons cling to each other. Science has discovered that if this force were 2 percent weaker, protons and neutrons could not stick together, giving us a universe of only hydrogen atoms (whose nucleus has no neutrons and just one proton). Of course, that's not much of a "universe." On the other hand, if the strong nuclear force were 0.3 percent stronger, protons and neutrons would stick together with such force that only "heavy" elements would exist, and there would be no hydrogen whatsoever. Neither a universe with only hydrogen nor a universe with no hydrogen can support life. So the strong nuclear force must be precisely what it is or the universe would not exist.

Speaking of supporting life, which is carbon-based, we know that a great abundance of the element carbon must exist for any life to exist. It's been postulated that there could perhaps be silicon-based life in the universe, but this idea by now has been generally dismissed as unworkable. For life to be possible anywhere in our universe, there needed to be vast amounts of carbon. In 1953, Sir Fred Hoyle—the Cambridge astronomer who coined the term "Big Bang"—discovered that the nuclear ground-state energy levels[9] of helium, carbon, oxygen, and beryllium had to be extraordinarily fine-tuned for enough carbon to be created. If any of the nuclear ground-state levels were just 1 percent different, there would not have been enough carbon in the universe to allow for the possibility of life. To Hoyle, an atheist, the notion that this perfect fine-tuning had "just happened" was statistically quite impossible. But what else could account for it? He later admitted that it was this discovery of these extraordinarily fine-tuned levels—and what

9. The lowest energy level of an element.

he saw as the overwhelming implication of a "guiding intelligence" behind them—that, more than anything else, had "greatly shaken" him and his atheism. He later wrote, "A common sense interpretation of the facts suggests that a superintellect has monkeyed with physics, as well as with chemistry and biology, and that there are no blind forces worth speaking about in nature. The numbers one calculates from the facts seem to me so overwhelming as to put this conclusion almost beyond question."

For any life to be possible in the universe, we need not only a superabundance of carbon but also the presence of at least forty different other elements. Of course we've got upward of a hundred. But forty are necessary, as a minimum. If we recall our high school chemistry, we remember that every molecule has a nucleus, composed of protons and neutrons, and that every nucleus is orbited by electrons. Creating different kinds of molecules requires electrons that can leave their orbits around one molecule and leap to another molecule. But if the electromagnetic force were any stronger, the nuclei would hold the electrons exactly where they are, not allowing them to pull away and join other molecules. On the other hand, if the electromagnetic force were slightly weaker than it is, atoms would not hang on to their electrons at all. In either case, life could not exist.

Theoretical particle physicist Paul Davies has himself said that "the impression of design is overwhelming." Another startling example of this fine-tuning concerns the ratio of the strong nuclear force to the electromagnetic force. Davies himself calculated that if the ratio between them had been different by just one part in ten to the sixteenth power, the universe as we know it would not exist. To put it in another way, if that ratio had deviated by .0000000000000001 percent, the universe would not be here. But, the ratio just happens to be exactly and precisely what it needs to be, and here we are.

Still, even these freakishly tall odds pale in comparison to the ratio of the electromagnetic force to the gravitational force. Physicists have calculated that if *that* ratio had been different by one part in 10,000,000,000,000,000,000,000,000,000,000,000,000,000, the universe would not exist. But somehow, it is just what it needs to be. Statistically this is quite impossible, but once again there it is and here we are. To explain why this is such an important ratio, we need to see that if it were that tiny fraction higher, only large stars would form; if it were that tiny superfraction smaller, only small stars would form. For life to be remotely possible in the universe, the universe must contain both large stars and small stars. That's because only in the centers of the large stars are most of the life-essential elements produced, and only a small star like our sun can burn steadily for billions of years, without which exceedingly steady burning, we couldn't be here. Again, that long number—one followed by forty zeroes, or ten to the fortieth power—is the maximum level of deviation beyond which even the possibility of life is ruled out. Of course that number is hard to comprehend. In his book *God's Undertaker*, Cambridge mathematician John Lennox says that the accuracy needed to hit a number that precisely is "the kind of accuracy a marksman would need to hit a coin at the far side of the observable universe, twenty billion light-years away." It's probably hard for us to think about a distance of twenty billion light-years, so let's consider another analogy of these same odds, given to us by Caltech astrophysicist Hugh Ross.

Ross tells us to imagine covering every square inch of the surface of North America with dimes. Once that is done, put on another layer. Take your time. Now put on another layer and then another. And one more. Continue this exercise until the dimes reach *the height of the moon,* which we've earlier said is about 238,000 miles up. This would constitute rather a large number of coins, of course. But we're far from finished. Once you've covered all of North America to the height of the moon, do exactly the same thing on another *billion* continents of the same size as North

America. If you are unable to locate that many other continents of that size, simply imagine doing that. Now randomly choose one dime in those billion 238,000-mile-high piles, paint it red, and put it back in the pile. Then blindfold a friend (no peeking) and ask him to pick out one of the coins from one of the billion continent-size, 238,000-mile-high piles. The odds of his picking out the red dime are ten to the fortieth power. Feel free to gulp.

The number of conditions like these only continues to grow. If any *one* of these conditions were not met precisely, the universe could not exist.

For example, we know that a proton has about 1,836 times the mass of an electron, but science has calculated that if that ratio were slightly larger or smaller, the universe would not exist. We also know that the average distance between stars in our part of the Milky Way galaxy is roughly thirty trillion miles, but we also now know that if this were much more or much less, our solar system could not exist. Everywhere we turn there is evidence of fine-tuning and design. It is as if almost every parameter we are able to measure turns out to be necessary for the universe to exist, as though every aspect of the universe is perfectly and intentionally interlocked with every other aspect in a way that challenges our imaginations to consider.

Before we go, however, let's touch on two examples of fine-tuning that are far more dramatic than the ones we have mentioned. The astrophysicist Hugh Ross explains that the expansion of the universe is governed by the mass density of the universe and the space energy density. Ross says that in order for enough stars and planets to exist for the *possibility* of life in the universe, the value of the mass density has to be fine-tuned to one part in ten to the sixtieth power. Are we surprised to learn that it is fine-tuned to that level? But Ross says that the value of the space energy density must be calibrated to a far higher level of precision. That value must be fine-tuned to less than one part in ten to the 120th power. Happily, it is.

The more science learns, the clearer it is that although we are here, we shouldn't be. Once we begin considering the details of it all, the towering odds against our existence begin to become a bit unsettling. When we come to see the superlatively extreme precariousness of our existence, and begin to understand how by any accounting, we ought not to exist, what are we to think or feel? Our existence seems to be not merely a virtually impossible miracle but the most outrageous miracle conceivable, one that makes previously amazing miracles seem like almost nothing.

It's as if someone logically convinced you that

the odds of being able to take your next few breaths were infinitesimally small. If we really believed it, we would begin to breath cautiously, perhaps even timidly and tentatively, expecting our next intake of breath to yield no oxygen. The slimness of our being here is so slim that it's enough to leave us goggle-eyed with terror—until in the next moment we realize we are indeed here and explode with gratitude for our very existence. This really can be the only proper and logical response to it all, to marvel and rejoice and rest in the genuinely unfathomable miracle of our being.

But there are yet two questions that must be answered.

The first is: Why haven't we heard any of this before? Of course a few people have heard some of it before, perhaps in a sermon by a hip, especially knowledgeable, apologetics-focused pastor. But the majority of people have not. Why haven't they? Mainly, because what the public comes to learn, whether via the media or via textbooks in the classroom, always lags far behind what science learns. So if in recent years new information has been discovered, it doesn't mean that this information will be disseminated to the public immediately. Even most scientists lag far behind on much of this new information and still cling to outdated concepts and theories. Each scientist focuses on his or her field and can hardly be expected to be up on the latest cosmological theories any more than a family doctor can be expected to know what is happening on the cutting edge of research on every disease. It's simply not possible. Finally, many scientists hold so strongly to materialistic assumptions that they are predisposed against these ideas and simply may not take them seriously enough to look further into them. The more time passes, however, the more evidence emerges supporting the fine-tuning theory, so the general scientific consensus grows broader each day, making it more difficult to justify dissent. Of course, this does not mean some do not try.

This leads us to our second question. What are we to make of what have been called the "anything but that" theories, which rather desperately try to find ways around the mounting evidence for—and implications of—a finely tuned universe? The most popular at present is the so-called multi-universe—or "multiverse"— theory, which postulates the existence of an infinity of other universes "that we cannot perceive." According to this almost comically clever idea, if there exists an infinity of other universes—and this is an infinitely big "if"—one of them must of course *by chance* possess all the variables perfectly right for everything to exist just as it does in fact exist—and would you be very surprised to learn that we just happen to exist in that one universe? How lucky for us. Of course, there is no scientific evidence for this theory, unless perhaps we simply "cannot perceive" the evidence. Of this multiverse theory, eminent physicist Sir John Polkinghorne has said: "Let us recognize these speculations for what they are. They are not physics, but in the strictest sense, metaphysics. There is no purely scientific reason to believe in an ensemble of universes." Philosopher Richard Swinburne put it less diplomatically: "To postulate a trillion-trillion other universes, rather than one God, in order to explain the orderliness of our universe, seems the height of irrationality."

So having answered these two questions and holding only to what science is able to tell us at the beginning of the twenty-first century, it seems impossible to avoid logically concluding that the existence of our universe is a miracle, one of impossible proportions. The more we know, the clearer it is that we should not be here to think about being here. We are a distinct mathematical impossibility. Do we simply shrug at this and move on, or dare we consider its implications? To simply say *It is what it is* or to prestidigitate the escape hatch of an infinity of universes is to ignore the sharp point of the assembled facts. To turn away or to tut-tut that one more time to think about it seems like intellectual dishonesty. Reason and science compel us to see what previous generations could not: that our existence is an outrageous and astonishing miracle, one so startlingly and perhaps so disturbingly miraculous that it makes any miracle like the parting of the Red Sea pale in such insignificance that it almost becomes unworthy of our consideration, as though it were something done easily by a small child, half-asleep. It is something to which the most truly human response is some combination of terror and wonder, of ancient awe and childhood joy.

# 6

## QUESTIONS ABOUT MIRACLES

As flies to wanton boys are we to th' gods.
They kill us for their sport.

—*KING LEAR*

In the summer of 1967, while diving from a raft into the Chesapeake Bay, my friend Joni Eareckson Tada misjudged the depth of the water and fractured the levels between her fourth and fifth vertebrae, becoming an instant quadriplegic. She was seventeen. It's one thing to consider this question abstractly, and another to think of it in a more personal way, as when it concerns someone we know, but in the more than forty-five years since the accident, Joni has been prayed for innumerable times, without any miraculous healing. Joni is herself a woman of profound faith. The question, then, is why hasn't she been healed?

Asking that—and asking why God would allow such a thing to happen to an active and vivacious seventeen-year-old in the first place—is to ask the questions behind all questions. These are probably versions of the questions most people plan to ask God when they get to Heaven. We are made in

God's image and so we long for meaning. Therefore it is natural and normal and appropriate for us to want to know such things. What happened to Joni reminds us that there are questions to which we have no real answers—at least no simple answers. Someone might say that it was God's way of bringing Joni to faith, which, in part, it seems to have been, but any sensitive person cannot help but wonder why God would need to do it that way. It doesn't make much sense to us, does it? In any case, it is inescapably difficult to think about. But while we are pondering these larger questions, here's something more.

In the moment that Joni's vertebrae fractured, she found herself underwater, completely unable to move her arms or legs. She was unable to push herself up from the bottom and would have drowned in a minute or two. But just seconds after she dove in and was paralyzed, a crab bit her sister's toe. Her sister had been on the raft a minute before but had already been on her way out of the water by the time Joni dove in. Her back was turned to Joni, and she wouldn't have looked back as she made her way out of the water, but because the crab bit her toe and it hurt she turned around to warn Joni that the crabs were out and in a biting mood. When she turned around to tell this to Joni, she noticed Joni's peroxide-blond hair waving underneath the water some distance away.

On a whim, Joni had the night before decided to

bleach her hair peroxide blond, and had done so, driving to the drugstore, buying a bottle of hair bleach, and dyeing it that night. Joni told me that if she hadn't done that the night before, her sister would never have seen her hair under the water at that distance. Joni's hair was always what she describes as a "mousy" brown that would have been perfectly camouflaged by the water and the color of the bottom—until that day when it was suddenly a bright white blond. So it was because of that crab biting her sister's toe at that moment and because she had decided to dye her hair peroxide blond the night before that her sister saw Joni in time to save her from drowning. As far as Joni is concerned, it was a genuine miracle that her sister saw her and saved her that day.

But of course we want to know what we are to make of a God who might be able to cause a crab to bite someone's toe so someone's life is saved, but who didn't do something to prevent Joni from being paralyzed from the neck down in the first place. She's been prayed for hundreds of times by well-meaning Christians who think their prayers will get her out of that wheelchair, but now it's been forty-seven years and she is still paralyzed. Two years ago she survived a battle with breast cancer. What kind of a God are we talking about?

Joni says that for the first two years after that accident, she struggled terribly with depression. She simply didn't want to continue living. She had been wonderfully athletic before, had ridden horses, hiked, played tennis. She would never be able to do any of these things again, and she knew it. Her will to live was nearly nonexistent, until one day about two years after the accident. It was then that she realized God might have a purpose for her. Indeed he did—as he does for all of us—and everything changed. She has been a bright light in the lives of innumerable people over the years. Joni is nonetheless unsparingly candid about how much she still dislikes being quadriplegic. She describes the routine she has to go through every morning when she wakes up: "bed bath," toileting, exercising, getting dressed. She can do none of these things on her own. Each of them must be done by someone for her or with someone. It's hard to imagine enduring that, day in and day out, for nearly fifty years. But she looks to God for strength and somehow gets that strength and continues to use it to encourage people struggling with disabilities. She is also an outspoken and effective activist and advocate on their behalf. Still, what exactly are we to make of this God who heals some and not others?[10]

---

10. I've known Joni from a number of meetings and have heard her talk about some of the things mentioned here. She's also written about them. But it was at the studios of 100 Huntley Street in Toronto that I first heard the details of her accident, after my on-camera interview of her.

## WHY DO MIRACLES HAPPEN TO SOME PEOPLE AND NOT TO OTHERS?

We have seen in the previous chapters that our very existence is miraculous. But when we typically think of miracles, we think about the ones that happen on a personal level, where God intervenes in a way that amazes us. Sometimes it's a miraculous healing. Other times it's a miraculous provision, as when someone suddenly gets a check for the exact amount they needed. But if we accept the idea that miracles happen— or that they *can* happen and sometimes do happen—then we must ask why they happen to certain people at certain times and not at others. And most practically speaking, why do they happen to this person but not to that person? Why was so-and-so miraculously healed of cancer, while that other person was not healed, even when so many people were praying? Why is my friend Joni still a quadriplegic?

In chapter 15 I tell the remarkable September 11 story of how my friend Lolita Jackson audibly heard God's voice directing her to safety just before the Twin Towers collapsed. But must we not wonder about her colleague who was with her and who perished? Must we not wonder about the fathers and mothers who died leaping from the flames to their deaths? How are we to make sense of that? We rejoice that one person was miraculously saved, but we can hardly forget about the others who weren't. Can we face these difficult questions? If we don't, what we think of as "the miraculous" becomes myopic and self-serving and unworthy of people claiming to care about truth.

How can we take the idea of miracles seriously if they seem to be so random, happening to this one and not to that one, happening here but not there? Is God merely capricious? In *King Lear*, Gloucester famously says: "As flies to wanton boys are we to th' gods. / They kill us for their sport." That is the pagan view of "the gods," who certainly don't exist, and who, if they did exist, obviously would not love us mortals. From what we know of them, they treat us indifferently and often downright cruelly, just as a "wanton boy" would pull the wings off a fly. But that is not the God presented to us in the Bible. The God of the Bible, if he exists, is a God who claims to love us and who knows us infinitely more intimately than we know ourselves. Jesus says that his father has numbered the very hairs on our heads. If we are talking about the God of the Bible, we must talk of a God who has himself suffered and suffered horribly—and who has died for us. And he would do it again and again and again. We must talk of a God who has been wooing us as a lover woos his beloved, chasing after her and doing all he can to win her heart. Though he will suffer for her and die for her, he knows this does not guarantee that she will reciprocate his love. But he does what he does still, for such is the nature of love.

Who God is and what he is like has everything to do with the subject of miracles. If God were some cruel tyrant in the sky, we wouldn't be surprised if he capriciously healed this one and let another die. But if God is who the Bible says he is, what should we make of *him* healing someone and letting someone else die? What do we make of *him* leading my friend Lolita to safety but letting others perish? How should we understand that?

Common sense suggests that any God who would heal one person and let another die an awful death doesn't seem to be a God anyone would want to worship, even if he really existed. That sort of God would seem loathsome, so wouldn't we be justified in hating him, or at least in avoiding him, as many people do? Thinking about miracles forces us to think about the nature of the God behind those miracles.

Miracles seem to attest to the presence of a loving and compassionate God, one who wants to help us, who wants to speak to us and encourage us. But as soon as we think of when miracles do *not* happen, we think the opposite is true, that God is indifferent and unloving and doesn't care if we are crushed and discouraged. So which is it?

If the latter is true, then it's safe to say that God really doesn't exist, because an indifferent and unloving God is hardly God in any real sense. And if he is sometimes loving and caring and at other times unloving and uncaring, in what sense is he any kind of God we could trust, with whom we would want to have a relationship?

It is at this point that most people shrug and walk away. It is sorely tempting to do so. If God is that complicated and confusing, it's hard to take an interest in him. But to walk away now is tragic, precisely because it's only by understanding this very thing that we can really get to the most important point of all. To walk away at this juncture is to be on the verge of what we seek—within reach of the breathtaking summit—but to lose our bearings and turn back, to miss out on taking those few last, difficult steps to something glorious.

So let's think a bit further.

It's only logical that if God *always* answered our prayers as we wanted him to, those answers to our prayers could hardly be considered miraculous. They would only be part of a predictable system that we could manipulate, if only we knew how. It really makes God not God, but a "God" or a god whom *we* are ultimately able to control through our efforts, whether via prayer or via our "moral" actions designed to elicit a favorable response. If that is the God in question, we who think of ourselves as his devotees are actually not worshiping him but rather a wished-for and prayed-for outcome, which is a fulfillment of our desires, whether noble or selfish. It follows that we are really quite indifferent to the God behind that outcome, if he is there at all. It is the outcome itself to which we are passionately devoted. So in this scenario, we are really treating God like a tool to be used, and we hardly acknowledge him any more than we thank the hammer or saw.

## IS IT "TRUE FAITH" OR "DEAD RELIGION"?

If the goal of prayer is really to "get the results we want," we have a strange, candy-machine idea of God. It is as though we need only to put something in and we get something back. It's a kind of trade. With this sort of a "God," there is no doubt that if I do *x,* then he *must* do *y.* In a way, he has no choice in the matter. If that's true, why would there be any gratitude on the part of the one getting what he wants? Hasn't he earned it by doing his part? If that's true, he owes God nothing, because he did what was necessary and now he simply expects what is coming to him. In other words, perhaps I say a certain prayer a certain number of times and perhaps I forgo this pleasure for a certain period of time, and in return I get what I'm after. It's a system that allows me to get what I want without the necessity of acknowledging God or having a relationship with God. Perhaps the thinking is that God is so rich it's no big deal for him to give me what I want, so why should I be grateful? Perhaps I know I am only using God because I despise him and only want to do what I must to get what I want. It puts me and what I want at the center of things and again creates a God who is no God.

This approach is what I've previously called "Dead Religion,"[11] which is contrasted with what I have called "True Faith," where the relationship with God is central, and the things we *get* from him are peripheral. We can think of it this way: If a child really loves her father and knows he really loves her, she trusts him. When he gives her what she wants, she is happy and grateful. But even when he doesn't give her what she wants, she knows that he has a reason for not giving it to her, and not just any reason but a reason that has her ultimate welfare and concerns at heart. So although it might take some effort, in the end she cannot help but be grateful. If we have that kind of a God in mind, then even when we don't get what we want or ask for, we can trust there is wisdom and real love toward us in *not* giving it to us.

---

11. In my 2012 National Prayer Breakfast speech, which may be viewed at www.ericmetaxas.com, I discuss the difference between "True Faith" and "Dead Religion."

There are many people who may talk about God and prayer and who outwardly look very religious, but they're really just performing rites and deeds and prayers so they can get what they want. If they felt that those rites or deeds or prayers wouldn't get them what they wanted, they would stop doing those things. So they are not really worshiping the God they claim to be worshiping. They are selfishly worshiping getting what they desire. For them, God is only a means to that end. If he doesn't give them what they want, they cut him off. Any parent understands that we don't want our children to treat us that way.

If we are talking about a loving God, we are talking about a God who asks us to trust him, whether we get what we ask for or don't. But he will never force us to trust him. That is entirely up to us. We have free will and we can accept his love or reject it, or claim it doesn't exist at all. We can trust him or distrust him as we like. But if he really and truly is the God of the Bible, who loves me with an unchanging and self-sacrificial love (agape), then I really and truly can trust him in all circumstances, which is tremendously freeing. In fact, I can go one step further than trusting him. To use a biblical phrase, I can rejoice in him.[12]

---

12. In his letter to the believers in Philippi, Saint Paul says, "Rejoice in the Lord always."

But is only possible if we really do know that God has our best interests at heart at all times. Of course, we have to decide on our own whether we believe that. But if we come to see that that is true and do allow ourselves to believe it, we are precisely where he created us to be: in his loving hands.

## IF WE THANK GOD FOR THE GOOD THINGS, WHY NOT BLAME HIM FOR THE BAD?

A good friend has often remarked that athletes publicly thanking God annoys him, because it follows logically that if they thank God for their successes they should also blame him for their failures, and why don't they? This is a very good question. We have all witnessed this phenomenon. I don't think there's anything at all wrong with thanking God publicly in that way. In fact, I think it's appropriate and right to do so, since it was God who gave us whatever we needed to accomplish what we accomplished. But to be fair to athletes who express their faith publicly, I have also heard a number of them say that even though they want to win, they are grateful to God no matter the outcome.

Therefore it actually does not follow that one should blame God for one's failures if one is grateful to him for one's successes. Rather, in a kind of Chestertonian inversion, it's correct to say that we cannot truly thank him for the good things *unless we also thank him for the bad things.* That way seems madness, but actually it makes perfect sense. This is because if we trust the God we know from the Hebrew Bible—and not some indifferent Greco-Roman deity, for example— then we know that he means well toward us at all times and in every conceivable way, so it follows that we actually can trust him with everything, including our failures and our difficulties, as we have just said. So if he is actually the God who loves us beyond anything we can imagine, even the bad things can ultimately be a blessing. In fact, Gods wants us to know that, because our sufferings will be easier to bear if we know God is with us in the midst of them, leading us toward something ultimately redemptive and beautiful.

The author of the hymn "Amazing Grace," John Newton, who once was a slave ship captain, and who became a Christian preacher and an enemy of the slave trade, once said: "I have reason to praise [God] for my trials, for, most probably, I should have been ruined without them." The author of *The Gulag Archipelago*, Aleksandr Solzhenitsyn, who suffered for twenty years in the hellish prison camps he describes in that book, wrote: "Bless you prison, bless you for being in my life. For there, lying upon the rotting prison straw, I came to realize that the object of life is not prosperity as we are made to believe, but the maturity of the human soul." This does not mean that Newton would have chosen to go through his trials, or that Solzhenitsyn in any way enjoyed the terrible suffering of his imprisonment. But it means that in retrospect they can see that God used those difficulties to bless them in the long run.

Of course, no one wants to suffer. Let's be clear about that. Let's also be clear that that is normal and healthy. We shouldn't want to suffer. But what we are talking about here is something else. It is understanding that as much as we wish to avoid suffering, there is more to life than merely avoiding suffering. In fact, good can come out of suffering. If we know this, it changes how we suffer. It gives it meaning. So what we desperately do want to avoid is not merely suffering but suffering without meaning.

If our suffering has a purpose, it is infinitely easier to bear than if our suffering has no purpose and no larger meaning. When a mother endures childbirth, she knows that it is leading to something life changing and glorious.

Viktor Frankl, who endured the death camps of the Third Reich, wrote about this in his famous book *Man's Search for Meaning*. He said, "In some ways suffering ceases to be suffering at the moment it finds a meaning, such as the meaning of a sacrifice." Frankl observed this in his experiences in the Nazi camps. He also wrote that "[t]hose who have a 'why' to live, can bear with almost any 'how.' "

Biblical theology is crystal clear on this, because there are a number of Scripture verses that address it directly. Perhaps the most direct one is from Romans 8:28. It reads: "And we know that all things work together for good to those that love God, to those who are the called according to his purpose." This is a very dramatic statement, and if you believe it, everything changes. Because it means that you can see everything that happens—both good and bad—as part of what God is doing to lead you toward the larger good. In other words, everything you do and experience, including suffering, has profound meaning. It is part of something larger that is happening and that is leading you toward something better. The J. B. Phillips translation of that verse makes the point even clearer: "Moreover we know that to those who love God, who are called according to his plan, everything that happens fits into a pattern for good."

So those who have faith in the God of the Bible can know that even if we don't get the miracle we are praying for, we can relax and trust that God is nonetheless leading us toward something through whatever it is we are enduring. That is an absolutely extraordinary concept, but if we believe that God can perform outrageous miracles, we should also be able to believe he can do that.

## ARE ALL MIRACLES FROM GOD?
## WHY SHOULD WE CARE?

Imagine that someone you love is deathly ill and another person you know offers to pray for healing. Does the identity of the deity to whom they pray matter? What if you learned that the dcity was a dark figure? What if the friend were to pray to the Prince of Darkness himself, and what if your friend said that the results were guaranteed, that your loved one would recover? It's tempting, but wouldn't a sane person be afraid to accept such a "gift" if that were really the source? Might not healing from this dark source come with serious consequences? We have all seen movies or know stories in which someone gets something extraordinary from the devil but must ultimately pay for it with his eternal soul. Don't we know there are some things not worth trading?

Even if we cannot believe in the existence of Satan, the concept is the same. If all we want is the gift—the miracle—and we couldn't care less who the giver is, we have not thought things through very well. If someone got what he wanted by doing the bidding of Adolf Hitler, what should we think of that person? If anyone were to give their loyalty to Hitler to get something in return, would not most people rightly regard that person as an immoral monster, who was in part responsible for all that Hitler did? Would that person not somehow partake of the evil of Hitler's deeds if they were to tacitly or openly assent to his doing something for them? Or can we shunt aside and ignore the sadistic horrors of the death camps if we get what we want?

We can consider the idea more broadly by asking whether it is immoral to accept a stolen car as a gift. If we do so, are we not complicit in the car's theft? Have we shielded ourselves from thinking about the person from whom the car was stolen? Do we not have a moral obligation to think about that person—and therefore an obligation to refuse the "gift"? Isn't it true that anything we get from a suspicious source isn't a gift at all but simply puts us in debt to the giver? If I accept a "gift" from a criminal, won't that criminal expect something from me in return? Am I prepared to give that?

The supernatural world is *not all good*. It is populated with angels and demons both. So to open oneself up to the supernatural realm without knowing exactly with whom we are communicating is not just foolish but also potentially extremely harmful. We have to admit that perhaps we don't know quite enough about the supernatural realm to gamble with it recklessly. If I am in touch with some supernatural power, I would do well to know just who wields that power and how they are ultimately disposed toward me. Are they giving me something to lure me down a path I would never take if I knew in advance where it was leading? We have to consider that if Satan exists, he is a supernatural being with the ability to use "miraculous" powers to deceive us. That's another good reason for us to be critical and careful and not to believe anything and everything.

We live in a culture that is for many reasons uncomfortable with speaking of evil or of Satan. One reason is that many people are embarrassed by the notion because it is often associated with the medieval idea of a red figure with hooves, horns, a tail, and a pitchfork. The Bible says nothing of anyone looking like that, but it does speak clearly of God's adversary, and the word "Satan" simply means "adversary." We have to be willing to separate such cartoonish notions from what actually exists. Even if we decide to reject this idea, let's be sure of what it is we are rejecting. Let's also be aware that many people we would regard as intelligent and sophisticated have taken the idea of a Satanic realm seriously. M. Scott Peck, who wrote the blockbuster bestseller *The Road Less Travelled*, also wrote a book titled *People of the Lie*. This Harvard psychiatrist did not take the idea of evil seriously either, until over the years he had encountered a number of patients in his practice whose behavior could not be explained in naturalistic terms. For anyone wishing a sober accounting of this subject, they would do well to start with that book.

## CAN PRAYER MAKE MIRACLES HAPPEN?

Even though prayers are not offered only to get a desired result, there is little doubt that most miracles are the result of prayer. God wants us to pray to him and ask him for things, just as any loving father and mother want their children to come to them with whatever is on their minds. But if our focus is solely on getting the outcome we want, the prayer will fail, precisely because our belief is placed in the wrong place. It's a great irony. If all we care about is the result, then we are effectively making that result our God, rather than God himself. So if we are praying to our "God"—the God of results—rather than to God himself, then we are praying to a "God" who is not God, and who is therefore powerless to help us.

Perhaps the best way to talk about this is to think about prayers for healing. How do *they* work, exactly? The shortest and most accurate answer to that question is *We don't know*. But we may indeed know something about how they work: For example, we can know something about the link between our thoughts and our prayers.

It is certainly possible that our mental ability to "visualize" a miraculous healing could have the ability to affect our body in a physical way. Though the link between one's mind and one's body is a deep mystery, we know there *is* a link. Someone who is relentlessly negative has a higher chance of falling ill than someone who is upbeat and positive. This does not mean that all illnesses are the result of our thoughts, but to deny any link whatever is to deny a great body of evidence. Honesty on this subject compels us to say that there is something there, but the details and the extent of that something are yet unknown to us.

Prayer obviously involves our thoughts, or certainly should. Whether we are speaking prayers out loud, or merely thinking them, our thoughts are meant to be engaged in our prayers. Even if we are praying prayers from a book or reciting a rote prayer, like the Lord's Prayer, we are supposed to be thinking them as we pray them, not just reading them or reciting them. We are not mynah birds or parrots. There's no magic in pronouncing the sounds in the phrase "Hallowed be thy Name" if we don't know what that phrase means. So our thoughts are vital to our prayers.

But there has been a tendency in recent decades to blur the line between prayer and thinking. One often hears the unfortunate sentence, *Our thoughts and prayers are with so-and-so.* Or we hear *We send our thoughts and prayers out to so-and-so.* What in the world do these statements mean? How exactly can our thoughts *be* with someone? Does this simply mean that we are thinking *about* them? But how can our *prayers* be with someone? Do we mean to say we are praying *for* them? Much more confusing is the idea that we can "send" our thoughts and prayers out to someone. We pray to God so that he might answer them. Why would we "send" our prayers to someone besides God?

It seems the reason people use this kind of elliptical and obtuse language is because they are confused about what prayer actually is. According to the biblical model, we pray to the God who is outside time and space, and that God reaches into time and space in answer. God is "outside the system" as we have said, and the miraculous is when he "reaches in" to our world from "out there," beyond this world. It's crucial we understand this. God created time and space but is *not* inside time or space and bound as we are. If someone has a narrowly materialistic view of the universe and believes there is nothing beyond time and space, their "thoughts and prayers" are hoping to get results from "within the closed system" of time and space.

Indeed, some believe that we are "gods" and partake of the divine in a way, so that we are essentially "praying" to ourselves or praying to the "collective unconscious," of which we are a part. But this is nothing like prayer to the God of the Bible who created the universe. Such people are really talking about using their own thoughts to provoke some kind of change or action, rather than appealing to a God—who is distinctly *other* and who is outside time and space.

We see this mistaken view manifested in roughly two ways, one we can call the "New Age Fallacy," and one we can call the "Religious Fallacy" or "Prosperity Gospel." Both of these fallacies trade on the idea of mentally visualizing what we want in such a way that we force "the universe" to make it appear. Both approaches believe they've found the hidden principles to the universe and have figured out how to make those principles work for them. Both look to us and our own efforts, rather than to God and what he would do for us out of his love for us.

The "New Age Fallacy" is what we find in things like Marianne Williamson's *A Course in Miracles* or *The Secret*. It's the idea that what we really need to do is get our thoughts in tune with the "universe" and good things will begin to come our way. But this is an idea that is bounded by time and space—that seeks answers from within the "universe." It does not bother with the God who created the universe and who is beyond the universe. It's about what is here inside time and space and how we can get it to work for us. It's about what we can accomplish if we only set our minds to it. It is not humbling ourselves before the creator of the universe, but about getting in tune with the universe itself, with "self-actualizing" and feeling "empowered."

But as we say, this is dramatically different from the historic and biblical view of prayer. According to the historic and biblical view of prayer, we pray to God, and God—not us or our positive thoughts or the "universe"—is the one who hears and answers prayer. The importance of the distinction between these two views of "prayer" cannot be overstated. To pray to the God outside time and space is different than simply thinking good thoughts or visualizing positive outcomes.

The "Religious Fallacy," while certainly invoking the name of God, nonetheless falls into a similar trap as the "New Age Fallacy." It puts all the emphasis on the faith of the person praying rather than on the God to whom the person is praying. This has also been called the "Prosperity Gospel," or "Name It and Claim It" teaching. It mustn't be denied that the faith of someone has some connection with the efficacy of that person's prayer. But if we push this idea too far, we end up believing that it is our faith that brings about the outcome. We think that if we can only believe strongly enough, we can make God hear our prayer and answer it.

Praying to God involves both us and God. God wants us to participate in what he is doing, and for sure one of the main ways we participate in what he is doing is by prayer. We can also participate in what he is doing by feeding the hungry and helping the poor and caring for the sick and giving of our resources to those who have little. God wants us to partner with him. So there is a paradox at work, and a mystery. On the one hand, the Bible says that apart from God we can do nothing. And yet, on the other hand, God invites us to do some things *with* him. This is at the heart of the mystery of prayer. God wants us to use our faith and to pray. But we can focus so much on the importance of our faith and our prayers that we forget about God and think it is our faith and our prayers that perform the miracle, rather than the God to whom we pray and in whom we have faith as we pray.

If we fall into that trap, we become convinced that if our prayer is not being answered as we would like it to be answered, it's because we aren't praying hard enough or long enough, or because our faith is simply weak. This puts far too much emphasis on our own role in whatever is happening or not happening. It will also inevitably lead to people saying that if you are sick and didn't get healed, it's because your faith wasn't strong enough. To blame the victim or the sufferer for his or her illness, and to suggest that if that person only had more faith and prayed harder, healing would follow is simply wrong. When I was in high school, I had a classmate who suffered from multiple sclerosis and over time she grew frailer and frailer. After our senior year she died. I knew that she and many were praying for her healing. But I also knew that some Christians were saying she was not healed because she did not have enough faith. This is bad theology.

Another version of the "Prosperity Gospel" or "Name It and Claim It" teaching has to do with finding a verse in the Bible and then "claiming" that verse. Proponents of this thinking believe that God *must* fulfill his promise to us in whatever verse we are "claiming" because what God says in his Word, the Bible, is true, and we can trust it to be true. So someone might pray: *God, your Word says in Isaiah that by your stripes we are healed and I know you are not a liar and that your Word is true and I claim that Scripture in Jesus's name and therefore I will be healed of this stomachache!* We need to have faith in what the Bible says, but we have to be careful that we aren't trying to force God to do what we want. That is arrogance rather than humility. God loves us, but we cannot demand things of him as though our faith is in charge rather than God.

If someone believes it is our faith that heals us

and forgets that it is God who does it, we should ask that person how much faith Lazarus had. Remember, he was decomposing in a tomb when Jesus raised him from death. His faith obviously didn't matter. It was all God. It is God and God's grace that heals, not our prayers and not our "faith." Though we are exhorted by God to pray to him, we cannot compel him to do what we wish.

## DO ALL CHRISTIANS BELIEVE IN MIRACLES?

In a word, no. Some Christians today, although holding to a conservative view of what the Bible says, nonetheless also hold to a doctrine called "dispensationalism," which essentially says that before the Bible was completed (around 90 A.D., when Saint John wrote the Book of Revelation), there was a particular need for miracles, so God gave us a special "dispensation" of the miraculous. But since then, now that God's Word exists in its complete and final form, we don't need miracles. As far as they are concerned, God doesn't need to reveal himself anyplace other than in the Bible, which is complete and sufficient. For these people, any "revelations" that go beyond reading the Bible are heretical and to be avoided and despised. As far as they are concerned, the Age of Miracles has been over for more than nineteen centuries.

But more typical of Christians who do not believe in miracles are those who hold to theologically liberal views of the Bible. These Christians do not subscribe to the dispensationalist view, which says that miracles happened up until the Bible was completed. They subscribe instead to the view that miracles actually never happened at all, including during Bible times. They are likely to try to find naturalistic explanations for Bible miracles, which we will touch on briefly in the next chapter. The difficulty with this view is that if all of the miracles in the Bible are explained naturalistically, we have to ask, *What in the Bible remains?* If we remove the idea of a supernatural God who is free to act in miraculous ways, we fall into the slough of despond inhabited by the scientistic naturalists. We essentially remove God himself from the Bible. Why anyone calling himself a Christian would feel the need to do this is complicated and mysterious, but much of this phenomenon seems to stem from embarrassment at being "out of step" with the wider secular culture. In other words, they have accepted the false view that pits "science" and "progress" against faith. Of course, tragically, in this desire to accommodate themselves to the surrounding culture, they have abandoned the very thing that can bring hope and healing to that culture.

## WHY IS IT SO HARD TO BELIEVE?

There are many reasons it is difficult to believe in miracles, but perhaps the principal difficulty in believing in anything has more to do with one's era and culture than with anything we might describe as "logical." We are inclined toward thinking that our objections to believing in something are "logical" objections, and therefore "objective" objections. But in truth our very ideas about logic and how one ought to come to conclusions about the nature of reality are informed by the usually unacknowledged presuppositions of the world in which we live. So the first step in trying to think about miracles is to see the presuppositions we bring to our thinking. This is itself difficult, perhaps because acknowledging them is a humbling project. Who wants to admit that we do not see clearly but through a cultural lens, darkly? Every culture and era flatters itself that we are finally seeing what previous eras and cultures could not see because of their own blinders and ideological lenses. To admit that we are in some sense no different from tenth-century peasants is unacceptable to most of us. It may be offensive. To accept it may take real courage.

Just because our ideological lenses are different—chronologically later and borne on more sophisticated "scientific" foundations—does not mean they are not ideological lenses. What is it about human pride that insists our generation is the one to finally see the unmediated and unadulterated truth? Cannot the utopianist horrors of the twentieth century (the War to End All Wars, the Maginot Line, the Gulag Archipelago, thalidomide) instruct us toward something like a greater humility? Wouldn't that be the wiser course?

Still, it's difficult. It seems self-evident that to reject all that is beyond the material world is the "scientific" way forward. But what if the evidence of science really does increasingly lead us to believe that perhaps there is something beyond the material world? Can we consider this? Or must we bow to the shibboleths of our culture, fearing scorn from people whose opinions mean so much to us? To believe in miracles in this day and age may require a real act of bravery. The hardest thing about opening oneself up to such beliefs is that it may reveal some unpleasant things about the people whose opinions we once took so seriously. But perhaps that is not such a bad thing, in the end.

# 7

## THE BIBLICAL MIRACLES

Then said Jesus unto him, Except ye see
signs and wonders, ye will not believe.
—JOHN 4:48

To speak of miracles without speaking of the
miracles in the Bible would certainly be odd, if
not perverse. Where but in the Bible should we
look for some template of what miracles are or
might be?

The most important point to be made about the
miracles of the New Testament in particular is
that they are all signs of things beyond themselves. Let's first consider the assumptions we
have when we think about miracles, whether from
the Bible or elsewhere. Most of us automatically
seem to divide miracle stories into those we
think plausible and possible and those we think
implausible and impossible—or perhaps even
ridiculous. If we accept that the God of the Bible
created the cosmos out of nothingness, we can
probably accept that he is capable of raising a
corpse to life or multiplying loaves and fishes.
Such things may strain our credulity, but they

don't seem to go beyond the limits of what most people would accept as within the realm of possibility for the creator of the universe. Sometimes, though, we hear miracle stories that for one reason or another simply do not seem right—but why don't they? The answer is that whether we are considering a work of art or a miracle story, each of us has an innate sense of limits and proportion, and this comes into play as we form our judgments.

## GOD CAN DO ANYTHING—BUT DOES HE?

Some years ago I translated a Grimms' fairy tale from the original German. It's titled "The Fisherman and His Wife" and is not written in the German of other Grimms' tales but in a dialect from Germany's northern coast, which makes sense since it's a story about a poor fisherman who catches a fish that can talk and grant wishes. But the fisherman's ill-tempered wife is never satisfied with what the fish grants them. After they get a big house, she complains that they should have one that's bigger still. She then demands a palace and wants to be queen, and then an even larger palace and wants to be emperor. Finally—reflecting the era in which the story originated—she demands that the fish make her pope, with power over all the kings and queens in western Christendom. But then came the difficulty for me. Because after the fish grants this wish, the woman is described as sitting on a throne "two miles" high. Before this detail, everything seemed to make sense. I had no difficulty accepting the outlandish idea of a talking flounder, or that it could grant wishes, but when I came to the detail of the throne's height, I balked. Something was amiss. But why could I accept everything else in the story but not this detail of the throne being two miles high? It simply seemed out of proportion, so I kept digging and eventually discovered a different, archaic definition of the German word "myle." That older meaning was not "mile," but rather "fathom," which is about six feet. So the throne, instead of being described as approximately ten thousand feet high, was actually being described as about twelve feet high. That was more like it. Somehow we intuitively sense what is within the logic and the limits of a story.

When we read the miracles of the New Testament, we bring this same instinct to the table. So for most readers, the healing miracles of Jesus don't especially strain our credulity, taken in context. Nor does turning water into wine. Nor even do the instances of his raising three people from the dead.[13] But when we come

––––––––––––––––––

13. Though not mentioned nearly as often, Jesus raised two others from the grave besides his friend Lazarus. They are the widow's son at Nain and the daughter of Jairus.

to something like Jesus walking on water, we cannot help but stop and wonder precisely how that was accomplished. It is somehow harder for the modern mind to comprehend or accept.

But once again reminding ourselves that God invented and created and sustains the endless reaches of the ever-expanding universe, that he created a reality whose surface the brightest humans only scratch when they explore the implications of quantum physics, can we not accept that if he were to be incarnated as a human being, he would be able to walk on water? If we accept that he can rise from the dead and that he afterward could appear and disappear as he pleased, passing through walls and then visibly ascending into the heavens, can we not accept that he has a relationship to the structure of matter that is necessarily different from the one the rest of us have?

But there are some miracle stories that are harder to accept, and with good reason. For example, in the apocryphal Gospel of Thomas, which is not in the Bible—and which the church and historians have always rejected as fictional and spurious—there is an account of the five-year-old Jesus fashioning sparrows from mud and then making them come to life and fly away. To most people, this sounds like an invention, but why is that? Why does it seem wrong in the way that a two-mile-high throne seems wrong in the context of that Grimms' fairy tale? How is it that we intuitively grasp that this anecdote is somehow different from the miracles attributed to the Jesus of the canonical Gospels?

Part of the reason is that most of us have read so many stories of so many kinds that we can sense which genre the story belongs to. This one invariably falls into the camp of stories in which fanciful miracles are attributed to saints, as in the story of Saint Patrick chasing all the snakes out of Ireland. We somehow know these things never actually happened, that they're just a bit of folklore and a bit of a tall tale. But there's more to our jaundiced view of this apocryphal childhood stunt. The idea of Jesus making sparrows from the mud also has something unmistakably show-offy about it, which is radically out of keeping with the character of Jesus we find in the rest of the Gospels. After all, what is the point of a five-year-old doing this if not simply to impress his friends on the playground? It seems to evoke the image of a crowd-pleasing tuxedoed magician more than it evokes the heroic and captivating Son of God we know from the pages of the New Testament.

Also, unlike other miracle stories, this one has the feeling of a cul-de-sac or appendix. Where does it mean to lead and what it is supposed to be saying to us on a deeper level? Every one of the real miracles attributed to Jesus is a sign pointing beyond the miracle itself. When Jesus brings sight to a blind man, he is signifying the idea that we are all spiritually blind and need God's help to see. He is also fulfilling the Old Testament prophecies about the Messiah. When he multiplies the loaves and fishes, he is doing something with many levels of meaning, the most fundamental of which is that he is feeding the hungry. But what exactly is the point of this playground sleight-of-hand involving sparrows? Even though we know God can do anything—and the Bible says "with God all things are possible"—we have a sense that Jesus simply wouldn't do this and didn't. It's out of character and somehow out of plumb, generally speaking.

God gave us common sense and he wants us to use our brains when we think about miracles. So it's a fact that even though we might believe that God *can* do anything, we know there are some things he *wouldn't* do. Some miracles would violate his character. But the idea that God has a character is itself interesting to consider. Many of us have an idea of what his character is like, but the question is where we got that idea from. Our ideas of who God is can often be formed by factors that have little to do with the God of the Bible. Some of us have an idea of God's character that we've cobbled together from bits and pieces of pop culture. Perhaps we think he's a bit like George Burns in the *Oh, God!* movies from the seventies. Or perhaps our idea of God comes from an overly severe and legalistic religious upbringing, or from the many portrayals of this kind of religiosity in TV and movies. Or perhaps we think God the Father is like our own fathers, who may not have been trustworthy or consistent or loving. So when we talk about God's character, the only standard to which we can consistently repair—and which is at all subjective—is the one we can see from the stories in the Old and New Testaments. These are the original sources, after all. So in keeping with this idea of God's character, when we hear any miracle stories, we want to evaluate them in part on whether they seem to fit with the character of the God of the Bible.

We know that unlike the gods in some stories from pagan folklore, the God of the Bible isn't a trickster or someone who "plays games" with us. For example, some people believe that the universe was created a few thousand years ago, but when confronted with geological evidence to the contrary, they respond that God "can do anything," including creating geological "evidence" that is deliberately misleading. When asked why, they say that he did that "to test our faith." Some have even maintained that God planted dinosaur bones in the rock strata for the same reason. Perhaps the single greatest difficulty with such arguments is that the character of this God of whom they speak is not consistent with the character of the God of the Bible. Jesus certainly never did anything intentionally misleading, nor does the Old Testament contain any examples of God misleading people along such lines. If you know the character of the God of the Bible, you are obliged to reject such ideas.

## THE GRACE OF GOD IN A FISH STORY

In chapter 17 of Matthew's Gospel, there is another story that stretches the boundaries of what seems possible and that speaks to us of God's character. It's the one in which Jesus tells Peter to pay the tax they owe by catching a fish, whose mouth will contain the necessary coin. Here is the passage:

> When they had come to Capernaum, those who received the temple tax came to Peter and said, "Does your Teacher not pay the temple tax?" He said, "Yes." And when he had come into the house, Jesus anticipated him, saying, "What do you think, Simon? From whom do the kings of the earth take customs or taxes, from their sons or from strangers?" Peter said to Him, "From strangers." Jesus said to him, "Then the sons are free. Nevertheless, lest we offend them, go to the sea, cast in a hook, and

take the fish that comes up first. And when you have opened its mouth, you will find a piece of money; take that and give it to them for Me and you."

Of all the miracles in the New Testament, this one is probably the quirkiest. What are we to make of it? To understand it properly, we need to look at the details.

The coin referred to in the passage is almost certainly a silver one-shekel coin, equal to two Alexandrine drachmas. We know the tax would have been one-half shekel per person, so the coin would have been precisely the right amount to pay for Jesus and for Peter. Speaking to the plausibility of this story, those who know something about fish can easily corroborate that if someone had dropped such a coin into the water by accident a fish might have quickly gobbled it, as fish often do when shiny things suddenly present themselves. Others have established that these fish—most likely what we now call tilapia—keep their young in their mouths for a time, and also pick up pebbles from the seafloor. Who can say what exactly was going on? But the detail that a fish had a silver coin in its mouth is not at all implausible. Nonetheless, the problem with "naturalistic" explanations is that they make the event seem plausible, while simultaneously "explaining it away," as though it weren't a miracle after all. In this case, however, that cannot be. Because even if we understand that a fish could have a silver coin in its mouth—and given Peter's years as a fisherman, he may even have seen such things many times—we still have to account for the further idea that Jesus tells Peter to go fishing, knowing that he will catch precisely that fish that has the coin in its mouth. Obviously that is the miracle. Of course, there's also the idea that Jesus would have known that the fish had the coin in its mouth in the first place. How could he know such things unless it were miraculously? The text makes plain that he did.

As with all the miracles Jesus does, there's more than meets the eye, and it is meant to point us to see something beyond the miracle itself. Certainly one of the most important aspects of this story is how it demonstrates a specific aspect of the character of Jesus, namely that of his unfailing graciousness. Jesus makes clear in what he says to Peter that they don't really need to pay the tax, but he says that they will do so anyway, "so that no one is offended." He wishes his disciples—and us—to understand that we must always go the proverbial "extra mile." We don't do what we are required to do; we do more. If we believe that God has given us much, we can well afford to give others more than is merely "just" or "deserved." God has been overgenerous with us, so we who are his blessed children should

137

also be overgenerous. God himself never gives what is our just deserts but rather gives out of the superabundance of grace, and so should we.

This idea of grace and generosity and unforced self-giving is at the heart of the New Testament idea of agape love and in the tiny detail of this story we see it once again. The most important and central illustration of this idea is, of course, in Jesus's death on the cross, where he sacrifices himself for others out of love, and not because we deserve this sacrifice. It is this grace that humbles us and makes us grateful to him, if we understand the situation. He didn't need to do what he did, but he did it anyway, not because we deserve it but because he loves us. To anyone not disposed to accept such a humbling gift, this idea is of course grating and off-putting, even offensive.

But Jesus always calls his followers well beyond the justice of "an eye for an eye; and a tooth for a tooth" and into this realm of agape love—of generous, gracious, selfless giving, borne out of the superabundance of a relationship with God. We even see this at the dawn of Jesus's public ministry, when he goes to the Jordan to be baptized by his cousin John the Baptist. If Jesus was the sinless Son of God, he certainly didn't need to be baptized, to have his sins forgiven and symbolically washed away. But Jesus wanted to identify publicly with the rest of us, who do need to be baptized and cleansed. He comes down among us not only by leaving the glory of Heaven to come to Earth but also by publicly entering the waters of baptism, humbling himself publicly. Jesus illustrates the same thing when he does the job of the lowest slave by washing the feet of his disciples. He over and over humbles himself in this way to show that if we want to be like him, we need to humble ourselves too. Paying the temple tax with the silver coin is one small example of that. So this detail makes this story consonant with the character of Jesus and with the rest of the New Testament stories, especially with his teaching that we love our enemies, that we walk the "extra mile," and "turn the other cheek."

It even links us to the famous story of the woman at the well, which gives us a visual image of the radical superabundance of God. In that story, Jesus talks with a woman who is all alone at a well, drawing water in the middle of the day. It is believed that she was somehow a woman of ill repute and was therefore there alone at a time atypical for drawing water. Jesus tells her that what he offers her is not just the cup of water we need to quench our thirst but a veritable gushing fountain that will overwhelm us with more than we can ever ask for or think about. He is not a utilitarian God, stingily parsing out the minimum we need for our sustenance. He is a God whose love and resources are boundless and who wants to shower us with them.

> Whoever drinks of this water will thirst again, but whoever drinks of the water that I shall give him will never thirst. But the water that I shall give him will become in him a fountain of water springing up into everlasting life. (John 4:13–14)

## THE FEEDING OF THE FIVE THOUSAND

The well-known miracle of the loaves and fishes illustrates the same principle of God's superabundant grace. It also illustrates the larger idea that each one of these miracles—or signs—Jesus did was meant to signify much else, and to point the people present—and us—to God himself.

Before Jesus performed this miracle, he had just heard of the beheading of his cousin John the Baptist by the evil Herod. He enters the scene filled with grief.

> When Jesus heard [the news], He departed from there by boat to a deserted place by Himself. But when the multitudes heard it, they followed Him on foot from the cities. And when Jesus went out He saw a great multitude . . .

Jesus is plainly in no mood to be overwhelmed with crowds of people desperate for his attention. He wants to be alone with his disciples, to grieve over the murder of his beloved cousin, who was not merely his cousin but who in Jesus's estimation was the greatest prophet of God who had ever lived. That the evil Herod had beheaded John to satisfy the whim of the woman with whom he was committing adultery—or her daughter—must have been overwhelmingly painful. But the innumerable miracles he had been doing had so captured the attention and imagination of people that by now literally thousands were moving through the countryside in the hopes of getting a glimpse of him, and then when he got out of the boat, heavyhearted and fatigued, he saw that this multitude of humanity had intercepted him. So the text says that despite his grief and all-too-human fatigue, he "had compassion on them and healed their sick."

We are often so familiar with what the Bible says that we skip past words and miss their meaning entirely. That Jesus "had compassion on them and healed their sick" is a staggering sentence, magnificent in its understatement. Jesus got out of the boat to see many thousands awaiting him. There was a wild desperation among them and Jesus was filled with compassion. But the verse says that "he healed their sick." A few verses later we see that there were five thousand men in the crowd, which means that there were probably fifteen or twenty thousand people in total. Many of them had traveled there specifically because they believed Jesus could heal "their sick," whom they had brought along, and in many cases had literally "carried" to this remote place. So when the text simply reads "he healed their sick," can we imagine how many miracles actually took place that day? It is likely that it was well into the hundreds, yet not a single one of them is mentioned in the Gospel accounts. We have a picture here again of the superabundance of God, and of the outrageous generosity of Jesus. The writers of the Gospels didn't feel the need to mention any of these healing miracles specifically, focusing only on the ultimate miracle of the multiplied loaves and fishes. In John's Gospel (21:25), using hyperbole to make the larger point, John writes, "Jesus did many other things as well. If every one of them were written down, I suppose that even the whole world would not have room for the books that would be written."

It is only after performing perhaps hundreds of miracles that we arrive at the miracle of the loaves and fishes:

> When it was evening, His disciples came to Him, saying, "This is a deserted place, and the hour is already late. Send the multitudes away, that they may go into the

villages and buy themselves food." But Jesus said to them, "They do not need to go away. You give them something to eat." And they said to Him, "We have here only five loaves and two fish." He said, "Bring them here to Me." Then He commanded the multitudes to sit down on the grass. And He took the five loaves and the two fish, and looking up to hcaven, He blessed and broke and gave the loaves to the disciples; and the disciples gave to the multitudes. So they all ate and were filled, and they took up twelve baskets full of the fragments that remained. Now those who had eaten were about five thousand men, besides women and children.

Before we can appreciate the richness of this great miracle, we should first strain out the gnat of an idea that this was not a miracle at all but merely an example of Jesus inspiring the stingy crowds to share with each other. That might sound funny, especially if you've never heard it before, but many have heard sermons along these lines, so it's worth explaining why this interpretation ignores the facts and must itself be ignored.

The notion that what really happened that day was a "miracle of sharing" maintains that in reality there was plenty of food but that people were selfishly hiding it from each other, until

Jesus somehow inspired or guilt-tripped everyone into sharing what they had, thus solving the problem. If our goal is to explain away the miracle with another "naturalistic explanation," or to promote communism, this interpretation does the job nicely. But if we wish actually to understand the passage, it simply won't do. In fact, this interpretation unravels with a single verse from Matthew's Gospel (15:32), where Jesus says: "I have compassion on the crowd, because they have been with me now three days, and have nothing to eat; and I am unwilling to send them away hungry, lest they faint on the way." Was Jesus kidding or playing games when he said that? What is there that would allow us to believe these people actually were hiding food? For sure, these were desperate people who had been following Jesus around the countryside, who now had been camped out for three days, being healed and hearing his teaching, and evidently giving little thought to their bodily needs. Jesus knows they have no food left and his disciples know it too. What other interpretation can we take away without willfully doing damage to the text?

In John's account of the story, Jesus asks Andrew: "Where shall we buy bread, that these may eat?" Jesus often asked rhetorical questions to make a point. He knew very well that it would cost infinitely more money than any of them had to feed this vast multitude. He also knew what he was about to do to feed them. So the disciples, discerning the problem, come to Jesus and essentially tell him that he must tell the crowds that the show is over, that they must now go away and take care of their bodily needs, because Jesus and his disciples simply didn't have the cash on hand to buy the food that would be needed.

But this is precisely when Jesus makes plain that the show is not over, that everything has been preamble to what he is about to do. The miracle of feeding the five thousand is the culmination of all that has gone before and it signifies a number of important things.

First, it communicates that Jesus's heavenly father cares about people's physical needs, not just their "spiritual needs." Just as he has compassion on the sick and heals them, he has compassion on the hungry and feeds them. He is not a God of disembodied spirits, but of flesh-and-blood human beings, and just as Jesus in his resurrected body ate food and made plain that he was not a ghost, so Jesus in this miracle makes plain that feeding hungry people is something that God takes seriously.

Second, Jesus once again gives us a picture of the superabundance of God. He is not a utilitarian God who only gives everyone what we need. After everyone is fully satisfied there are twelve large baskets left over. He wants to overwhelm us with the blessings of Heaven.

A third point being made in this great miracle of "multiplication" requires that we remember what most people present would have known, namely the other miracles of multiplication in their Scriptures. Many of them in witnessing Jesus's miracle would have instantly recalled that the prophet Elisha had famously multiplied olive oil, as recounted in 1 Kings 4–17. As that story goes, a widow who was in debt had only a single jar of oil. Elisha asks for it and then proceeds to fill jar after jar with oil, which is then used to pay her great debt. Later in the same chapter he miraculously multiplies twenty barley loaves to feed one hundred men. The text itself is similar to the account of Jesus feeding the five thousand.

Then a man came from Baal Shalisha, and brought the man of God bread of the firstfruits, twenty loaves of barley bread, and newly ripened grain in his knapsack. And he said, "Give it to the people, that they may eat." But his servant said, "What? Shall I set this before one hundred men?" He said again, "Give it to the people, that they may eat; for thus says the Lord: 'They shall eat and have some left over.'" So he set it before them; and they ate and had some left over, according to the word of the Lord.

Those present would have understood that what Jesus did was like what Elisha had done, but dramatically superior, since many thousands were fed. This miracle would have indicated to them that he was a prophet of God, like the great Elisha, but they would have also understood that he was something far beyond Elisha.

The fourth point being made concerns another parallel. The Jews knew that one day a Messiah would come who was like Moses. They of course knew that Moses had fed the multitudes in the wilderness with manna, which appeared miraculously every morning and which was called "the bread of Heaven." So what Jesus did that day would have explicitly reminded people of what Moses had done and would have linked him in their minds to Moses.

The fifth point Jesus makes in this miracle is one that would have been lost on all present, but it would not be lost on anyone familiar with what he later did at the Last Supper. Jesus's praying and breaking the bread that day amid the vast multitudes was a prefigurement and a foreshadowing of his breaking the bread in the Upper Room, which in turn was a prefigurement of Jesus's body being broken on the cross and through Communion being shared through the centuries with all generations.

Finally, the number of baskets left over—twelve—is almost certainly intended to remind us of the twelve tribes of Israel and of the twelve Disciples, who by being the first followers of Jesus represented the "church" of all his followers through history, and who were meant to be the "new Israel."

So the story of Jesus feeding the five thousand, like all of his other miracles, is not a nice "naturalistic" story about sharing our food, nor is it a mere magic trick performed by a sorcerer to delight and impress. It is rather first and foremost a sign pointing beyond itself to the identity of the one behind it and behind all other miracles. Like every miracle that ever was, it is a sign from beyond this world, pointing us to the God beyond this world, to the God who came into this world to lead us back to himself and who is himself the way back.

## LAZARUS RAISED FROM THE DEAD

The story of Jesus raising Lazarus from the dead is in many ways a miracle of miracles. It gives us a picture of God entering and acting in our world in a kind of unadulterated way, in a way that is as simple and unmistakeable and dramatic as anything within the pages of Scripture. The story is regarded by most Bible scholars as the very culmination of all Jesus's miracles in the New Testament. Everything that has gone before builds to this scene, which takes place just before the end—before Jesus's entrance into Jerusalem amid shouts of acclamation and before his death on the cross a few days later.

To understand the significance of this miracle, we have to understand the context in which it takes place. First of all, we must remember that Jesus was very close with Lazarus, and with his sisters, Mary and Martha. So when Lazarus became very ill, his sisters immediately sent word to Jesus, believing he would swiftly come and heal their brother. Jesus was many miles away at this time, but when he finally received word of Lazarus's illness, he said, "This sickness will not end in death. No, it is for God's glory so that God's Son may be glorified through it." The disciples, when they heard this, assumed that Jesus knew Lazarus would not die (but of course they didn't understand this fully), so they didn't try to push him to go to Lazarus right away. They assumed he had the timing of it all under control, which of course he did. Jesus did not hurry to Lazarus but remained where he was for two more days. It is, of course, clear in retrospect that Jesus knew Lazarus would indeed die, and that Lazarus's death would give him the opportunity to perform the greatest of all his miracles and to glorify God more powerfully than he had yet done.

So two days after he learned that Lazarus was sick, Jesus decided it was time to go to Bethany, the village where Mary, Martha, and Lazarus lived, less than two miles from Jerusalem. His disciples knew that the chief priests in Jerusalem had been threatening Jesus with death, so they were worried that he should go near Jerusalem. But Jesus was not worried, although he knew what he was about to do would only infuriate the chief priests all the more.

As he began the journey, Jesus made things plain to his disciples: "Lazarus is dead, and for your sake I am glad I was not there, so that you may believe." Jesus knew that this would be more powerful than all that had gone before. It would dramatically build the faith of his disciples, and many who did not yet believe in him would come to believe in him as a result of what was about to occur.

When Jesus arrived in Bethany, he heard that Lazarus had already been in the tomb for four days. There was a Jewish belief that the soul stayed near the body for three days, so this detail that he had been in the tomb for four days made it clear that there was no possibility of anything like mere resuscitation. The other two people Jesus raised from the dead had been dead for a very short time: The son of the widow of Nain was being carried from his house, having presumably died, and Jairus's daughter died a few hours or perhaps even mere moments before Jesus arrived. But Lazarus had been lying in the tomb for four days and was by now decomposing. His sisters had hoped Jesus would return in time to heal their brother. They also knew that Jesus had raised two others from the dead, so even after Lazarus had died they likely still had faith that Jesus might arrive in time to restore him to life. But now that he had been in the tomb for four days, they had almost certainly given up any such hope.

When Jesus met Martha, he told her, "Your brother will rise again," and she replied, "I know he will rise again in the resurrection at the last day." But Jesus had not gone there to remind them of what they already knew. He had gone there to show them something new, something that would startle them like a thunderbolt. He had come to reveal to them and to the world the unbridled, unfathomable power of God.

In this conversation with Martha, Jesus made a truly staggering statement. He said: "I am the resurrection and the life." Such words are either sheer unparalleled hubris or they are madness—unless they are true. He then said: "The one who believes in me will live, even though they die; and whoever lives by believing in me will never die. Do you believe this?"

The reason that those who believe in him will never die is because Jesus is himself the source of life. He is the one who created the universe and who created life. Although the disciples and Mary and Martha believed he was the Messiah, they did not yet seem to have grasped that their friend was the creator of the universe and the source of life itself. But as he approached the end of his days on Earth, it was time to reveal these things, to speak them and to demonstrate them.

But first we would see the other pole of who he is. We would see the humble humanity of Jesus when—seeing his friends and others weeping— Jesus himself wept. The verse is two words: "Jesus wept."[14] These words show that the one who is life itself is not some impersonal energy force but a person, one whose heart breaks for the sadness of his friends, and one who was likely also weeping at the power that death still has in the broken world he has come to restore to wholeness.

Even as Jesus approached the tomb, he was riven with emotion. The text says he was "once more deeply moved." But then he did what he had come to do. "Take away the stone," he said. Martha protested, saying, "[B]y this time there is a bad odor, for he has been there four days."

Jesus said, "Did I not tell you that if you believe, you will see the glory of God?" They took away the vast stone from the front of the tomb and Jesus then prayed loudly: "Father, I thank you that you have heard me. I knew that

---

14. Of the 31,102 verses in the Bible, it is the shortest.

you always hear me, but I said this for the benefit of the people standing here, that they may believe that you sent me." He did not want the meaning of what he was about to do to be missed. As with all miracles, it was what God was communicating through the miracle that was most important. So this was not merely about restoring his beloved friend Lazarus to life; it was about revealing his true identity such that many will come to bclicve in him, and it was their belief in him that would restore all of them to true life as well.

"Lazarus, come out!" he cried. It is a strange thing to command a corpse. But this is the one who had cursed a fig tree. This is the one who had rebuked the boisterous wind and waves, saying to them, "Peace, be still!" We recall that the fig tree withered and the wind and the waves obeyed him—and now we see Lazarus too obeying the creator of the universe. In a moment, he came out of his tomb, alive and still wrapped in his grave clothes.

Because Bethany was so close to Jerusalem, there were many mourners present that day to witness Lazarus emerge from his tomb. All who saw it must have become unhinged. Who can imagine what one would think in seeing someone dead four days obey the command to leave death and the darkness of the tomb for life and the light of day? We know that it was Jesus's intention to show forth the power and the glory of God, and we know that he knew what would be the result. He knew that those who saw it would tell everyone they encountered, that the news of this miracle would spread like wildfire and would ignite passionate faith in many. But he also knew that the religious leaders would now be so infuriated that they would know they must kill Jesus. Amazingly, the word of this event led so many to believe in Jesus that the religious leaders even planned to kill Lazarus.

The miracle of Lazarus's resurrection illustrates a number of things, the first perhaps being the simple existence of evil. How can it be that when Jesus raises a man to life, the religious leaders should seethe with anger? What good person could fail to rejoice that a young man dead four days had returned to life? But we know that these men were thinking only of their own power, which was gravely threatened. They had allowed themselves to be blinded by their own power and were not thinking about God and about life, but about themselves, and the logical culmination of such thinking ends in murderous thoughts, in evil acts.

The second is that God really does perform miracles to communicate with us. Jesus wanted to demonstrate God's power specifically so that people might see who he really was and come to believe in him. Even though he did what he did out of compassion and love for Lazarus and his sisters, nonetheless he said to his disciples, "[F]or your sake I am glad I was not there, so that you might believe." If Jesus were interested only in keeping his friend Lazarus alive, he could have returned early and healed him. Or he could have returned slightly later and raised him from the dead an hour after he had died. But Jesus waited deliberately. He wanted to magnify the effect of the miracle so that it would point people to him as the Messiah and so that God would be glorified.

This leads to the third point: that for God to be glorified, it sometimes means first allowing something unpleasant to transpire. Jesus could have saved Lazarus from dying, or could have raised him from the dead immediately, but he did not. In a sense this miracle shows us that we can trust God, and if we do trust him he might take us on the long and difficult road, but it's only to bless us the more in the long run. So we must consider the implications of this. Can it be that God allows us to go through things specifically so that we have an opportunity to trust him and then to see him do something we wouldn't have expected, something beautiful and extraordinary that wouldn't have been possible if we had had our prayers answered when and how we wanted them to be answered? If this is true, wouldn't it follow that any difficulty we encounter is an opportunity to trust God, to see how he might bring something glorious out of our trial?

Wouldn't it also follow that if we did not look to God in our difficulty we would be missing the opportunity to see him do something more wonderful than merely taking away the difficulty? Or perhaps it tells us that if we really know who God is, we will want to trust him, and we will allow him to bring us into difficulties or suffering, knowing that if we let him, he will use these things to bless us and to do something beautiful that wouldn't have been possible otherwise.

The story of Lazarus—because it is a picture of starkest contrasts—gives us a picture of what all true miracles really are: God acting alone, without our help. Lazarus did absolutely nothing to cooperate with Jesus. He was as inert and passive as a stone. As a corpse. As such, he was by definition incapable of helping. Lazarus did not have the ability to "exercise his faith" or "trust in Jesus" or "believe." Because the text says he had been in the tomb for four days, we are not even given the luxury of supposing that his "spirit" was hovering nearby and only reentered his body as we might have supposed with the other two whom Jesus raises to life. Here in the final days of Jesus's life and ministry he gives us an unadulterated picture of what a miracle is: God acting from beyond this world. We see clearly that it is all God and all God's grace. This in turn gives us a clear picture of our spiritual condition:

*We are spiritually dead.* Apart from God and the spiritual life that God imparts to us, we have no life. We are not merely spiritually sick and in need of God's healing. We are spiritual corpses who need the resurrection life that only God can give us. We cannot give it to ourselves and we cannot even help God give it to us. It is a picture of our total and abject dependence on God.

This miracle shows us what we talked about in chapter 4: God is the reason for life. We see it in Jesus's raising of Lazarus, but it is presaged in his superlatively powerful declaration, "I am the resurrection and the life," which, in a way, is a chilling statement. Can we believe that this dear soul who loved his friends and who wept when they wept is the same one who created the moon and the sun and the stars? Jesus declares that he is "the resurrection and the life" and then he demonstrates it by raising a four-day-old corpse to breathing, walking, conscious life. In raising Lazarus from the dead, Jesus wanted all to see the thing that it seems no one had yet seen: that he was God, the very author of life. Once we can fathom this, we not only think of Jesus differently, we think of life differently as well. When we see trees bursting into leaf and when we see eggs hatching to produce birds that fly through the sky, we think of him, the man weeping by his friend's tomb. The miracle of Lazarus is God's way of forcing us to see that apart from this Jesus, there is no life. He—that humble man who would die a horrible death in a short time—is the one who spoke the world and life into being and who has sustained it ever since and sustains it now.

# 8

## THE RESURRECTION

Death, be not proud, though some have called thee
Mighty and dreadful, for thou art not so;
For those whom thou think'st thou dost overthrow
Die not, poor Death, nor yet canst thou kill me.
From rest and sleep, which but thy pictures be,
Much pleasure; then from thee much more must flow,
And soonest our best men with thee do go,
Rest of their bones, and soul's delivery.
Thou art slave to fate, chance, kings, and desperate men,
And dost with poison, war, and sickness dwell,
And poppy or charms can make us sleep as well
And better than thy stroke; why swell'st thou then?

One short sleep past, we wake eternally
And death shall be no more; Death, thou
shalt die.

—JOHN DONNE

The great English poet John Donne, in his
famous poem, declares what Christians have
always believed: that Death was murdered in a
tomb, and that Death and the tomb can hold us no
more. Donne doesn't refer specifically to that
tomb because he doesn't need to. As an English
bishop, it is what he and what all Christians have
believed, that the resurrection of Jesus opened the
door, leading the way from that tomb and death to
freedom and eternal life. Even though Death still
lingered through the centuries, it ultimately died.
Even though each of us will die, we may now all
live again, forever. This belief has informed
Western civilization for nearly twenty centuries,
but it is a belief that is so radical it can easily be
taken for granted, can be ignored as metaphorical,
as something akin to saying that each spring
brings new life, or that "life springs eternal." But
we mustn't take it for granted. The death of Death
is not about the recurring cycle of spring. On the
contrary, if the resurrection happened, it is that
event—simultaneously historical and mythical—
of which the recurring cycle of spring itself is a
mere shadow and type.

The real defeat of Death hangs on an event as

implausible as anything imaginable: In a hewn rock tomb just outside Jerusalem, the cosmos itself—and not just the material cosmos, but the temporal universe too, which is to say space and time both—pivoted and reversed course, undoing the curse of Death that had been upon us since the Garden of Eden. Is this a beautiful myth, or did something miraculous literally happen?

How is it possible that a human being that has really and truly died—that has become an inert corpse, with all the attendant unpleasant attributes of congealed bodily fluids and rigor mortis— could reverse course and again become a living, breathing, walking, talking, and eating human being? There can be no question that it's impossible, so for it to happen would require no small miracle.

## THE CENTRALITY OF THE RESURRECTION

The claim that this happened is not merely important to the Christian faith, it is superlatively central and crucial. According to the apostle Paul, if it did not actually happen, there is nothing more to discuss of Christianity at all. What Paul said was that if Christ was not actually and literally raised from the dead, Christian faith is useless. If that did not happen, our sins cannot be for-given and washed away, so the central idea of Christian faith, that Jesus's death and resurrection fundamentally transforms and redeems each of us who put our faith in him, evaporates. If he did not rise from the dead, we do not rise from the dead—and Death wins. In fact, Paul pointedly says that if Jesus did not rise from the dead, "[W]e are of all people most to be pitied."

Some scholars in the last century or so seem to have missed or discounted the passage where Paul makes this so explicitly clear. They seem to want to say, *Er, um . . . let's not be so hasty. We can work with this. If Jesus did not literally rise from the dead—because science is now advanced enough to tell us that none of these things could have happened—all is not lost! On the contrary, let's see what we might salvage from this wreck.* They would then talk movingly of how Jesus had not risen bodily but had risen *spiritually,* whatever that might mean. They would say he had risen "in the hearts of his disciples"! But this is nothing more than a rhetorical dodge and a linguistic fudge; it is, practically speaking, meaningless. It's as though I would say to my wife, *Let me help you with those heavy packages—metaphorically speaking.* Or as though I would tell my landlord, *The rent check is in the mail. Spiritually speaking.* Or as though I would say to my daughter, *I love you so much I would die for you. Figuratively speaking!*

So how can scholars say such things? It is no great mystery. From where they are, they have no choice. They are materialists who have dismissed the very idea of a literal resurrection, and with it every other kind of bona fide miracle. But in overemphasizing the materialistic world and dismissing the idea of anything supernatural, they ironically inflate metaphor beyond the bursting point. They say that this cannot happen literally, because all there is is the natural, materialistic world. So to somehow get beyond the material world without *literally* getting beyond it, we will just put all of our supernatural eggs in a *metaphorical basket.* They will simply take all of that stuff that we think of as unreal—because we have arbitrarily limited reality to our physical and natural and sensory reality—and put it in a basket that exists only *in our minds,* which is actually not real, but which we will inflate to the point of a *kind of* reality. We will do an end run around our circumscribed definition of reality and voilà, we will square the circle. But this too they have only done in their minds. Their circle is still as circular as ever it was.

But it seems clear from what he writes that Paul has somehow heard this all before, centuries ahead of his time. So he has definitively pre-empted this kind of thinking with that famous passage. And the Church Fathers and the Church itself in its councils has ratified his thinking as canonical. There is no escape. It's all or nothing. Christians do not have the option of hedging their bets on this one. Our entire belief is predicated on this miracle. We can ignore what Paul wrote or try to marginalize it somehow, but if we do that, we marginalize ourselves from the great river of Christian thought over the last two millennia. We claim a tiny tributary as the "true river" and paddle alone into a swamp.

In looking at Paul's famous passage, we see that Paul not only says what he says, but he then underscores it dramatically by teasing out the fatal implications of it. He seals the gate and then double and triple seals it. He says if Jesus did not rise from the dead we are left with precisely nothing, and less than nothing, because not only wouldn't we have no forgiveness of sins or anything else, we would be the most pitied of all people in the world; we would be pathetic. He is saying that if Jesus did not rise bodily from the dead we are far worse off than pagans and nonbelievers.

What Paul does in that passage is like what Elijah does in the Second Book of Kings. Elijah has a kind of contest with the priests of Baal, in which they both build piles of wood and then ask their respective gods to light it on fire, except Elijah pours gallons and gallons of water on his pile, as if to say, *If God is God, I think that not only can he light wood on fire, he can light it on fire if it's soaking wet.* Which of course God does. It's an effort to underscore things, to raise the stakes dramatically, and that is precisely what

Paul is doing in that passage. He's saying we cannot have it both ways. Either Jesus rose bodily from the dead or he didn't, and if he didn't we lose everything—and then some. So let's not kid ourselves.

If someone says that the miracle of the resurrection doesn't matter, remember that Paul says that it matters more than anything; and two thousand years of the Church has said the same. If someone tells us that Jesus "rose in the hearts of the disciples," we are obliged to smile and say, that's a nice idea, but unfortunately it cannot work. It's a fundamental contradiction of what Paul and all Christians have been saying since the first century.

So that's the biggest question: Did this miracle *really* happen?

Before we answer that, here is John Updike's wonderful poem "Seven Stanzas at Easter," in which he makes the same point:

> Make no mistake: if he rose at all
> It was as His body;
> If the cell's dissolution did not reverse,
>     the molecule reknit,
> The amino acids rekindle,
> The Church will fall.
>
> It was not as the flowers,
> Each soft spring recurrent;

It was not as His Spirit in the mouths and
   fuddled eyes of the
Eleven apostles;
It was as His flesh; ours.

The same hinged thumbs and toes
The same valved heart
That-pierced-died, withered, paused, and
   then regathered
Out of enduring Might
New strength to enclose.

Let us not mock God with metaphor,
Analogy, sidestepping, transcendence,
Making of the event a parable, a sign
   painted in the faded
Credulity of earlier ages:
Let us walk through the door.

The stone is rolled back, not papier-mache,
Not a stone in a story,
But the vast rock of materiality that in
   the slow grinding of
Time will eclipse for each of us
The wide light of day.

And if we have an angel at the tomb,
Make it a real angel,
Weighty with Max Planck's quanta, vivid
   with hair, opaque in

The dawn light, robed in real linen
Spun on a definite loom.

Let us not seek to make it less
   monstrous,
For our own convenience, our own sense
   of beauty,
Lest, awakened in one unthinkable hour,
   we are embarrassed
By the miracle,
And crushed by remonstrance.

## DID THE RESURRECTION REALLY HAPPEN?

The idea that there is enough evidence to make an informed decision on something as outrageous and as long ago as the resurrection of Jesus from the grave is itself startling and hard to believe. Many persons (this author was one of them) believe that we can never know much more about it than about where Adam and Eve are buried or whether Cain and Abel had freckles, or what Noah's voice sounded like. But the life and death of Jesus took place well within historical times, which these other things certainly did not. The *Iliad* and *Odyssey* were written seven centuries earlier. The complex and brilliant plays of Euripides, Sophocles, and Aeschylus were written more than four centuries earlier and all we know of Alexander the Great and Aristotle and

Socrates happened centuries before Jesus's birth.

We know so much about what happened in Jesus's time—about the Roman Empire and about what took place in Palestine during the Roman occupation and about Jewish life and customs in that time and place—that while we may not have a surfeit of knowledge and evidence, we've at least got a hatful. So let's see if we can determine whether this miracle of miracles probably happened or probably didn't happen—or whether it's truly impossible to say.

We should begin by simply citing the great controversies and arguments that swirled around this epic event in the reign of Pontius Pilate. From these alone it's clear that Jesus really lived and was crucified and laid in a tomb and that on the third day, that tomb was found to be empty. On those points there is almost zero doubt. The doubt only comes in on how Jesus left the tomb. Our only two options in answering that are whether he left the tomb through resurrection or other, less dramatic means.

## DID SOMEONE STEAL JESUS'S BODY?

At the time that these events happened, there was a fierce contingent who insisted that Jesus's disciples had stolen his body. Others claimed that the Romans had stolen it. Still others said that the Jewish religious leaders who had opposed Jesus had stolen his body. It's very easy to make these claims. It's even easier to simply say that the body was stolen, because in using the passive voice, one's attentions are focused on the verb of "stealing" and distracted from the subject of "who." Because when we home in on that, the idea that his body was stolen becomes dramatically less plausible.

So let's examine each of the proposed thieves in turn, beginning with the idea that it was the Romans who took the body from the tomb. They would have been the only ones able to actually do it. Who else would get past the armed guards stationed outside the tomb? To appreciate what was at stake here, we should understand something of what this tomb was like and who was guarding it. Here is the passage from the Gospel of Matthew:

> On the next day, which followed the Day of Preparation, the chief priests and Pharisees gathered together to Pilate, saying, "Sir, we remember, while he was still alive, how that deceiver said, 'After three days I will rise.' Therefore command that the tomb be made secure until the third day, lest his disciples come by night and steal him away, and say to the people, 'He has risen from the dead.' So the last deception will be worse than the first."

Pilate said to them, "You have a guard; go your way, make it as secure as you know how." So they went and made the tomb secure, sealing the stone and setting a guard.

In the Roman world, "sealing the stone" was something done officially, with the full force of Roman law. Once the giant wheel of stone had been put in place, covering the mouth of the tomb, the Roman soldiers put a cord across it with an official wax seal bearing the imperial Roman mark. There would have been official, legal witnesses to this. This seal was infinitely more forbidding than the plastic yellow tape that reads: POLICE LINE. DO NOT CROSS. It was also more forbidding than the vast stone wheel sealing the tomb. This is because anyone daring to break a Roman seal would risk death. It would be like spitting at an image of Caesar. Besides this imperial seal, there was a Roman guard, which does not mean there was a single guard but rather an official number of sixteen, four of whom would stand for the duration of their shift, with the remaining twelve sitting in a semicircle around the four.

That anyone would be able to get past these sixteen armed soldiers to roll away the massy stone and steal the body is preposterous. Some have said that perhaps the guards were bribed, but can we imagine it never occurred to the Roman authorities that guards might be bribed? Human nature has not changed in two millennia. The Roman authorities well knew such temptations existed, so if a guard in such a position were discovered or even thought to have taken a bribe, he would have been put to death in a gruesome fashion: by being crucified upside down or by being set aflame in his own clothing. If a policeman in our world takes a bribe, there will be a trial and he might lose his job and perhaps go to prison for some time, but he will not be put to death. But Roman soldiers knew death was nearly certain if they failed in their duties, and were mightily disinclined to take a bribe. Even the most beef-witted of them understood that money could not be enjoyed by the dead.

But besides asking *whether* someone might steal the body, we have to ask *why*. What might be their various motives?

## MOTIVES FOR STEALING THE BODY

Starting with the Romans, we know that their reason for consenting to have Jesus executed was to quell the unrest that was always threatening to explode among the Jews in Jerusalem. At Passover, this threat was dramatically increased, so if throwing a sop to the Jewish religious leaders by executing this popular upstart would give them a way to keep their people in check, why not do it? But they knew that if the body were to be stolen, it would be far worse than if Jesus had not been executed in the first place, so they took every precaution to prevent its being stolen. To understand the extent of these precautions is to know the idea of theft is too flimsy to take seriously.

But for argument's sake, we may imagine that by some unforeseen and unimaginable fluke the body could have been taken. We already know the Romans had no motive to do this, so what might be the motives of our other two candidates for this theft?

The Jewish religious leaders were in the same position as the Romans. For them, keeping Jesus dead was the very point of going to the considerable trouble of having him killed. Proving that he was not the Messiah, and proving that his disciples were religious nuts unhinged by the patently ridiculous idea that their Lord would rise from the dead was a large part of the reason for having Jesus executed. But it was also the way to end the unrest Jesus and his followers had been causing them. He had been a troublemaker of the first order, had thrown sand in the gears of the well-oiled political order of which they were an integral part. But as Jesus became more prominent and daring and troublesome, they saw that the only way to deal with him was by having him executed in a way that seemed legitimate and legal. When Jesus had entered Jerusalem on a donkey to the adulation of the palm-strewing crowd, he had dared to identify with the Messiah prophesied in their Scriptures. This was too much and now there was no other way: He must be executed. Once dead he must be shown beyond any doubt to have remained dead. The slightest whiff of his possible resurrection would upend all of these best-laid plans.

In fact, that was the only risk in having Jesus killed, that someone might afterward say that he had risen from the dead, as he had reportedly claimed he would do. So what could be the motive of the religious leaders for stealing his body, were that possible? Also, if they had for some reason stolen the body, wouldn't they eventually have produced it to silence everyone who was claiming that Jesus had risen from the dead? If the religious leaders or the Romans had produced his corpse, they would have ended everything once and for all. That could be the only reason they would have stolen the body, if ever they did. But if they didn't produce the body, why didn't they? We must conclude they didn't produce it because they didn't have it—and were themselves bamboozled by its disappearance. So the only thing they really could do when the tomb was shown to be empty and the body nowhere to be found was to claim that the disciples had stolen his body, to claim that the disciples had done this to create the impression that Jesus had in fact risen from the dead.

The third candidates and certainly the most oft-cited for this supposed theft were Jesus's disciples themselves. They would have had a far harder time penetrating the Roman guard than the Romans or the Jewish religious authorities. But once again, for argument's sake, let's assume they somehow succeeded in this. The question remains: Why would they have done it in the first place?

The religious authorities said that they would have done it to keep the magic going, so to speak, to keep the "movement" alive. But what movement was that? This was not a political movement or a "cause" of some kind. The only disciples who might have thought of it as a political movement was Judas, who by this time had already taken his life. The remaining disciples and the many other followers of Jesus devoutly believed he was who he said he was: a king from another kingdom. Why would they all suddenly leap to the idea that it was okay to throw away all they believed for the sake of continuing something? If Jesus was dead, what was there to continue? If they believed he was dead, which they obviously did, they would have been crushed, which by all accounts they were. What could be the point of trying to fool the world that he had risen from the dead if they themselves didn't believe it? What in their previous actions would lead us to believe they were hucksters of that sort?

But once again, for argument's sake, let's assume that this wild idea somehow made sense, that these earnest devotees had suddenly changed everything we know about them and had tried to "keep things going," whatever those things were. Wouldn't one or more of them have told the truth *eventually?* Can we really believe that in all the years that followed, through all the horrific persecutions, not one of them would have changed his story? It's also a well-established fact that the more people involved in a conspiracy the harder it is to keep it quiet. If this were a conspiracy, it would have involved scores of people. But human beings crack under torture and under threat of death and, as the years pass, under the weight of their own consciences. So how could it be that these many disciples and the other devout followers of Jesus could have all continued to lie along the same lines for years and years? With the exception of John, all of the disciples were put to death for claiming these things. Can we really imagine that not one of them would have recanted, would have spilled the proverbial beans to save his own skin?

Can't we see from their own reactions to the news of Jesus's resurrection that they themselves didn't believe it was possible, that they were flabbergasted when they heard about it? Can't we see from all the narratives of this period that they were not conniving and canny revolutionaries, but guileless followers of someone beautiful and good and true, whom they really thought God's promised Messiah, who would lead them into the kingdom of Heaven—but who was now dead, for they had seen him killed and sealed in a tomb, and who could lead them no more, breaking their hearts beyond breaking?

But if Jesus really had actually risen from the dead, despite their initial and obviously understandable skepticism toward it, can we imagine these disciples behaving any other way than exactly as they behaved? If they had seen him resurrected, and then had seen him in his resurrected body many times, and if upward of five hundred had seen him in the forty days that followed and were all talking about it, can we not imagine that nothing could have deterred them from telling the world about it, even though they were persecuted and murdered one by one over the years that followed?

## THE "SWOON THEORY"

One other theory that now must raise its bald, sunburned head is the so-called swoon theory, or, to dignify it even further, the swoon hypothesis.

This was first proposed and popularized about two hundred years ago. It maintains that Jesus never really died but just went into a "swoon" or temporary coma. Although this is generally now—because of medical science and other evidence—thought risible, we should compose ourselves to consider it, because it still makes its appearance in books every few years.

It is important to recall that Jesus was scourged horrifically and must have bled considerably as a result, so much so that he was too weak to carry the crossbeam to the site of the crucifixion. A scourging by cruel Roman soldiers armed with a flagellum is not something anyone should wish to contemplate. The flagellum had a number of cords, at the end of each of which was affixed a piece of bone or metal, which would hook and tear the flesh of the person scourged. The third-century historian Eusebius tells us that the "veins were laid bare, and . . . the very muscles, sinew, and bowels of the victim were open to exposure." We don't get the impression from history that most other victims of crucifixion were first scourged and brutalized this way. Many of the poor souls who were crucified lived in agony for two to four days or more upon their crosses. Jesus is said to have died in six hours, so that when Pilate himself heard of it, he marvcled that Jesus was already dead. (Pilate's reaction to hearing of Jesus's death is one of many such details in the

Gospel narratives that seems too quirky to be invented.)

We also know that Jesus's hands and feet were nailed to the cross with spikes. Can we imagine that these spikes piercing his hands and feet would not have drawn considerable blood? We also know that because sundown was approaching on that Friday afternoon, the soldiers wanted the three crucified victims dead before sundown. Actually, we should clarify that the religious authorities wanted them dead before sundown, because to have them on the crosses on the Sabbath would, in their eyes, have desecrated the Sabbath. So it was because of this monstrous religious fussiness that the men crucified on either side of Jesus now had their legs cruelly broken at the shins, the soldiers smashing them with a heavy iron mallet. Having their legs thus broken made it impossible for these men to push up in order to draw breath, so they would have suffocated much sooner. But the Roman soldiers would only do this if the victim was still living, of course. To their eyes, Jesus appeared to be dead, but to make sure, one of the soldiers stabbed him in the side with his spear. Jesus did not flinch, so it seemed clear that he was indeed dead. At least it was proof enough for the Roman soldiers, for whom this detail was very important, and who had much experience along these lines. As further proof to us that he was dead, the

Gospel writers say that something that looked "like blood and water" flowed out of the wound. Two thousand years ago the eyewitnesses to this and the Gospel writers would have had no idea what this signified, but medical science today tells us that after someone has died the blood inside the body begins to clot, so that the blood separates from the watery serum. So we can now know what they did not: that by the time the Roman soldier stabbed Jesus with his sword, he already had been dead for some time.

We also have to think about what happened after Jesus was confirmed to be dead. Most victims of crucifixion had their bodies left on the crosses, where birds would eat their flesh. These gruesome sights served as a warning to anyone thinking to defy the Roman authorities. If and when these bodies were taken down, they would be thrown into a pit, where dogs and other animals would eat them. But we know that Joseph of Arimathea, who was very wealthy, worked up the courage to approach Pilate himself and "beg" for the body of Jesus. Pilate granted this and Joseph of Arimathea then accorded Jesus the dignity of being buried in a tomb that he himself had owned. Conveniently, the tomb was nearby.

Taking a dead body down from a cross could not be easily done. The great spikes must be removed. If there were the slightest life in Jesus, surely Joseph of Arimathea or Jesus's mother, Mary, or

179

the others on hand would have witnessed it, indeed would have strained to see it. But how could that be possible, given what he had been through, and given that the Roman soldiers were satisfied that he was dead? The text tells us that they were in a hurry to bury him in the tomb, because sundown was coming. Jesus died at three in the afternoon, so there wouldn't have been much time to take him down from the cross and transport him to the tomb. The normal procedure for a body being buried would be to anoint it with spices, but although Mary and some other women did what they could in the short time they had, they couldn't finish it, so they planned to return as soon as possible after the Sabbath was over, which is to say at sunup on Sunday morning.

So we have to see that all that the Gospels record makes sense. Where are the holes in those accounts? They are all logical, given everything we now know. If fact, because we know so much more today, we can say that these accounts are far more logical now than they would have seemed two centuries ago when the Swoon Theory was first proposed.

## SUNDAY MORNING

We may also consider the several accounts of what happened early that Sunday morning. Everything we can know about that morning points to the fact that on that Sabbath, all of Jesus's disciples considered him dead. There isn't any inkling that anything else was possible, and given his having spoken of his resurrection, this is itself strange and sad. Whatever faith they might have had in this direction seems to have evaporated by the events of the previous days. In accordance with this assumption, Mary Magdalene and Jesus's mother and a woman named Salome proceeded sadly but dutifully to the Garden Tomb at sunup on Sunday, to finish what they had been unable to finish on Friday evening. If any of the disciples had spirited him away, surely these women would have known it. But they expected to find Jesus's body there. In the first verses of chapter 4 in Mark's Gospel, they ask one another who will help them to roll away the stone. We know that it was a very large stone, entirely covering the entrance, which was itself four and a half to five feet high. Some have suggested it would take many men to move it. But when the women arrived, the stone had been rolled away already.

The four Gospel accounts vary in a few details. In the Gospel of Matthew it says that there had been a great earthquake and "an angel of the Lord descended from Heaven and came and rolled back the stone." The text continues, saying that his "appearance was like lightning and his clothing white as snow. And for fear of him the guards trembled and became like dead men."

One has to wonder what these guards would have thought if there were a tremendous earthquake, followed by an angel in blazing white descending and rolling away the huge stone. Surely they hadn't expected this, and surely their innate sense that something overwhelming and genuinely supernatural was happening would have turned their training to jelly. In the Gospel of Mark it says that when the women came to the empty tomb and saw the angel in the tomb, they were themselves frightened. After the angel had spoken to them, "they went out and fled from the tomb, for trembling and astonishment had seized them." Is it any wonder? We are obliged to realize that these guards and these women were no more used to seeing such things than we are today. Would we be surprised to surmise that these guards had befouled themselves for fear and had then run into Jerusalem to tell the chief priests "all that had taken place," as the text tells us? What were their options after the tomb had been opened and the dead man they had been charged to guard had flown the coop with seismic and angelic fanfare? The text goes on to say that the Jerusalem elders gave the guards enough money to guarantee that they would stay mum about what they had seen and would thenceforth say that the disciples had stolen the body, an effective canard bruited about for centuries and still today.

We also learn that it was these women who

informed the disciples that Jesus was not in the tomb, who told the disciples that an angel had appeared to them and had told them what happened. In that patriarchal culture, it makes little sense to put this detail in the Gospel accounts unless it had actually happened as described. If this were made up, surely the women would be the last ones entrusted with being the first to see the tomb. In fact, in keeping with what we might expect, after these women run to tell the disciples what happened, even Peter and the others do not believe them. To the disciples, "these words seemed to them an idle tale and they did not believe them." This underscores the simple fact that at this point no one thought Jesus could be anything but dead.

There are so many difficulties with each of these theories that as crazy as it might sound and does sound, the most plausible alternative, following the facts we know and the logic that flows from them, is that Jesus rose from the dead. Unless, of course, one dismisses this idea out of hand, which many certainly do. But if one does so, and dismisses the possibility of all miracles, what then can the explanation be for all that we now know? And how is dismissing this idea out of hand any different from accepting it or any other idea without thinking it through critically and examining all the alternatives? On what basis can we do this?

We again and again must remember that resurrection from the dead was as implausible then as it is today, and we must remember that it was as staggering to those who came to believe it as to those who did not believe it. This and only this can account for the sudden boldness with which those who did believe it spoke of it. It is only because they had witnessed an outrageous miracle that they had the courage to talk of it incessantly, despite being threatened with death if they did not stop. For them, the reality of the resurrection was how the authority of God manifestly trumped all earthly authorities. It wasn't merely a theological idea but a reality to which they were eyewitnesses. They had themselves witnessed the power of God—and the person of God—in the resurrected Jesus of Nazareth. After that, nothing in this world could dissuade them from believing it, and no authority in this world could frighten them from proclaiming it. They had no fear of death because they had seen Death itself triumphed over by the one who claimed to be "the resurrection and the life." They might have claimed to believe it before, but after the crucifixion and resurrection, they had no doubt.

What can you do with people like that? As the Romans learned, not much. Part of the miracle of the resurrection is that it so empowered a ragtag band of fishermen and tax collectors that they were emboldened to stand against all earthly authority and power, and ultimately would upend the once inviolable order of the mighty Roman Empire. History tells us that this happened. So what better explanation can be offered for how it happened? Unless we have missed something, there exists none. And if there exists none, we are invited to submit to the logic of what we now know: that this most celebrated and most scorned miracle of miracles actually happened—and, perhaps most miraculously of all, can even be understood to have happened.

# PART TWO

## THE MIRACLE STORIES

# INTRODUCTION
## TO THE MIRACLE STORIES

In his book *Mere Christianity*, C. S. Lewis rather famously said that when it came to deciding who Jesus Christ was, we really only had three choices. First, we could say he was a liar, that all of the things he said were simply lies. Second, we could say he was not a liar but a lunatic, so he couldn't be held responsible for saying the things he said. And third, we could say he was actually who he said he was, the Lord of Heaven and Earth.

Lewis said that there were no other options besides those three—Lord, liar, or lunatic— because Jesus hadn't left us any other options. To regard Christ as a wonderful moral teacher is not possible, because he said so many things that a sane and wonderful moral teacher would never say, such as when he cursed a fig tree or raised people from the dead or said that he was the promised Messiah of the world, or when he forgave sin or healed the blind, to name a few examples. Socrates didn't do any of those things or claim to do any of those things, but if he had claimcd to, we would rightly say he was an outright liar or a fraud—or simply non compos mentis. And so it must be with Jesus. He can hardly be someone who pronounces deeply sane and wise things on the one hand and a madman or deceiver on the other. We are forced to choose. Lewis here holds our feet to the logical fire.

I believe that when it comes to the stories I will tell in the following chapters we are faced with a similar situation. We can perhaps imagine that the people telling these stories are simply lying for the purposes of self-aggrandizement or for any other reason. Or we can perhaps imagine that they are simply deceived, so that they are themselves convinced that these things happened, although they didn't. Or finally, we can conclude that as difficult as they might be to make sense of, they are nonetheless true stories.

The people telling these stories (I am, of course, one of them) must be carefully considered as either trustworthy witnesses to events or as untrustworthy witnesses to events (or nonevents). We must consider whether what they are saying is an embellishment in toto or an embellishment in part—or no embellishment at all, but simply factual. We must consider the source, as it were, because in a court of law, as one tries to determine the facts of a case, one has to speak to the reliability of the witnesses. If one has a reliable witness, it's a strong indicator that what that witness is saying actually happened. If one has an unreliable witness, one simply has no way of knowing whether what they are saying happened.

This is why I've chosen to limit myself to telling the stories of people I know personally. This adds a level of trustworthiness to these people, because I am not having to take someone else's word for it that they are trustworthy. I've eliminated a layer of confusion. Had I chosen to tell the stories of people whom I do not know, I might have found far more exotic and incredible miracle stories, but I would not have the satisfaction of knowing that the person telling the story was really and truly trustworthy. So what we have in these pages is limited in scope: stories told to me by people I know personally, and because I know them personally, stories I believe are true.

But I don't believe they are true simply because I trust the people who told them to me. I have been told many stories over the years, but not all of them are true. We have to try to get to the bottom of things that people tell us, and I have tried to include only those stories that I believe withstood my initial skepticism and questions. Just because some miracle stories are true doesn't mean that they all are true.

The following stories illustrate that these kinds of experiences are not only for mystics—or only for nuns or monks or priests or "certain" people. They illustrate that the God of the universe wants to communicate with every single one of us and that there is not only one way in which he does that. Because he created each of us differently, he will communicate with us individually. Though he is the same God for every one of us, in his tenderness and desire to reach us he is able to speak to us in ways that are very specific to us. The story of my conversion in the next chapter is a particular illustration of that idea. God will never demand that we speak his language; on the contrary, in love he condescends to speak ours. He uses vision and dreams and words and circumstances and experiences to communicate with us, and he wants us to expect that—not to demand it but neither to be closed to it.

# 9

## CONVERSION MIRACLES

I once was lost, but now am found, was blind, but now I see.
—JOHN NEWTON, FROM
THE HYMN "AMAZING GRACE"

Christian conversion . . . is a supernatural, radical thing. The heart is changed. And the evidence of it is not just new decisions, but new affections, new feelings.
—JOHN PIPER

I changed. I have been turning into a different person since that half minute.
—JOY DAVIDMAN

Until you have given up your self to Him you will not have a real self.
—C. S. LEWIS

I have often heard people say that the biggest miracle of all is someone's conversion from nonbelief to belief, or that the greatest evidence of a miracle is the changed life that results when someone goes from nonbelief to belief. But other people are of the mind that people can't change, that we are who we are and that's that. When someone claims to have changed, they assume he is probably kidding himself or, more likely, trying to fool others. Examples of this view arise when convicted criminals claim to come to faith. *How convenient for them!* the cynics cry, assuming the actual point of these claims is to persuade the judge or warden or parole board to be lenient with them. This can surely be the case, and yet I can think of several people who really did genuinely come to faith after committing crimes. What shall we make of them?

One was my dear friend Chuck Colson. Chuck was the special counsel to Richard Nixon, one of the infamous "president's men" who took amoral political ambition to new heights, and who eventually fell spectacularly in that historic debacle and "long, national nightmare" known as the Watergate scandal. Chuck was called the White House "hatchet man" and was said to be willing to "run over his grandmother" to get the president reelected. But just before everything fell apart in public, things were falling apart privately for the former marine. Something in him began to wonder about God, and in the summer of 1973, over the course of a few weeks, he was dramatically converted.

But when word got out that the take-no-prisoners tough guy had become a born-again Christian, the news media had a field day. No one would believe this nasty political operative had really changed his stripes. He was lampooned in political cartoons and on late-night television. But, mirabile dictu, it really had happened. In fact, Chuck was so serious about his newfound faith that he refused to take a plea bargain to avoid prison, because he would have to lie. His lawyer thought he was out of his mind to refuse it, but Chuck wouldn't back down. And so he went to prison. After he got out of prison he decided that God wanted him to spend the rest of his life helping prisoners, which he did when he founded Prison Fellowship. Instead of rebooting a very lucrative legal career with big-name clients, he chose to go back into prisons, and that's what he did for the rest of his life. You don't do something like that for thirty-five years just to fool people into thinking you've changed. But many still doubted he had changed, and even some of his obituaries didn't seem able to see the reality of his changed life after all those years. But I knew him personally and saw who he was. His conversion to putting God and others first in his life, to loving his enemies, and to behaving in a way that would glorify God and bless those around him was as deep and authentic as anything one can hope for.

Still, the belief that someone is inherently bad

and utterly beyond the possibility of change persists. If you've ever met someone who is really awful—or who at least seems pretty awful—you struggle to imagine they could really turn their lives and their sins over to God and be forgiven and change dramatically. I can see why some thought that about Chuck, and I can think of a few people who fit this bill in my life. I especially remember when I was not yet fifteen, working for a few hours each Friday and Saturday night as a busboy in a Greek diner near our home. Since I was not yet sixteen it was under the table, for tips only, but I needed some cash to buy backpacking equipment, so I'd asked my father if he knew anyone who could use me. He'd suggested a diner not far from our home. It was owned and run by—no kidding—a corrupt Greek Orthodox priest, who had once been our parish priest but who had been sent packing by the parish council. In later years I learned from friends that he had chased waitresses, and eventually he went to prison for tax fraud. Who can doubt that he drove people away from God?

But as bad as he was, the short-order cook in the diner was worse. He was a short, nasty, brutish Greek named Manolis, who every time I entered the kitchen with my basin of dirty dishes would say vulgar, sexual things to me about women, real and imaginary. He trafficked in nonstop dirty talk, so I didn't take it personally, disgusting as it was. "Eric, you have gell-friend?" he would ask, leering like a satyr. "You have gell-friend?" Actually I didn't have "gell-friend," but to get him off my back I said that I did. Of course, this only stoked the fire. "Eric! Eric! You gell-friend she give you somethin', eh?" On and on it went. One day Manolis was in the process of suggestively asking me if I knew the priest's teenage daughter and began effusing over her looks when the priest came in through the swinging doors and overheard it. But Manolis was a decent enough cook, so the priest only snapped at him: "*Ela, sar-rap, vre Boubouna*!" So don't ask me why, but when I think of the sort of unregenerate person whom I cannot imagine ever really changing, for some reason, I think of him.

But if you purport to be any kind of Christian or person who regards the Bible as divinely inspired, you cannot take that position. According to the Bible, no one is ever really past the possibility of God's grace. Besides, who are we to know who is and isn't beyond it? Aren't there too many examples of people we thought beyond the pale who were not beyond it after all, who really changed and surprised everyone around them?

The reason so many people regard genuine conversions as miracles is because of the dramatic changes often witnessed in the lives of those converted. As I've just said, Chuck Colson went from being a tremendously prideful, hyper-aggressive political zealot, to someone humbled and humble who served the poor and the disenfranchised with all of the talents and energies he had once used to claw his way to the top. How had that happened? What could account for that? More dramatically, David Berkowitz, infamous for the "Son of Sam" murders in New York in 1977, years ago had what anyone close to him describes as a deep and thorough conversion to Christian faith, so much so that he refuses to appear before his parole board, believing he doesn't deserve to be released for what he did.

Another conversion worth talking about is the conversion of C. S. Lewis, the Oxford don whose writings after his conversion touched many millions of lives.

## THE MIRACLE OF
## C. S. LEWIS'S CONVERSION

Conversion is often thought of as something that happens instantly, and it sometimes does happen that way. But it often doesn't. Even when it happens in a way that appears instant, there is often more to the process than meets the eye. Later in this chapter, I tell of my own experience in being transformed literally overnight, but I can also remember steps along the way to that night, steps that were crucial and that were a part of my having that overnight experience. So on the one hand it happened overnight, and on the other hand it took years. William Wilberforce described his own conversion as "the Great Change," which I write about in my book *Amazing Grace*. It consisted of a period of almost two years in which Wilberforce continued to change. But he never references any particular moment when he crossed the line of "conversion." For all we know, the line he was crossing was so wide that it took him two years to cross it. Who can really say?

The conversion of C. S. Lewis is a bit like Wilberforce's. Except for him it doesn't look as much like a long process as a number of distinct steps. He writes about the culmination of it in his autobiographical memoir, *Surprised by Joy*. One day he got into the sidecar of his brother Warnie's motorcycle and they took off for the Whipsnade Zoo. When he got into the sidecar, Lewis says, he did not believe that Jesus Christ was the Son of God, but when he got out of the sidecar at the zoo, he did. At what point, then, in that one-and-a-half-hour motorcycle journey did Lewis cross the fabled line from unbelief to belief? Or was the whole journey of thirty-five miles the crossing of that line? Or was this ride in the sidecar that day simply the final leg of a longer journey? Once again, it's impossible to say. Lewis himself certainly didn't know the answer.

But in *Surprised by Joy*, Lewis recounts what happened before he got into that sidecar. For him there were several levels of unbelief and belief, and it seems that this is the case with most people who experience conversions, although usually it's hard to see these steps and articulate them. Lewis was about as perceptive and articulate as anyone who ever lived, so he did write about what he perceived of this journey. But even the great Lewis could see it only dimly.

Lewis tells us in *Surprised by Joy* of how as a child he experienced a deep longing for something beyond himself. He uses the German word "*Sehnsucht*," but also translates it as the English word "joy." By way of context, Lewis's mother died when he was nine. He had prayed hard for her recovery, but she had not recovered. The years that followed were not pleasant ones. The boarding schools to which his father sent him were awful. Then there was the terrible experience of being a soldier in the Great War. Lewis's time in the trenches, amid the bombs and poison gas and carnage—and seeing his closest friend killed—only hardened his heart toward whatever it was for which he had longed as a child. He became a confirmed atheist. He may not have been especially happy about it, but he simply came to feel that that was the way things were, and he must face them. He was too old to believe in any God. His memory of praying for his mother's healing, followed by her death, was enough to settle things in his mind.

But Lewis's disinterest in the God of the Bible didn't close him off to the world of fairy tales and myths. He particularly enjoyed and even loved the old Norse sagas. Something in him resonated with them, though he never asked just what that was, and he was sure they were just stories, that they had no bearing on the material world in which we all live. In *Surprised by Joy*, he writes:

> On the one side a many-islanded sea of poetry and myth; on the other a glib and shallow "rationalism." Nearly all that I loved I believed to be imaginary; nearly all I believed to be real I thought grim and meaningless.

Lewis loved poetry and myth so much that early on he hoped to become a poet. This was in the first decades of the twentieth century, when poetry was still widely read and enjoyed. Lewis wrote under various pen names and even tried his hand at longer verse, including *Dymer*, an epic poem written in the style of Homer. As a student at Oxford University, Lewis scored an almost unheard-of "triple first" and afterward became an expert in medieval literature, teaching and writing at Oxford about such masterworks as *Sir*

*Gawain and the Green Knight* and Spenser's *Fairie Queene.*

While at Oxford, Lewis became friends with J. R. R. Tolkien, who was a devout Roman Catholic. In time, Lewis's atheism turned to a kind of theism, but it went no further than that. How this happened he hardly knew, but he had put off its happening as long as he could. It was not something he had desired. In a letter to his friend Arthur Greeves, he said: "I gave in, and admitted that God was God, and knelt and prayed: perhaps, that night, the most dejected and reluctant convert in all England."

There his faith remained until one night when he, Tolkien, and their mutual friend Hugo Dyson took one of their late-night walks on the long wooded path behind Magdalen College in Oxford. The name of this path is "Addison's Walk" and it is still there, just as it was more than eight decades ago when they frequented it. On September 19, 1931, at one or two in the morning, they were walking on Addison's Walk when their conversation turned to the subject of myth. Tolkien suggested to Lewis that the story of Christ dying and then rising from the dead was indeed a myth, just as the stories of all those young gods who died and then rose from the dead were also myths. But he suggested to Lewis that the myth of Christ was also true. He suggested that it was the one time in history that a myth had actually happened. This was why he believed it and he encouraged Lewis to think about this as well.

A true myth. It was something Lewis had never considered. But was it really true? Could it be? That was another story. But there was enough evidence to it that he must at least consider it. If a genius like Tolkien believed it was true, and if the brilliant G. K. Chesterton, whom he so admired, believed it, and if the great writer George MacDonald, whose stories he so admired, had believed it, he must at least consider it.

Nine days after that walk with Tolkien and Dyson, on the sunny morning of September 28, Lewis and his elder brother Warnie decided to take a trip to the Whipsnade Zoo. Why they did this is lost to history, but what happened that day changed history, because Lewis says that it was during the course of this journey that everything changed for him. It was whilst driving along the roads to the zoo that he crossed the invisible but ultrareal line from not believing into believing, though he knew not how. It was no conscious decision, and yet it happened. He knew that it did. "I have just passed on from believing in God," he wrote, "to definitely believing in Christ—in Christianity. I will try to explain this another time. My long night talk with Dyson and Tolkien had a good deal to do with it."

Who can say how such a thing happens? But the

effect this had on Lewis over the years to come was profound and extraordinarily far-reaching. For one thing, after he came to faith, he began to articulate that faith in an endless spate of books that have been read by many millions around the globe. His books on apologetics, such as *Mere Christianity*, have awakened millions to the rationality of Christian faith, while his books of fiction and fantasy, such as the Chronicles of Narnia, have awakened people to the imaginative and mythical side of it. It seems that after these two sides of the faith came together in Lewis's conversion, he spent the next decades of his life sharing both of them with the world.

## MY CONVERSION

My own conversion, which I recount in this chapter, was not the classic kind of conversion, although I've come to think that there really is no such thing as a "classic conversion." In my case, my conversion didn't make me feel especially grateful that Jesus had died for my sins. I didn't really feel any particular sense of repentance. I didn't think about what Jesus had done on the cross. I certainly believed in all those things, and knew they were deeply important, but there was no deep sense of those things that led to my conversion as many often describe. Some people would say that I cannot have been converted if those things—which they insist upon—weren't ticked off on whatever mental form they use to determine who has experienced an actual conversion and who hasn't.

But that's just not what I experienced and there are innumerable instances of conversions that don't involve these feelings. Perhaps I already knew Jesus in some way and perhaps this was just a big and important step in embracing him fully and wholly. Who knows? God knows. All I know is that in that dream he revealed himself to me in a way that changed everything and from then on I have had no doubt that he is exactly who he says he is and that I want to give him my whole life.

Paul's truly classic conversion on the fabled and proverbial Road to Damascus was not one where he was delivered from a load of guilt and sin. We have no record that he rejoiced that he had been forgiven and that Jesus's death on the cross had delivered him from his sins, that it had paid his debt to God. Surely he would come to understand and feel those things eventually—and help all of us since to understand them—but when he was blasted off his high horse that day, none of these things seems to have entered the picture. It was simply an encounter—and a humbling encounter—with Jesus himself.

Actually, I have come to think of conversion not as crossing a finish line but as crossing the starting line. Only once we know God and invite him into our hearts can we begin to run the real race we were meant to run all along. And once that happens, all kinds of things begin to change in our lives. Sometimes those changes are very fast; for example, I have heard of many people who suddenly experienced a sudden lack of desire for something to which they were previously addicted. They are suddenly freed from a desire to do crack or heroin. It's clearly miraculous and what Christians call a "deliverance." But others continue to struggle with addictions for many years, or for the rest of their lives, despite a genuine commitment to God and a desire to be relieved of that addiction, or that besetting sin, whatever it is.

In my case, the only thing that seemed to change quickly was my attitude toward sex outside of marriage. I suddenly knew that I couldn't have any part in that any longer, despite a long-term relationship with someone I loved and thought I would marry. I suddenly knew that it was incompatible with the new person I had become, and that to honor God I had to give that up. But the miracle for me was that giving it up was suddenly second nature. I felt that God's holiness was much more important and I wanted to be close to him and to give him full rein in my life, so this was not difficult. I suddenly felt a desire to want to channel this toward marriage.

But it was so powerful a change that I knew it really was miraculous. It was as if I could somehow feel God inside me, filling up whatever part of me had sought him in that direction. I suddenly didn't want what I had previously wanted. I knew that God was the answer to all my desires. I wanted God.

## WHY THESE MIRACLES ARE SO POWERFUL

Some of the strongest evidence that genuine conversions are indeed genuine—and therefore miraculous—is that they often overwhelm the one who has been converted. We've all met people who couldn't shut up about their faith, who suddenly become insufferable, as though every single conversation has to be about God and the Bible. Sometimes its merely annoying and evidence of something that God has little to do with, but in many cases it's evidence that that person has had an overwhelming transformative experience that they themselves can hardly make sense of. It's often been compared to falling in love. Someone head over heels in love is wont to make an idiot of himself or herself, gushing about the object of their love at every opportunity. Much of that has to do with a volcano of emotions they're hardly at liberty to stop from erupting. When someone finds God in a real and powerful way, the effect is often the same. They talk about God and just can't stop talking about him or thinking about him.

I can speak from personal experience. I'm sure in the months and first years of my conversion many of my friends and relatives thought I had flipped. And to some extent I had flipped, depending on the meaning of the verb "to flip." Practically speaking, as with any torrid love affair, it will eventually simmer down to a manageable boil. In my case, it really did take years. I eventually got much better at learning how to channel my faith and my zeal for God in a way that wasn't entirely and quickly off-putting. I'm not fooling myself into thinking it's not still off-putting at some times to some people, but I know I've made progress.

During my first few years as a believer I not only couldn't shut up about my faith, I was sometimes judgmental toward some of those who didn't share it. But on the other side of that equation, I remember having powerful feelings of love and empathy toward total strangers, a sense of God's love for them, and a desire to do anything I could to show them his love, to bless them, to help them. It was all somewhat overwhelming, but I'm happy to say that most of it was on the positive side of this equation.

I was often hardest on those who were already in the Christian world but whom I felt were not as zealous as they could be in reaching those who didn't know God. As is typical, I was hardest on my own—my family and my childhood church, the Greek Orthodox Church. I saw it as an institution that had essentially failed to prepare me for the wide world and for the secularism of that world. I waded into a swamp full of alligators and when God finally pulled me out to safety I wondered why my childhood faith had not at least armed me with a shotgun or something to protect me.

I remember having conversations with Father Peter Karloutsos, the wonderful Greek Orthodox priest at the church in which I grew up, who is a dear friend. But I know that many of the things I said to him must have made him think I had become a religious fanatic or joined a cult. I was a young man and very ardent about my new faith in Jesus, and in my broken way I was trying to communicate this to him. But I don't doubt half of what I said came across more as judgmental toward him and the ancient Orthodox faith, and I'm sure after a few of these conversations he decided just to give up on me, for his own mental health. At least for a while. I'm sure it was fatiguing for him. I'm glad to say that after fifteen or so years we came to understand each other and have a love for each other, as we should, considering we've known each other for almost forty years. But back then I wouldn't have predicted that.

But I was in a pickle. My conversion to faith in Jesus had been so powerful that I felt I had to go wherever he was leading me, and at that time he was leading me toward evangelical expressions of my faith, and not to the ancient Orthodox church. But for many Greek Orthodox, the church is the only connection to their ethnicity. For me it was the community in which I had grown up. I hadn't stopped being Greek or loving the people I knew in that community. So sometimes when it came to the church from which I felt exiled, I felt like a robin in winter, wishing I could come in, sit down by the hearth, and perhaps eat a souvlaki and drink a shot of ouzo.

I remember about three years after my conversion, I woke up one Saturday morning and was just praying about the day ahead. I had no particular plans and as I prayed I felt God nudging me to drive up to Danbury to help out with the Greek Festival. It was that weekend at the Assumption Church. So I got dressed and drove the forty-five minutes north and offered my services. They couldn't turn me away, could they? I had gone to this church my whole life, and my parents still went. These were my people. Just because I didn't attend on Sundays was no reason I couldn't help out at the festival. When I arrived, Father Peter's welcome was tepid, but when I asked how I could help, they put me on what I think of as the front lines of every Greek festival—the souvlaki booth. It's the hottest and loudest and busiest place to be. But I was thrilled to be there, helping out in my community. I wanted to repair the breach I had created by some of my arrogant statements and at least show that even though I might be attending another church, I was still Greek, and I was still part of this community.

It was exhilarating working there and as firm a proof of one's Hellenic bona fides as anything could be. A few hours into my time, wilting from the heat under the tent of the souvlaki booth, smelling of pork smoke and oregano, I overheard some people talking about something controversial. As I continued listening, I gathered that there was someone at the front of the church driveway handing out Christian tracts, someone who had nothing to do with the Greek Orthodox Church. Father Peter was nearby, and I heard him say in a clearly derisive tone that it was some "born-again Christian." It stung a bit to hear this, because for all I knew he had wanted me to hear it, but in a few minutes it dawned on me that I ought to go over and see who this person was and what they were handing out.

I walked the thirty or so yards down the church driveway to where the man was standing. He had positioned himself so that almost anyone coming to the festival would pass him. He was handing out evangelistic brochures or what

Christians call "tracts"—which many mis-pronounce as "tracks." But here was the real surprise: He was Greek! Evidently he thought it clever to come to the festival and tell his fellow Greeks about what he had found, about being "born-again" and having a personal relationship with Jesus instead of a meaningless and nominal "religion" that consisted only of attending church. He desperately wanted to communicate that and he thought this would be just the place to do it. In some ways I found it funny, and secretly couldn't help cheering him on. How wonderful if all the people he was talking with would find what he had found—and I had found!

I didn't know who he was or where he had come from, but what he was doing clearly rankled the leadership of the church. Then one of the members of the church parish council came out, a short man with a mustache. I had seen men like this over the years. They had little patience for this sort of thing. "Go on and get outta here!" he said to the man. "We got our own religion! Our religion is the oldest religion there is!" I understood what he meant to be saying, that Greek Orthodoxy was in some ways the original form of Christian faith. To some extent that's correct. I understood that what he said came from a place of pride, both good and ill. It's good to know about your heritage and to take pride in it, but the man had no sense of what this other man had experienced, that this man had evidently found nothing in the Greek Orthodox Church but empty tradition, and now that he had found the joy and the peace of a real relationship with God, he wasn't going to shut up about it.

I went back to the souvlaki booth, chuckling to myself. Later on I drove to my parents' house. We planned to return to the festival for the evening, when there would be Greek dancing. My brother and his wife showed up too, and around six we decided it was time to drive to the festival. But in the hours since I had left, I had been strangely haunted thinking about the man handing out tracts. For some reason I kept thinking I knew him. I wouldn't get the chance to find out anyway, since it had been many hours since I was there and for sure he had left. But when we drove up Clapboard Ridge Road toward the church, I was thrilled to see him still handing out the tracts and talking to people about his faith. We parked the car and I immediately hustled over to him. Now that I was up close, I saw that he seemed to have a positively angelic glow about him, a joy. He wasn't an angry man; there was a kindness and gentleness to him. He wasn't someone with a theological ax to grind; he seemed to embody the peace of God, the way Christians are supposed to but so often don't. As I looked at him, he still reminded me of someone, and I was by now burning to find out if I was correct. I asked him a few questions about his work history and within seconds I had the unbelievable answer: It was Manolis, the short-order cook from the Hilltop Diner. I hadn't seen him in thirteen years. He was so different from the man I had last spoken with in 1978 that it was downright startling. Whatever he had been, he was no longer. He was profoundly changed. Christians often quote the Scripture verse that says God makes us a "new creature in Christ," and this man was the most vivid example of this that I ever could have imagined.

Of course, I asked him what had happened to him to account for the change and he told me. His wife had become a born-again Christian. At first, he had rejected it entirely, but over time he came to see that her own conversion was genuine and positive, and he had eventually followed suit. From my point of view, that day and forevermore, it was nothing less than a miracle. It is the one instance in my life of seeing the miraculous transformation of a human being, of seeing just how very miraculous a real conversion can be. I am sure that I will never get over it and will never stop talking about it until the day I die.

The remainder of this book is, of course, comprised of miracle stories. I thought it would be right to have the first of these stories, which now follows, be the extraordinary story of my friend Ed Tuttle's conversion. Ed is the person to whom this book is dedicated and is the person whom God in his mystery and grace used to bring me to faith in the summer of 1988. A conversion is often called a "second birth," and those who come to faith often say they are "born-again." With all such spiritual births, just as with physical births, they do not only bring one person into being but often portend the future births of others. So Ed's being born-again was the preamble to my own second birth, as my second birth has been the preamble to the second births of others, and so on and so on, just as it should be, world without end. Amen.

## BECOMING THE PERSON YOU WERE MEANT TO BE

I met Ed Tuttle in the fall of 1987 when I began working at Union Carbide in Danbury, Connecticut. Our friendship dramatically changed my life, as I tell in the story after this one.

Ed Tuttle grew up in Southington, Connecticut, in what could reasonably be described as a very Catholic home. When his parents were courting, Ed's father made Ed's mother a crucifix-shaped box for her rosary beads. Ed remembers that there was a small chapel in their house, which one saw immediately upon opening the front door.

Jehovah's Witnesses and other visitors wouldn't need much time to know what they were dealing with.

As a young boy, it was Ed's great ambition to become a paleontologist. Ed attended St. Mary's Elementary School in Waterbury and one day in the fourth grade he had an overwhelming experience that changed his dreams and ambitions in a moment. He remembers sitting in the fourth row back, near the window, when suddenly, and quite unrelated to anything being said by the teacher, a powerful wave seemed to come over him that he knew instantly was a call to serve God. It was so overwhelming that he immediately tapped on the shoulder of the girl in front of him (like an overwhelming percentage of girls from that era, her name was Dawn) and flatly told her that he was going to be a priest. Dawn shrugged at this confession and turned back to face the front. But Ed knew what he had experienced. As soon as he got home he told his mother that he knew that he wanted to be a priest, which, given his upbringing, was the only possible interpretation of being called to serve God. His mother proudly recalled his announcement very often for others in the years that followed.

After eight years at St. Mary's, Ed attended four years at a Catholic seminary high school in Cheshire, Connecticut. After graduation, to pursue his studies to become a priest, Ed decided to continue at a seminary college in the Northeast run by the same Catholic order as his high school. In accordance with seminary requirements, Ed was pursuing his BA in philosophy.

The years at the seminary were increasingly confusing. Ed was so bright that he skipped a grade in grammar school, and he was only seventeen when he began his freshman year. He soon found the atmosphere at the seminary difficult to comprehend in some ways. He had girlfriends at this time, but was strongly discouraged from seeing them because it would interfere with his calling as a priest. Still, he knew that on weekends many of his fellow students would go with some of the younger priests to gay bars in Boston. In the confused thinking of the seminary, this was somehow considered acceptable because it wouldn't lead to marriage.

One weekend in his sophomore or junior year, one of the priests who had befriended Ed took him to the Cape on a weekend night. The priest, who was about thirty, bought Ed dinner and strongly encouraged him to drink. Later that night Ed woke up and was startled to find the priest next to him in bed with his hands where they shouldn't be. Ed hadn't seen this coming at all, so he was very upset and confused by it. Ed remembers that the head of the religious order who oversaw the seminary flew in and had a conversation with Ed about this incident, telling him that he shouldn't be too hard on the offending priest; after all, everyone is different and he shouldn't make too much of it. The message Ed took away from this was that he must not talk about it with anyone, and it was only years later that Ed was able to tell his parents about it.

This incident and atmosphere, coupled with what had been a very difficult relationship with his father for some years, only added to Ed's depression and confusion, both sexually and theologically. He knew that spiritually and morally he was drifting, but he knew not where.

One night as he sat quite depressed on the bed in his dorm room, Ed found himself staring at a tall oak tree just outside his window. He remembers thinking that if that tremendous tree had grown out of a tiny acorn, God really was powerful and could do anything. Ed continued thinking about God when all of a sudden the room was filled with a presence so powerful that it nearly paralyzed him. He felt that he almost couldn't breathe or move. But he knew it was God. Then he heard an audible voice say: "I've taken care of you for these eighteen years. I'm not going to stop now." It was unlike anything he had experienced since the wave that had come over him in fourth grade. It so affected him that when he walked down the hall of the dorm his friends asked what had happened to him.

Ed never forgot this experience, but the effects of it faded. After his junior year at seminary, he decided he couldn't go back. He finished his degree at Merrimack College and lived in the dorm there. That year, Ed met his future wife, Donna, who was the same year as he and soon became his friend. Donna had grown up in New Jersey and was pursuing a degree in chemistry, with a minor in biology.

It was only at their graduation in 1978 that Ed realized his feelings for Donna went well beyond friendship, but by then she had already accepted a good job working as a lab technician in Southern California. If Ed wanted to continue their relationship, he would have to move there. Ed had by now realized that he wanted to pursue art and become an illustrator, so he applied and was accepted to the prestigious Art Center College of Design in Pasadena. He moved to Southern California and continued his relationship with Donna, which soon became serious.

But no sooner had Ed taken a few classes than he came to understand that almost none of the credits from his philosophy BA at Merrimack were transferrable, so he would need to entirely redo his bachelor's degree. He knew that couldn't work, nor could he afford it, since there was little financial help to get a second BA. So after a short time he dropped out, and in 1979 he moved in with Donna. They lived a block and a half from the beach in San Diego. Ed led what he recalls as a pretty crazy life, smoking pot and drinking in much of his spare time. But at some point they thought they should settle down, so they planned to move back to the New York area to be closer to their families. Donna landed a job with American Cyanamid in Connecticut as a research chemist, and they moved to an apartment on Second Street in East Norwalk in 1981. In June 1982 they were married. Ed had landed a job at the design agency run by Tom Fowler, considered one of the top designers in the country. Seeing only a stack of drawings and ads, Tom was sufficiently impressed with Ed's talent that he moved him out of the layout department and took him under his wing. This enabled Ed to earn a good living over the next few years, and more than made up for his being unable to continue with his art studies.

On the surface, as they say, all was well. But Ed's inner restlessness could not be assuaged by his fulfilling job and his marriage to the woman he loved. In fact, within about six months of marriage, Ed decided that he wanted to leave Donna. As Ed recalls, he "wanted what he wanted" and refused to see beyond that. He was actually involved with various strains of New Age spirituality at that time and the people he encountered on that path were encouraging him to "actualize" himself and "pursue his own journey," come what may. So even his selfishness—at the cost of devastating Donna—seemed to him the true and most "spiritual" path. He sat her down on their bed and flatly told her that he was tired of her. Her tears seemed to have no effect on him at all.

One night, not long after this talk, Ed had an extraordinary experience. Their apartment comprised the first floor of a three-family house. Ed had been using the second bedroom as his studio space and was working there one night, listening to David Bowie on the stereo. Donna was asleep in the other bedroom. Ed remembers that he was both proud of himself and grateful to be working on what was a fairly important project for General Foods, a major corporation.

Then, suddenly, up in the corner of the room he saw an extraordinarily bright light. Ed says that as soon as he saw it the stereo music went dead quiet. Whether it was just his perception as he was enveloped by this overwhelming presence or whether the stereo actually turned off, he didn't know, but suddenly there was only this powerful light and total, heavy silence. Ed recognized this presence as the same presence he had encountered as a fourth grader and then in his dorm room when he was eighteen, so it didn't frighten him at all. He said that for a time he talked to this presence and whenever he stopped talking it would "breathe" on him. It was clearly some kind of interchange, and he felt total peace and comfort. He knew this was not connected to the New Age things he had been dabbling in. "This was the real deal," he says. "I would talk to the light and the light would respond by breathing on me." He said he knows it sounds corny, but that's exactly what happened.

At one point, Ed said, "Why are you here for me?" and suddenly the light vanished and the silence lifted and he heard the stereo again. But it had been so wonderful that Ed now completely panicked. "I freaked out," he said. "I thought, You've got to be kidding!" He simply had to continue the conversation, but instead of turning the stereo down he ran out into the kitchen to escape its sound. He got a glass of water and stood facing the sink, trying to get his thoughts together. Then he turned around and the bright light was right there in front of him, not high up as it had been in his studio but down at about his eye level.

Ed said that once again the light began breathing on him. He was thrilled and excited it was there again. But then, all of a sudden, as though someone blew out a candle, there was a final burst of breath and in that moment, Ed felt something hit his heart. In that moment the light vanished and Ed fell to the kitchen floor in a crumpled mess, sobbing and wondering what this all meant. "For the next year and a half," he explained, "I was a madman." For the first time in his life, he had a strong hatred of his sins: the way he was treating Donna and taking her for granted, the pot, and the porn. He suddenly knew these things were all wrong, but at the same time that he suddenly hated them, he felt that they were all pulling on him more powerfully than ever. He said that during this time, he felt that he was in the middle of a tug-of-war over his soul, as though he were being torn in two.

He became so desperate to reconnect with what he had lost in the kitchen that he tried every and any spiritual path he could find. He was at one point about to experiment with "astral projection," although somehow that fell through. But he remembers being desperate and half-crazed during this period. During this time, he and Donna decided to move up to the Waterbury area. Both of them had secured jobs there and found a place to live. So they ended their lease in Norwalk and packed their things. But then, in lightning succession, Ed's new job fell through, Donna's new job fell through, and the place they were about to move into fell through. They found themselves with all their belongings in a moving truck with nowhere to go and no jobs. So they ended up moving in with Ed's parents. A good friend of Ed's from high school, Tom Vaichus, let Ed and Donna store their things in his basement.

This period was tremendously humbling for Ed and Donna, but their friendship with Tom and his wife, Susan, was a bright spot. Tom and Susan had become born-again Christians. Ed and Donna were clearly not on the same page, but Tom and Susan were kind, friendly, and emotionally healthy. Ed was devastated to find himself jobless and living with his wife in a small bedroom in his parents' home, but Tom and Sue helped them deal with it. At one point Tom gave Ed some books he thought might help. Ed didn't agree with all of it, but some of what he read pierced his heart and made the time a bit easier.

One day, Tom and Susan told Ed and Donna about a weeklong series of Christian events that would be happening up in Springfield, Massachusetts, an hour and a half away. There were events every night from Monday through Thursday, and Friday and Saturday were all-day affairs. Ed and Donna loved Tom and Sue enough that they agreed to go and give it a chance. But as the week passed, Ed found himself getting increasingly angry. He came to the conclusion that what he was hearing was "Christian garbage" that was not only foolish but also extremely dangerous. By Thursday evening he was simply furious. On the drive back, he was practically yelling at Tom, and when they got out of the car in Waterbury he stood toe-to-toe with Tom, literally poking him in the chest and telling him that he would never, ever be dragged back to this thing. Ed told him point-blank, "It's wrong. It's dangerous. And I'm done. There is no way I would even think about going back."

As it happened, because of work, Tom and Sue couldn't go up the next day. At least not until the evening. And for some reason Donna didn't want to go up either. As for Ed, despite his powerfully passionate protestations the night before—for no reason that he could fathom at the time or in the years since—he decided to get in the car and drive up by himself.

During one of the sessions, the man on the stage began speaking about how a man ought to treat his wife. He was speaking on the verse in Ephesians where it says "Husbands, love your wives as Christ loved the church." The speaker was making it clear that husbands should not selfishly be looking to their wives to have their needs met. They should instead be giving themselves wholly to their wives in love and should be trying to meet their wives' needs. Ed suddenly felt as though the man were pointing right at him, as though he was saying everything just for Ed's benefit, as if every word were intended for him alone. He couldn't believe how powerfully it affected him. He knew how he had been treating Donna was wrong and he was overwhelmed. Immediately after the session was over, they gave people in the audience an opportunity to stand, to say a prayer, and to give their lives to Jesus. Ed didn't hesitate. He stood up and prayed along with the man on the stage, publicly giving his life to Jesus. What happened at that point he can never forget. He says that suddenly everything looked completely different to him. "It was as if shades had been over my eyes and now they were lifted, and I could see," he says. "I wish I could explain it better. It was as when Dorothy steps out of her house in the Land of Oz and suddenly now everything is in color." Ed says that he felt that all he could see was Jesus, although he didn't see Jesus literally. But he knew when it happened that it was Jesus, that suddenly he could see Jesus, where before he had been blind to him.

These events were held in the big sports coliseum in Springfield, and after this happened, Ed left his seat and walked around in the hallway, staggered by what he now saw and felt. He thinks that he must have looked like a zombie, staring at everyone in sheer awe and amazement at what he was seeing and experiencing. Immediately after this he said he felt a surge of love for Donna unlike anything he'd ever felt before, as though that day for the first time he knew what it was like to love his wife. This was Friday, July 27, 1984.

That evening Donna did come up with Tom and Sue, and she saw the change in Ed, that he was no longer burning with anger but was instead taking copious notes of what he was hearing.

From this period forward, Ed experienced an insatiable desire to read the Bible and for some time was reading it from five to seven hours a day. Donna wasn't sure what had happened and feared the whole thing was just another phase for Ed, so she just kept watching and waiting to see when the phase would end. The good news is that she's still waiting. They've now been married thirty-two years and have four grown daughters and a grandson.

# THE GOLDEN FISH

What happened to me in the summer of 1988 changed my life forever. It's the miracle that opened the door to so many other miracles in my life. It happened sometime around my twenty-fifth birthday, although I can't remember the exact date. I had a dream in which God spoke to me in what I've called "the secret vocabulary of my heart." But in order for that dream to make sense to anyone besides me, I'll have to reveal that vocabulary.

If someone had investigated my life at that time to determine the basics of who I was, they'd likely have settled on three main themes at the heart of my identity: first, being Greek; second, freshwater fishing; and third, the life of the mind and the search for meaning.

My parents are European immigrants (my dad is from Greece, my mother from Germany) who came to New York in the mid-'50s, met in an English class in Manhattan, and married. I came into the world in 1963 at Astoria General Hospital and attended a Greek Orthodox parochial school through fourth grade. In 1972 we moved to the relatively rural environs of Danbury, Connecticut, where I went to public school and attended the Greek church every Sunday.

For Greeks in America, being Greek is important, and perhaps because I am only half-Greek, it was especially important for my dad to communicate this to me. Once, when he saw a chrome fish on the back of a car he was excited to explain that this was from the Greek word "*IXTHYS*," meaning "fish," because the early Christians used this word as an acronym—*Iesus Xristos Theos Ymon Sotir*—Meaning *Jesus Christ Son of God Our Savior.* It was their secret symbol.

My only real hobby besides watching TV was freshwater fishing. I fly-fished for trout and panfish, sometimes tying my own flies, but I mostly fished for bass—both large- and smallmouth. I was once even in a bass tournament. I had ice-fished too.

At Yale I was exposed to what is sometimes

called the life of the mind. I knew from freshman year that I wanted to be an English major, but not just because I loved words. I loved meaning too, or the idea that through the symbols and ideas in literature you were actually discovering the meaning of life itself.

I never took seriously the idea that our lives are meaningless, but neither did I ever settle on any particular alternative. I had dismissed Christianity as hopelessly parochial. Yale was aggressively secular, and I came to think that if there were truth in the universe then perhaps the Christian faith touched upon it, but it had to be something much larger, something that probably included all religions.

Sometime after graduation I came up with a kind of answer, involving the symbolic image of drilling through ice on the surface of a lake. It was a vaguely Jungian/Freudian idea that said the goal of life and all religions was to drill through this ice, which represented the conscious mind, in order to touch the water beneath, which represented Jung's "Collective Unconscious," a rather vague "God force" that somehow connected all of humanity. It was an Eastern and impersonal idea of God, making no particular claims on anyone, and how one was supposed to go about "drilling through the ice" was another story. I had no clue, but I liked the idea of it.

Graduation itself was like stepping off the top

of the ladder I'd been climbing my whole life. Good grades got me into and through Yale. I majored in English, edited the Yale humor magazine, worked in the dining hall, and sang in some musicals. At graduation I was Class Day speaker, preceding the main speaker—my future friend Dick Cavett—and I received several awards for my short fiction. What could lie ahead but success?

But instead of success I was launched into a stepless void, unable to climb toward what I thought I'd wanted to achieve, which was success and acclaim as a fiction writer. For the next few years I tried—mostly in vain—to write short fiction, and I sold some literary humor pieces to the *Atlantic*. I spent aimless and unproductive months at the elite writers' colonies of Yaddo and MacDowell. I lived in sublets in the Boston area and insecurely clung to a perpetually foundering relationship. One might say that I floated and drifted, which inescapably and inevitably leads to that singularly humiliating cul-de-sac of moving back in with one's parents, which I did. I was twenty-four.

The parents of my Yale friends saw that I was trying to "find myself," but my own parents— who'd never had the privilege of a college experience and who had worked very hard to finance my own—preferred that I simply "find myself a job." It was a seriously awful time. My now long-distance relationship was going down for the third time and I took the only job I could get: proofreading chemical manuals and other nonliterary arcana at Union Carbide's world headquarters. My cubicle seemed to be about a quarter of a mile from the nearest window.

But it was there, alone in the belly of this corporate whale, that I finally considered the question of God. In my misery I now befriended a bright graphic designer, who began to engage me on the issue of faith. Ed was older—already married with kids—and one of those born-again Christians I'd been trained to steer well clear of at Yale. I was perpetually wary, but in my pain and longing for relief I was desperate enough to keep the conversation going—for weeks and then months. To avoid real engagement or controversy, I half pretended to agree with him and his positions. But whenever he invited me to church, I demurred. One day at lunch, Ed said, "Perhaps you don't really know God as well as you think, Eric." I was offended. Who did he think he was and how could anyone claim to know God? Anyone with a brain knew that even if it were all true, we certainly couldn't *know* it, and so would have to content ourselves with that, with agnosticism. It was the only logical choice. But I wasn't content at all. Ed once told me to pray that God would reveal himself to me, but I thought praying to a God I wasn't sure was there didn't make any sense. And it didn't. But in my confusion I sometimes did ask for some sort of sign.

It was an unpleasant time in my life, generally. Driving through the miles of traffic on I-84 to Union Carbide every morning was real drudgery and added to my depression. I would listen to the local FM rock station and one of the songs in the Top 40 at that time was Robert Plant's "Heaven Knows." I remember in my desperate reveries about life I would sometimes wonder whether this song or that song might be a sign to me from God. It sounds ridiculous now, but at the time I was desperately hungry for something, for anything to reveal itself to me, to show me the way forward. One day I was listening to Robert Plant sing "Heaven Knows" and I remember wondering, *Does Heaven know? Does God know? Does he know who I am and that I'm down here listening to this song and wanting him to speak to me? If he exists.* The song had just come on as I pulled into the vast cement complex of Union Carbide, and as I drove through its long, depressing concrete tunnels toward the parking garage, I listened to the lyrics and continued to wonder. I pulled into my parking spot and waited for the song to finish, and the moment it finished, I turned it off. But I remember that then I thought: *Okay, God, if you're real, let that song be playing when I turn the radio back on.* It's embarrassing now that I would think that, that such a thing would have meaning to me, but I was grasping at straws. I really desperately wanted to know if "Heaven knew." I had never been any kind of Led Zeppelin fan, but the song's lyrics seemed to goad my thinking along these lines. I was desperate to know if God was listening to my thoughts and was real. But I needed a sign, so that's what I prayed, if it can be called a prayer, and in retrospect, I think that it can, that any such thoughts directed to God, even speculative thoughts toward a God who might or might not be there, are prayers.

Eight hours later, fatigued from another day in that crushing corporate atmosphere I dragged myself to the car, got in, fired the ignition, pulled on the seat belt, and shifted into reverse to pull out of the parking space. I clicked on the radio out of habit and the song that was playing was Robert Plant's "Heaven Knows." I had completely forgotten that eight hours earlier I had thought that thought, or prayed that prayer. It hadn't crossed my mind once since I had left the car that morning. But now I was in the car and there it was. I remember being overwhelmed. Had God answered my prayer? Was there a God? Was he real? He was! He was real! Heaven *did* know. It was true! I remember driving out of that parking lot through the maze of concrete ramps and looking up and shouting as I drove, "You're real! You're really real!" I was beside myself.

But here is the most amazing thing. After that, I did nothing. I'm sure I forgot all about it within a few days. It just evaporated. I didn't tell Ed Tuttle about it. I did nothing, and it simply evaporated. Perhaps I thought the ball was now in God's court or something, but within a few days I was as unsure of God's existence as I had been before it happened. Maybe I was embarrassed at my enthusiasm and now thought that it was just a coincidence. After all, it was a Top 40 station and that song was near the top of the Top 40, even hitting number one at some point. Was it really a miracle? I guess I came to conclude that it wasn't. But I will never forget that feeling that God was real, that he knew my thoughts, that I could talk to him. It only lasted for a short time, but it was amazing. What if it was actually true? But at that point I wasn't at all convinced that it was.

A couple of months later—in June 1988—my uncle Takis, who is my father's elder brother, had a stroke and went into a coma. Naturally my family and I were very upset. I mentioned the situation to Ed and a day or two later, he said that he and some friends were praying for my uncle. I was astounded at the kindness of the gesture. And I was also astounded at the thought of these people who clearly believed there was a God who heard prayers like theirs and could do something about it. The idea that they were praying to a God who was "out there," who was not "us" or some form of "us," but who was really "other," hit me. This was different from trying to be in touch with our own "collective unconscious" or the "divinity within us."

A few days later, Ed asked if he could pray for my uncle *with* me. I was a bit taken aback, but because I so wanted my uncle to recover, I agreed and followed Ed into a ghastly fluorescent-lit conference room not far from where my cubicle was. I'd never done anything like this before, but I knew that it certainly couldn't hurt. So we sat in chairs, side by side, and I closed my eyes as Ed prayed aloud—and as he did, something transcendent seemed to take place. It wasn't anything physical or deeply mystical. But inside me there was a subtle shift as he prayed, as though a window had been opened onto another realm and I'd felt the faintest touch of some heavenly breeze. When it was over, I opened my eyes. *What was that?*

Around this time a slight shift was taking place in my mind too. I had picked up M. Scott Peck's book *People of the Lie*, and this prominent Harvard psychologist's compelling accounts of dealing with real evil got my attention. He hadn't himself believed in the existence of real evil, but over the course of a number of experiences, he felt that there was nothing else that could account for what he had seen and heard. Based on what I read in his book, I agreed. And I reasoned that if real evil existed, there must be an alternative. Would that be God? I was also reading Thomas Merton's *The Seven Storey Mountain*, the classic account of a brilliant Columbia graduate who finds his way to faith and then enters a Trappist monastery and writes about it. And around this time I was reading Bonhoeffer's *Cost of Discipleship*, which Ed had given to me, though I cannot remember if I was reading these before or after the dream. Ah yes, the dream.

Some days after my twenty-fifth birthday, I had a vivid dream. I dreamt I was ice-fishing on Candlewood Lake in Danbury, Connecticut. Candlewood Lake is a man-made lake, created in the 1930s, to provide a backup source for the Housatonic River's hydroelectric dam. I had spent a lot of time on Candlewood growing up, had swum there and had fished there from boats and from shore, and I had ice-fished there too.

In the dream I was standing on the ice and I vaguely remember that my childhood friend John Tomanio and his father were with me. It was a spectacularly bright and beautiful winter day, so bright that you had to squint because of the whiteness of the snow and ice. I looked into the large hole we had cut into the ice and saw the snout of a fish poking out, which of course never happens. I reached down and picked the fish up by the gills and held it up. It was a large pickerel, perhaps even a pike. And in the dazzlingly bright sunlight shining through the bright blue sky and off the white snow and ice onto the bronze-colored fish it appeared positively golden. But then in the dream I realized that it didn't merely *look* golden, it actually *was* golden. It was a living golden fish, as though I were in a fairy tale. And suddenly in the dream I understood that this golden fish was *IXTHYS*—Jesus Christ the Son of God Our Saviour—and I knew immediately that God had one-upped me in the language of my own symbol system. I had wanted to touch inert water, to touch the "Collective Unconscious," but he had something more for me: He gave me his son, a living person, Jesus Christ. I realized in the dream that Jesus Christ was real and had come from the other side to me—to *me*—and now I was holding him there in the bright sunlight and I was flooded with joy at the thought of it. At long last my search was over. It was over. And it was true. There was a God and Jesus was God and he had shown that to mc in a way that only I could understand, in a way that utterly blew my mind. God knew me infinitely better than I knew myself, and he had taken the trouble to speak to me in the most intimate language there was: the secret language of my own heart. That was that.

When I went to work the next day I told Ed about the dream. He asked what I thought it meant, and I said to him what I never would have said before to anyone—I would have cringed to hear anyone else say it. I said that I had accepted Jesus. And when I spoke those words I was flooded with the same joy I had had inside the dream. And I've carried that joy with me for the last twenty-six years.

I've told the story of my dream of the golden fish innumerable times. I don't tell it in public very often, but about a year ago I was speaking at Lee University and the campus chaplain thought that I should share my story of coming to faith. So instead of talking about Bonhoeffer or Wilberforce, I gave my testimony, as Christians sometimes put it. I remember that the connection with the students that day was extraordinary. There were about two thousand of them in the auditorium for that chapel and I cannot recall a crowd being more plugged in and responsive. I walked out of there on a cloud, so happy that my story had been received as it had.

But early the next morning I woke up and opened my computer to find an e-mail from one of the students who was there that day. He had e-mailed me via my website earlier that morning. He said that he had been in the audience the day before and that, frankly, he hadn't been impressed with my talk. He went on to say that he thought it was a bit pretentious or something. He also said that on the way out of the auditorium he had cracked a sarcastic joke with his friend, saying, "Yeah, maybe God will speak to *me* in a dream!" You can imagine that reading this was getting my attention. Why was someone who didn't appreciate my talk e-mailing me and giving me all the details of how he didn't appreciate my talk?

But the next sentence explained everything. He said that that night, God really *had* spoken to him in a dream—and that's why he was e-mailing me. I could hardly believe what I was reading, but I could tell from the way he said everything that he was on the level, so I e-mailed him immediately and asked him if he might tell me more. He e-mailed me back a few hours later and told me his story and the story of the dream. He said he was from England and was a freshman at Lee. He said that he had lost his mother to suicide just three months before. He wasn't any kind of Christian and had really only ended up going to this Christian university because of a sports scholarship. Then he told me the dream. One thing was clear when I read his account of it: It was God speaking, all right. It was an amazing dream. And he too had no doubt that it was God who was speaking to him. He explained some of the details and said that he clearly understood that God was telling him he needed to accept Jesus so that he could bring that peace and comfort to his stepfather and eleven-year-old stepbrother, who were obviously hurting badly from the loss of his mother, who had only been forty-one when she'd taken her life.

I connected him with the campus pastor. Recently I was in touch with him and am happy to report he is thriving in his newfound faith. The idea that God would respond to someone's sarcastic crack about a dream by visiting him in a dream that night and changing his life in the same way is something that will encourage me for a long time.

## "I AM YOUR LIFE"

My friend Frederica Mathewes-Green is a great writer. I don't merely mean great as in "totally awesome," but in the sense that she is a writer's writer, someone whose observational abilities, insights, and ability to turn well-crafted and compelling sentences are all superlative. Frederica is known mostly as someone who writes about her faith, so it's all the more extraordinary for me to think that long before I met her or read her writing, she was not a person of faith. In fact, Frederica says that when she was in college in the early seventies, she was contemptuous of Christian faith and downright hostile to it.

Frederica was raised in a nominally Christian home but rejected her parents' faith in her early teens. She was not a materialist, however, and remained open to other avenues of spirituality. She says that while in her teens the essence of her "homemade belief system was 'the life-force.'" She had concluded that it was somehow the "raw energy of life itself . . . [that] was the essence of God, and the various world religions were poetic attempts to express that truth." She would simply take from each tradition what she liked and ignore what she disliked. But during her senior year in college she gained an insight into herself that startled her. "I realized that my selections were inevitably conditioned by my own tastes, prejudices, and blind spots," she says. "I was patching together a Frankenstein God in my own image, and it would never be taller than five foot one. If I wanted to grow beyond my own meager wisdom, I would have to submit to a faith bigger than I was and accept its instruction."

This is when she chose Hinduism as the one faith whose tenets and conditions she would submit to. She was at the University of South Carolina at the time. "I chose it in part because I thought it would look really cool on me," she says. "I enjoyed the vivid poetry and mythology of the faith, but can't say I engaged it deeply. When all the world's religions were coquetting to be my choice, Christianity didn't even make the lineup. I considered it an infantile and inadequate religion. I found it embarrassing, childish— probably because I associated it with my own naive childhood. A rhetorician could have told me which logical fallacy this was, to presume that since I was immature when I was a preteen Christian, the faith itself was immature."

Not many years after graduation, Frederica met and married her husband, Gary, in a charmingly typical "hippie" wedding of the time, in the woods, with Frederica wearing flowers in her hair and sandals. "You can picture it," she writes, "the women in tie-dyed dresses and floating batik scarves, the jovial black lab with a red bandanna around his neck, the vegetarian reception under the trees."

Immediately afterward, she and Gary took off for Europe. They'd saved enough money that they planned on extending their honeymoon three months. They would hitchhike, live on wine and cheese, and generally do whatever else they could to keep costs down. On June 20, 1974, Frederica and Gary took a ferry from Wales to the Irish coast and then hitchhiked up to Dublin. They found a cheap hotel and later that afternoon decided to take a walk and see some sights.

They were in what seemed like a business district when they stumbled upon a church and decided to take a look inside. Frederica separated from Gary and admired the stained glass windows and stonework in the dimly lit building. "Eventually," she says, "I came upon a small side altar. Above it there was a white marble statue of Jesus with his arms held low and open, and his heart exposed on his chest, twined with thorns and springing with flames." Frederica explains that the statue depicted an apparition that a French nun had witnessed in 1675. The nun heard Jesus say, "Behold the heart which has so loved mankind." Frederica will never be able to explain exactly what happened next. But suddenly this young woman so hostile to Christianity found herself on her knees in front of the statue. "I could hear an interior voice speaking to me," she says. "Not with my ears—it was more like a radio inside suddenly clicked on. The voice was both intimate and authoritative, and it filled me."

It said, "I am your life. You think that your life is your name, your personality, your history. But that is not your life. I am your life." It went on, naming that "life-force" notion I admired: "Beyond that, you think that your life is the fact that you arc alive, that your breath goes in and out, that energy courses in your veins. But even that is not your life. I am your life. I am the foundation of everything else in your life."

After this, Frederica stood up feeling rather shaky. She says that it "was like sitting quietly in your living room and having the roof blown off. I didn't have any doubt who the 'I' was that was speaking to me, and it wasn't someone I was eager to get to know. If someone had asked me a half hour earlier, I would have said I was not sure the fellow had ever lived. Yet here he was, and though I didn't know him it seemed he already knew me, from the deepest inside out. I kept quiet about this for a week, trying to figure it out. I didn't even tell Gary, though he must have wondered why my eyebrows kept hovering up near my hairline."

Frederica says that it wasn't the kind of "woo-woo spiritual experiences where everything goes misty and the next day you wonder if it really happened. It was shockingly real, as if I'd encountered a dimension of reality I'd never known existed before." She explains that years after this experience she read C. S. Lewis's gemlike novella, "The Great Divorce." It begins, she explains, "with the charming idea that every day a bus crosses the great divide from Hell to Heaven. Anyone who wants can go, and anyone who wants can stay. The thing is, Heaven hurts. It's too real. The visitors from Hell can't walk on the grass, because the blades pierce their feet like knives. It takes time to grow real enough to endure Heaven, a process of unflinching self-discovery and repentance that few are willing to take. At the end of the day, most of the tourists get back on the bus to Hell."

She says that the experience that late afternoon

in that dimly lit Dublin church was "real like that, like grass that pierces your feet. In that explosive moment I found that Jesus was realer than anything I'd ever encountered, the touchstone of reality. It left me with a great hunger for more, so that my whole life is leaning toward him, questing for him, striving to break down the walls inside that shelter me from his gaze."

# A BROOKLYN DRUG DEALER FINDS GOD

I first heard about "Cisco" through my friend Joel Tucciarone, fellow Yale man and longtime marketing consultant, who lives in Bay Ridge, Brooklyn. For years Joel has attended a men's Bible study meeting in the back of a diner and composed of Brooklyn "regulars," including a number of ex-cons, some of whom were once involved in organized crime. For example, one of them, Mr. V, was part of what is known as "the Family" before he found God. After he came to faith, he went to the head of the Family and asked to be released from his line of business, which, uncharacteristically, the capo did, as Mr. V had taken the oath of familial loyalty. Cisco was a member of this Bible study as well and was known to be what is often called a "prayer warrior," someone who spends hours in prayer and whose prayers are known to have a particularly powerful effect.

Whenever I was facing something particularly arduous, Joel would say that he'd call up Cisco and ask him to pray. A few times I even got on the phone with Joel and Cisco together, and I was able to hear Cisco pray his wonderful prayers, which were both respectful and like someone speaking to his best friend. Through Joel I eventually heard a little bit about Cisco's story, and when I began writing this book I knew I may want to tell it, so one very cold late December night, I met Joel and Cisco in the back booth of an Italian restaurant in Bay Ridge. That's where Cisco told me his story.

Cisco—short for Francisco—Anglero was born in Puerto Rico in 1944. His family came to Brooklyn in 1949 and they were the first Puerto Ricans to live on Coney Island, which at that time was predominantly Irish, Italian, German, and Jewish. As a little boy in this very tough part of Brooklyn, Cisco's dark skin and inability to speak English made him a target for the other kids. He told me that he would "catch a beating" almost every single time he left his house, which was more than once a day, to run errands or go to school. His father taught him a type of French foot-fighting called savate, but strictly forbade him from ever using it on the other kids in the neighborhood, so he simply took the beatings, more afraid of what his father might do if he fought back and badly hurt one of the other kids.

In 1953, on his ninth birthday, Cisco's father gave him a baseball glove, which was promptly stolen by two neighborhood bullies, sixteen and seventeen years old, respectively. When Cisco's father found out, he seemed to have finally had enough, and he gave his son permission to defend himself. Actually, he went much beyond that. Knowing Cisco to be far outmatched by these older kids, his father handed Cisco a baseball bat, sent him out the door, and made it clear that he had better come back with his glove—or else. As an added impetus, he said that if Cisco didn't return with the glove, he would turn the bat into splinters over Cisco's back. Cisco doesn't believe his father ever intended to carry through with that threat; he felt that it was one final encouragement to do what he needed to do to stand up to these older boys. So Cisco promptly went to the homes of each of these bullies, lured them outside, and unleashed the rage that had been building inside him for years, smashing each of them across the knees with the bat in brutal fashion, especially given his age. Needless to say, he brought the glove back and after word got out that he would defend himself, he was given a wide berth.

Over the next few years, Cisco's reputation as someone to be feared only grew. At age eleven he and a friend named Cookie began lifting weights, and pretty soon, Cisco became obsessed with it. He became tremendously strong and by his late teens was as big as some of the best bodybuilders in the world. At seventeen, he boasted nineteen-inch biceps, a fifty-inch chest, a thirty-two-inch waist—and he could bench five hundred pounds. By the time he was twenty-two, although he was only five eleven, he had a fifty-three-inch chest, twenty-one-inch arms, and weighed 245. He lifted at a gym frequented by Lou Ferrigno, and although he never competed in any formal bodybuilding contests, he once beat a renowned bodybuilder who became Mr. Universe, in an informal contest. Unsurprisingly, the hulking young man was hired as a bouncer at various Brooklyn clubs and was later hired to be a bodyguard to some of the organized crime leaders in the area. Eventually they used him to collect their debts. Finally, he was drawn in to dealing drugs. By any account, Cisco led a strange life. He had a regular day job, driving a refrigerated dairy truck—something he did for thirty-eight years—but at night he led another life entirely, in the world of organized crime.

Cisco remembered that during all those years as a teenager, whenever he would return home from his late-night adventures, his mother would greet him in her familiar rocking chair, the one his father had made for her. Her father had been a Pentecostal pastor in Puerto Rico, and whenever his mother wasn't cooking or cleaning she could be found in her chair, praying and reading the Bible. Cisco said that when he walked in, she would tenderly ask how he was feeling and tell him that she was praying for him to come home. She would then look up to the heavens and thank God for her son's safety. Cisco shrugged it all off. He loved his mother, but this was not the sort of thing a tough guy on Coney Island was supposed to be interested in, and he wasn't.

Actually, Cisco had contempt for anything to do with the church. Much of the reason had to do with someone in the neighborhood who had become a pastor. Cisco remembered that this man had a church in the middle of Coney Island, but what Cisco knew of him didn't comport with the image he had of how a pastor should conduct himself. Most Sundays, Cisco went to the house of his friend Tito to hang out and play dominoes. This pastor often showed up there with cocaine, and he tried to seduce the friends of Tito's sisters, who were all of twelve, thirteen, and fourteen years old. Cisco knew that this pastor was in his midtwenties and had a wife and kids of his own. How could he live with himself?

Because she had bad asthma problems, Cisco's mother began spending a lot of time in the warm climate of Florida. Even there she had bad asthma attacks and went to the hospital, but after a few days she always recovered, and life went on. This happened so often that it became a predictable pattern. But one day in 1968, when Cisco was twenty-four, he learned that his mother had died. Cisco hadn't been prepared for this. It came as a tremendous shock. His mother had only been fifty-two years old. The news hit him so hard that Cisco began crying uncontrollably. When he walked out on the street to go home, still sobbing, he suddenly saw the twentysomething pastor. That this hypocrite should be walking down the street alive, when the one person he loved most in the world was gone, tore at Cisco. He suddenly found himself cursing God over and over. "Why did you take my mother?" he screamed. "She used to go to church all the time. She worshiped you and praised you and you let her die! And this hypocrite pastor who's always trying to molest kids, you gave him a church and he's walking around like everything's okay!"

After that day, Cisco turned his back on God completely. He even became a hit man, killing for hire, although during our meeting that night in the Italian restaurant, he made it clear that he didn't feel free to give me any details about that darkest part of his life. During these years, Cisco also became more and more involved in dealing drugs. At one point he was the drug lord over a significant neighborhood in Brooklyn. This went on until 1988, when he was arrested and sent to jail for two years. But no sooner was he released than he was arrested again. Eleven days after he had been released, Cisco was home, watching a Yankees game. Realizing he had nothing to drink in the house, he drove down to the liquor store on Brighton Beach Avenue and bought some beer. But as he exited the liquor store, he saw that two narcotics officers had blocked his car with their own cars.

"What do you want?" he asked them. They told him they were going to search his car. Cisco was very careful never to have drugs with him. He might have been one of the biggest drug dealers in Brooklyn, but he wasn't about to get caught with drugs in his car. So the officers didn't find anything and Cisco was about to get in his car and leave, but just then a police sergeant pulled up in a van. The sergeant asked the officers what they had found. When they told him nothing, he told one of them to go to the back of the van, get a kilo bag of coke, put it under his police vest, and search Cisco's car again. This was all said right in front of Cisco.

So the officer went to the back of the van and returned to search Cisco's car, this time producing a kilo bag of coke, which he held up so that all the bystanders could see it and be witnesses in court. Cisco knew there was nothing he could do. This was the rough justice of that time and place. In the cops' eyes, they knew Cisco was a notorious drug dealer, so framing him to get him off the streets was perfectly acceptable. The cops took him to central booking, and that day he started what was a journey of six years in the New York State correctional system.

After he was booked, they took Cisco to a main correctional facility in Brooklyn, which was located in the old Brooklyn Navy Yard. Cisco was taken upstairs to the fifth floor, where he saw a phone. He asked if he could call his wife, who of course had no idea why her husband had never returned home. But a group of prisoners quickly made it clear that he could not use the phone. Cisco was baffled. "Why?" he asked them. "Is it broke?"

"No," they said gruffly. "Nobody can't use nothing unless we tell them." Three of them got very close to Cisco in a threatening way. A bit later he spoke to some other prisoners, who informed him that that was the "house gang." The cops had essentially given them the run of the place. While Cisco was sitting at the edge of his bed, quietly incensed that these men had prevented him from calling his wife, he noticed something. Next to each bed were small metal lockers. When Cisco accidentally leaned against one, he saw that it wasn't attached to the floor. It was large and heavy enough for what he had in mind. That night when everyone was asleep, Cisco lifted one of the lockers and smashed it with all his considerable might over the sleeping head of first one and then another of the men who had threatened him.

The third one woke up, but Cisco managed to smash the locker across his head as well. The fourth man, who was farther away, saw what was happening and ran screaming to the "bubble," which was what they called the Plexiglassed area where the COs were stationed. He shouted that he was about to be killed. In a moment all the lights came on and the COs appeared. As they tried to determine what had happened, the captain saw that there was blood on Cisco's locker and asked Cisco if he had been the one to do all this. "Are you kidding?" Cisco said. "This is my first time here. Why don't you wake them up and ask *them* who did it?"

The five members of the house gang were taken away, four to the infirmary. When Cisco got up the next morning, he asked the remaining men whether he could use the phone and they quickly informed him that the phone was all his—that it "belonged to him now." Whether because of the beating they had witnessed, or because word had gotten out that Cisco was connected to organized crime on the outside, or most likely because the five members of the house gang had vanished, things were now dramatically different. Cisco could use the phone as much as he liked. But he knew there were a lot of men there who had never been allowed to use the phone. So he asked them, "How many of you never get to talk to your families?" About ten hands shot up. "Come here," Cisco told them. "Get on the phone and call your family." He told them they could have as much time as they liked.

Not long afterward, Cisco bumped into one of the captains of the organized crime family he had been working for who was doing time there. The man had been told to take care of Cisco, and he found him a job in the mess hall. Cisco had been working there for four or five months when two old friends from his neighborhood walked in. It was Hector, a Puerto Rican, and Frankie, an African-American. He hadn't seen them in some time and they all greeted one another warmly. No sooner had they done so than the two of them asked Cisco if he wanted to go with them to church services upstairs. There were services every week in another part of the jail. Cisco thought they must be kidding. "Go where?" he said. He made it clear he was not interested. Then the three of them sat down and Cisco told them how he had come to be there, beginning with his mother's death and his anger at God and the downward spiral into becoming a hardened drug dealer.

Over the next weeks it became abundantly clear that Hector and Frankie had "found God" in prison. Every chance they got they asked Cisco if he wanted to join them at the church services and each time Cisco adamantly refused. "Forget about it," he said. "This might be for you, but it's not for me." They continued to invite him. One day Cisco had had enough. He exploded. "No!" he said emphatically. "You ask me every week! Leave me alone! You're driving me crazy!" At this point he went to turn on his Sony Walkman, to tune out his annoying friends. But for no particular reason it wouldn't work. He then asked Hector, "Could I use your Walkman?" Hector gave his Walkman to Cisco, but for some reason it didn't work either. Cisco would not be deterred He asked Frankie if his Walkman was working. Frankie said yes, that he had put fresh batteries in that morning. So Frankie gave Cisco his Walkman, but when Cisco tried to turn it on, it refused to work as well. Cisco couldn't figure out what was happening. He was frustrated and angry. It was mystifying. At about this time, Hector and Frankie left for the service, leaving Cisco alone on his bunk, surrounded by men listening to their own Walkmen or sleeping and snoring. He thought he would turn on the TV, but that wouldn't work either. Now, he was furious. What in the world was he supposed to do with no music and no TV and a room full of snoring men? At this point, Cisco thought he might as well go to the service. Anything was better than listening to these snoring men. So he went up to the service and saw that the minister was none other than Dr.

Matthews, his bronchial doctor. Like his mother, Cisco suffered from asthma, and Dr. Matthews had been treating him. But here she was playing the role of minister too. Hector and Frankie were thrilled to see that Cisco had come after all. "Do you feel it?" they asked him. Cisco said he felt absolutely nothing. What was he supposed to feel?

Again, the next week they asked him whether he wanted to go with them. He didn't. His Walkman was working now, so he turned it on and lay on his bunk. But five or so minutes after they had gone, Cisco began to feel tremendously agitated. He was normally calm and cool, but for some reason at that moment he felt extremely worked up and out of sorts, as though his heart might come out of his mouth. He began pacing up and down the room. For no reason he could make sense of, he felt compelled to go upstairs to the service.

Since everyone had already gone up, Cisco went to the "bubble" to ask for permission. But the CO said it was too late. He said Cisco would just have to wait till Wednesday. But Cisco couldn't wait. So he asked the CO to call up the captain. Cisco had done a fair amount of dirty work for this captain, who was himself connected to the organized crime family Cisco had worked for. Anytime someone crossed him or got out of line, the captain would send Cisco to their cell to give them a beating. For that, he got fifty dollars. "Tell him I want to go up to the service and you won't bring me," Cisco said, hoping the captain could get him permission. As it happened, he could.

So Cisco went upstairs to the service. But as he looked into the room now, he had a strange feeling. Everyone was singing as they had been the previous week. It wasn't his cup of tea, but it had been hard to get up here, so he finally went in and stood at the back since there were no chairs at all there.

He was standing about thirty feet from the front where a group was leading worship music from a small low platform. That's when he looked up and saw someone on the platform that he recognized—she looked just like his mother. She was part of the worship team.

Cisco said to himself, "That's my mother. . . ." Then he thought, "But my mother is dead." At that moment, he started to cry and could not stop.

Hector and Frankie came over to him and Hector asked, "Did God touch you? . . . You feeling something?" Cisco told him, "If you don't want to get smacked in the face, just leave me alone. . . ." The two of them got the message and drifted off.

When the worship music was over, there was a call to come forward to pray and receive Jesus. Cisco looked and saw his mother waving for him to come forward to the altar. She was smiling at him with the same smile that he had always loved. He went forward, his eyes still filling with tears. At the altar, Cisco got down on his knees and Dr. Matthews, who was ministering, came over to everyone gathered and prayed what she called the "sinner's prayer." Everyone repeated it, including Cisco. She finished and everyone stood up. When Cisco got up, he wondered to himself, "Where's my mother?" and began to look around for her.

Just then, an African-American woman, seeing Cisco rather obviously looking around, approached him. "Are you looking for someone?" she asked. Cisco said, "Yes, there was a woman I saw a few minutes ago who looked like my mother. She was waving for me to come forward from my seat and she was smiling at me. But I don't see her now." Then the black lady said, "That was me waving to you to come forward. It was me that was smiling and waving for you to come down and accept the Lord."

Now, Cisco's mother was fair-skinned, but this woman was extremely dark-skinned, so dark that Cisco said her skin seemed to shine. His mother was only five feet tall and this woman was five foot six or seven. Cisco's mother was a skinny woman, a little over one hundred pounds, while this woman was rather heavyset, and probably weighed more than one hundred and fifty pounds.

While they both had black hair, this woman's hair was quite kinky. Cisco's mother's hair was straight. And his mother had a gold tooth among her other teeth, but Cisco saw that this woman had no teeth at all. Cisco hardly knew what to think. He said to himself, "If that was not my mother, what did I see?"

At this point, Cisco started to walk away, quite confused. But Dr. Matthews saw him and called him back.

"Here, Francisco," she said. She had obviously been waiting for this moment. She handed him a large brand-new Bible. Cisco opened it and looked at it. "It's nice," he said, and handed it back to her. But she said, "No, it's for you. With this Bible you're going to start your ministry." Cisco had no idea what she was talking about. What did she mean by "your ministry"? How would she know whether he would ever have a ministry, whatever that meant? Nonetheless, he took the Bible and left. Cisco still has that Bible, with the date it was given to him written inside it: September 25, 1990.

After that day, Cisco went back every time there was a service. What happened to him in that service had changed him forever; it still affects him deeply. After retelling this story, he said, wiping tears from his eyes, "I was twenty-four when my mother died and I had not seen her since I was twenty-two. Looking back now at the age of seventy, you can see how I still feel about her. God did something to my eyes that day in the chapel. Because I loved my mother and because of the way I had cursed God, he gave me the vision of her, knowing that was the only way I would come to him. And he knew the purpose of my life, of what he had in store for me."

# 10

---·◆·◆·◆·---

## HEALING MIRACLES

I am the Lord that healeth thee.
—EXODUS 26:15

Then great multitudes came to Him, having with them the lame, blind, mute, maimed, and many others; and they laid them down at Jesus' feet, and He healed them.
—MATTHEW 15:30

When people talk about miracles, they typically think of healing miracles. That's probably because there's something fairly tidy and binary about them. One day the tumor is there; the next it's not. Someone prays for a blind man and he regains his sight. A televangelist prays for a woman struggling on crutches, she tosses the crutches away and leaps about. Whether such miracles happen is a separate question, but when someone mentions the word "miracle," most of us think of these sorts of scenarios.

In this chapter I will tell five stories of healing miracles, although as I asked friends whether they had experienced miracles, many more than these five offered stories of miraculous healing. They are more common than I ever thought. I remember my own grandmother telling me how she had prayed for her own leg, which was hurting, and "felt a sizzling" and was instantly healed. This was in the 1970s. My mother was at work and my grandmother was taking care of my brother and me over summer vacation. She told me that she spoke to God, saying, "I can't take care of these children today unless you heal me," and as she was talking to God—which is to say, as she was praying—she felt a warmth in her leg and it was healed, just like that. She was not a woman given to hyperbole. Although there's nothing dramatic about it, I mention it because I have heard many stories like it over the years. Most of them aren't especially dramatic, but all of them are in a way nonetheless amazing.

Though I myself have prayed hundreds of times for healing, I cannot recount any answers to these prayers. I recall in the summer of 1990 being on the hot streets of the South Bronx. Some friends from Times Square Church and Saint Paul's Church in Darien, Connecticut, were doing an "outreach" in that impoverished area, praying for people and talking to them about God. An elderly black man leaning against a storefront asked us to pray for him, lifting his shirt and revealing a hideous growth. After he replaced his shirt, we "laid hands" on him and prayed, in faith, in Jesus's name. Whether a healing happened we will never know. But just because these things don't happen as we would like them to happen, doesn't mean we shouldn't pray, knowing that God can heal. The Bible says clearly that God wants us to ask him for help when we need it, and it is clear that asking for healing when we are sick is part of that. Whether he heals us is another story, but if we don't ask for it, we are preempting the very possibility that it might happen. So we should ask. And as the following stories illustrate, God really can heal us.

## CISCO AND HECTOR

In the previous chapter, I told the story of how Cisco Anglero found God. But that wasn't the end of what happened to him. In fact, while he was still in prison, God used him in a dramatic way.

Cisco remembered that one day about six weeks after his dramatic conversion experience (see page 245), he was walking back to the dorm from his job in KK—what they called the officers' cafeteria—when he saw that his friend Hector was in bed, shaking and shivering. It was about 75 degrees out, but for some reason Hector was wearing his boots and socks, a sweater, his heavy coat, and a thick winter blanket. Cisco asked him what was the matter. "I don't know," Hector said. "It feels like I'm dying." In Cisco's remembrance, Hector had always been around 215 pounds and very muscular, but the moment Hector and Frankie had arrived Cisco saw that Hector was noticeably thinner. But he never asked him why. Cisco had always been taught to mind his own business: If someone wanted you to know something, they would tell you. But the truth was that Hector had contracted AIDS. He was perhaps 180 when Cisco first saw him a few months earlier. Now he was even thinner.

Cisco had no idea how to respond to what his friend had said, so he just sat on his bunk nearby and opened his Bible. But then Hector called to him: "Cisco, come here."

"What's the matter, Hector?" Cisco said, coming over to his bed. "What can I do for you?"

"The Holy Spirit told me that if you pray for me, what I feel now is going to be gone." Cisco had no idea what to make of what Hector had just said. After all, he had been a Christian for only six weeks.

"If I pray for you?" he said. "I don't know how to pray." But Cisco loved his friend and wanted to do what he could. One thing he had learned was that prayers were more powerful if the person praying didn't have any unconfessed sin. So he said to God, "Lord, if I'm doing something you don't want me to do, show me. But I don't want my friend to be like this." After that, right there by his bedside, Cisco began praying for Hector in the only way he knew how. His prayers were simple but deeply heartfelt.

Suddenly, Cisco told me, a very bright light—"as bright as the sun," he said—covered the two of them, "like a halo. It was a circle." They were on the second floor of the facility, so it couldn't have been actual sunlight. Cisco said that when he finished praying the light went away and he went back to his bunk and sat down. Then, suddenly, he saw Hector stand up, take the blankets off, and take his coat off and the sweater too. And then Hector began jumping up and down and saying over and over, "Thank you, Jesus! Thank you, Jesus! Thank you, Jesus!"

One of the corrections officers saw what was happening. He knew Hector had been in very bad shape, so he immediately called up Dr. Matthews in the infirmary and told her that Hector had taken everything off and was jumping up and down. A few minutes later Dr. Matthews showed up and asked Hector what had happened. He told her everything. Then she examined him and said that it didn't seem that anything was wrong with him. For no reason anyone could divine other than the prayer that Cisco offered, Hector was suddenly feeling fine.

What happened that day was clearly mystifying and dramatic, but it didn't halt the overall progress of the disease. Hector continued to lose weight and grow weaker.

About two months after the day he prayed for Hector, Cisco had a terrible argument on the phone with his wife, Christine. It so affected him that he stopped reading the Bible and praying. It was a very dark period for him.

One day during this time, Cisco walked into the dormitory and saw that they were taking Hector out in a wheelchair. Cisco learned they were taking him to Kings County Hospital, where Dr. Matthews was in residence. Hector's weight had by now dropped down to about 145 pounds. Dr. Matthews was with Hector and she took Cisco aside and explained there was nothing more they could do for Hector. They were taking him to the hospital to make him more comfortable while the disease took its inevitable course.

About ten days later one of the officers came over to Cisco and told him he had a visitor. Cisco absolutely never had visitors. He had made a point of telling his wife, Christine, never to visit him, so he was sure it wasn't her. His brothers lived in Puerto Rico, so he knew it wasn't either of them. His sister lived in Florida. Cisco had no idea who it could be. But he went to the visiting room and saw a woman coming in. She sat down and told him that she was Hector's mother. Cisco asked how Hector was doing and she said not well. He was on many medications and had

IVs all over him. His weight was down to 120 pounds.

But Hector's mother told Cisco that Hector had told her the story of how Cisco had once prayed for him and how his symptoms had vanished instantly. She told Cisco that Hector had said that God had spoken to him again. God had told Hector that if Cisco prayed for him again, he would be healed completely. Not just the symptoms, but the disease itself. Cisco again had no idea what to make of this. How could he pray for Hector? He was in prison. He certainly couldn't go over to Kings County Hospital and pray for his friend in person. The only thing he could think of was to go down to the infirmary and talk to Dr. Matthews. Perhaps she could call Kings County, since she was a resident there. Perhaps they could get Hector on the phone and Cisco could pray for him that way.

Cisco told Hector's mother he would do whatever he could. So he went downstairs to the infirmary and found Dr. Matthews and explained the situation. He said that he felt he needed to pray for Hector over the phone. Dr. Matthews said she would see what she could do. So she called Kings County immediately and asked to be put in touch with Hector. But that wasn't possible. They told her she could speak to the doctor in charge, or to the head nurse, but not with Hector himself. She could visit him in person if she liked, but talking to him over the phone was simply not allowed. They were at an impasse. "I don't know what else to do," she said to Cisco.

Just then, for the first time in his life, Cisco heard God speak to him, telling him to get the phone number Dr. Matthews had just dialed. So he asked her for it.

Dr. Matthews didn't know what Cisco thought he could do with the phone number. She explained to him that if they wouldn't let her speak to Hector, they certainly wouldn't let Cisco speak to Hector. But Cisco knew what he had heard. God told him to get the number, so he persisted. Finally she relented and gave it to him. Cisco immediately left the infirmary and went upstairs to use the phone. But as he was doing that, God spoke again, telling him, not yet, to wait. So he obediently went to his bunk and waited. Phone use was restricted, and there were no calls allowed after 10:00 P.M. But it was just after ten when Cisco heard God speak the third time, saying, *"Now. Go."*

So Cisco walked over to the "bubble" and knocked on the glass and said to the CO that he had to make a call. The CO laughed, figuring Cisco was kidding around with him. But Cisco made it clear he wasn't kidding at all. "I need to make a phone call," he said. "I need to call Kings County." But the CO said that wasn't possible.

The phone was already shut down for the night, and he wasn't about to lose his job by letting Cisco use it.

Cisco said that at this point "something just came over me and I said, 'If you don't give me the phone, then it's on your head.' " Cisco later thought that it must have been God speaking through him, because he wasn't sure why he said that, but the urgency was powerful. Those words shook up the CO somehow, and he immediately changed his mind and gave Cisco the phone. But he said, "Please just make it ten minutes. If you're on longer and they catch you, I'm going to get fired!"

So Cisco dialed the number. A nurse answered. She asked if he was Hector's relative. Cisco said that he wasn't, that he was a friend. The nurse said she was sorry, but if he wanted to speak with the patient he had to be a relative. But he was welcome to come there in person. Cisco explained he couldn't come there in person because he was calling from prison. The nurse said that was even worse, and he might as well forget about talking to Hector.

But for the second time, a tremendous boldness came over Cisco. "If you don't put Hector on the telephone," he said to the nurse, "God says that he will punish you." At this point Hector, whose bed must have been nearby, said something to the nurse. Cisco could hear his voice through the phone. Hector obviously knew Cisco was on the phone because of what he heard the nurse saying on her end. Finally, the nurse relented. "Okay, okay," she said, "but you can only talk for a few minutes, because I'll get in trouble." She handed Hector the phone.

"What happened, buddy?" Cisco asked. Hector said that the Holy Spirit had spoken to him again. "He told me that you were going to pray for me," Hector said, "and that he was going to heal me." Cisco knew that what Hector said the last time had happened just as he had said it would happen. There wasn't much time, so right then Cisco prayed for Hector's healing over the phone. After he finished praying, he told Hector that he loved him and hung up.

That Friday the COs told Cisco he had another visitor. He went down to the visitors area and saw Hector's mother walking in. From the look on her face Cisco assumed she was there to tell him that Hector had died. He braced himself. But when she got to the table, her expression changed. She was beaming. She told Cisco that what happened when he prayed was a miracle. She said that a few minutes after he finished praying and hung up, Hector's whole body began shaking violently, so much so that all the intravenous needles came out of his body. He then fell off the bed, got up, and started jumping up and down, over and over, thanking God. It was a miracle. She told Cisco that the Kings County doctors had been checking Hector for the last three days and they couldn't find any evidence of the AIDS virus in his body. They decided to keep him there for a few more weeks, just to make sure that he was okay, but after that, they would release him.

That was the last Cisco heard of Hector for about five years.

Not long after Hector's healing, Cisco was sleeping in his bunk when suddenly he woke up, sweating. He didn't know if it was in a dream or in a vision, but God had spoken to him, telling him that he was going to prepare Cisco to become the director of a men's ministry to alcoholics, drug addicts, people with mental illness, ex-cons, and homeless men.

After some time, Cisco was transferred to a prison upstate, and then to Rikers Island. After Rikers he went to Ulster County Jail and then to Eastern Correctional. He finally got out in 1992, going back to his home and his wife, Christine, on Coney Island. Cisco began attending a church nearby called Coney Island Gospel Assembly. The pastor who founded the church was a man named Jack San Filippo, who had died not long before, so his daughter had become the pastor and Cisco was a deacon. One Sunday after church, Cisco was sitting in the pastoral office when a phone call came in for the pastor from Larry Johnson, the director of Victory Outreach.

He explained that seven homeless men had been staying at the Victory Outreach church but could no longer do so for various reasons. "Would Coney Island Gospel Assembly be willing to take them in?" Larry asked. The pastor asked Cisco if he would be able to take responsibility for them. "I'm not a babysitter!" Cisco shot back. But then, Cisco felt "something like a bolt of lightning" hit him in the back of the head. And he heard a voice telling him, "Remember!" It was God jogging his memory of when he had told Cisco that someday he would run a ministry for the homeless, ex-cons, alcoholics, drug addicts, and people with mental illness. So Cisco changed his mind and those seven men eventually turned into a ministry that he ran for nine years.

A year after that, Cisco was at DeKalb Avenue in Brooklyn, meeting with his parole officer. On the way home he stopped into a restaurant to get a soda when he bumped into someone who knew his old friend Hector. It had been five years since he'd prayed for him over the phone and he hadn't heard anything since. So he immediately asked the friend about Hector. Had he heard any news of him? The friend told Cisco that Hector was completely healthy. In fact, he was at that time in Bible college, training to become a minister.

Cisco's ministry to the men of Brooklyn thrived too. Over the next few years 1,200 to 1,500 passed through it. The journals kept by Cisco and the pastor documented that during the nine-year period more than eight hundred of them gave their lives to God, went back to their families, and found work. Cisco's been ministering to men in Brooklyn ever since.

# A SIMPLE HEALING PRAYER

I've known my friend John Alan Turner for about ten years now, and every time we meet I marvel at how similar we are, especially in our taste in literature and our sense of humor. John studied at Pepperdine University, Pacific Christian College, and the London School of Theology, and then went into the pastorate. One day John told me the story of something that happened in the spring of 2000. It was during a Sunday morning worship service in Columbia, Maryland.

John was then thirty, and he pastored the church—the Columbia Church of Christ. The congregation was a relatively small congregation, with about 125 attending each week. But this was in one of the least "churched" counties in America. "We were struggling to keep the lights on and our hopes up," as he put it. There was no church building, so they met in the local community center, which they rented for Sunday worship. According to John, the room where they met was depressingly generic, "the kind of place where people might have all kinds of events, from a wedding reception to a child's dance class." Every week the church volunteers had to show up early to set up and then tear it all down afterward.

In his congregation there was a soft-spoken parishioner named Michael who was a psychiatrist. Michael was part of the group who had volunteered to be in the rotation to lead worship and that week, it was his turn. But Michael's father—with whom he had had an incredibly tumultuous and painful relationship—had died recently. His father had been physically abusive, with a harsh religious streak. John said he was "the kind of Catholic who believed kids needed to be spanked periodically for no good reason other than it helped beat the original sin out of them and taught them how to suffer like Jesus." So Michael's father's death was sudden and unexpected, and John could see that Michael was having a very difficult time reconciling his decidedly mixed emotions. More than once Michael said: "I don't know how people process stuff like this without a church family. I suppose that's what keeps guys like me in business."

So that Sunday, John walked into the room where they gathered for worship when Michael, who was already there, approached him. John saw that he was wearing a sling and walking gingerly. For some reason, John had a bad feeling about it. "John," Michael said, "I've pinched a nerve in my neck. It's made my arm go all pins and needles. It started Friday and was so bad I had to cancel all my patients for the day. I went to my doctor and thought it would be better by now. But it's throbbing. I can't lead worship today. I'm sorry."

Michael's eyes were shining, and John could see that it was from tears. He was in real pain—physically, emotionally, spiritually. Obviously playing guitar and leading worship was out of the question.

John's mind began racing immediately. He had a service to lead in a few minutes. But he didn't want to lead the music portion of it and preach too. He thought it would look too much like a one-man show. In mentally scrambling to figure out what best to do, he was probably a bit dismissive with Michael. He told him everything would be fine and said he should get some rest and that he hoped he would feel better soon. A few quick conversations later, he found someone to fill in for Michael. Then he took a deep breath and the service began.

The services always began with a song, after which John would greet everyone, share a few announcements of upcoming events, and have the congregation stand to greet one another. This week, after the first song, as John brightly said,

"Good morning!" to the congregation, he saw Michael sitting off to the side, obviously wincing in pain and discomfort, though he was trying to look pleasant.

John realized he couldn't continue. He stopped everything and did something he had never done before. In fact, he never deviated from the plan at all, but he now felt something welling up inside him that he couldn't ignore. So instead of what was scripted, he simply said, "Folks, you know Michael. Your program says he's supposed to lead us in song this morning. But he can't. He's got a pinched nerve in his neck. It's causing him a lot of pain. It actually cost him patients on Friday. You know what? Let's just pray for him right now."

John asked Michael to come out of his pew and step forward to where John was standing in front of the congregation. John placed his hand on Michael's "good" shoulder and then prayed spontaneously:

"God, thank you so much for Michael and his servant's heart. You know what a rough year he's had with the death of his father. And you know how much pain he's in right now—inside and out. God, I don't believe this is your best for him. I don't believe you like seeing Michael suffer like this. The pain of grief never goes away in an instant, but the pain in his arm could. You could do that. We'd all love it if you would. But if you don't, continue to make Michael brave and strong—and help us to know how to be better friends and neighbors to Michael and to others around us. I pray all this in Jesus's name. Amen."

Michael was visibly moved. John was too. With that, Michael returned to his seat, and they moved back into the planned schedule of the service, which at this point consisted of more worship.

Then, about ten minutes later right in the middle of one of the songs—the mild-mannered and soft-spoken Michael literally started jumping up and down. Over and over. He then came sprinting to the front, waving his previously "bad" arm all over the place like a wild man.

"He did it, John!" Michael said. "He really did it!"

Michael was never exuberant, but he now actually grabbed the microphone from one of the singers up front and said, "Folks, I don't know how to explain this, but as I was sitting there during worship just now my arm started feeling really warm and then it felt like it just kind of breathed a sigh of relief. And now look at this!" He waved the arm all over again. The congregation wasn't at all used to this sort of thing happening on Sunday mornings in their church, but neither were they skeptical that something extraordinary had indeed just happened. They knew Michael well enough to understand this was a bona fide miracle, and they all spontaneously began clapping and shouting.

After things calmed down and Michael went back to his pew, John proceeded to preach his sermon. But how do you follow something like that? Who could think of anything except what had just happened? John now says he probably should have skipped the sermon and just had everyone continue praising and worshiping and then all go home. As far as he was concerned, the miracle of Michael's arm was all the sermon anyone needed that morning.

Today John and Michael live in different cities, but on those rare occasions when they bump into each other, Michael tells anyone in earshot about "the time John healed my arm." And every time he says it, John corrects him, saying that it was "the time God healed Michael's arm and I just happened to be standing there."


## ALLERGIC TO EVERYTHING

I met my friend Lucy Schafer in the midnineties through mutual friends at Redeemer Presbyterian Church on the Upper East Side in Manhattan. Lucy was at the time working long hours as an associate producer for a major news program.

It was a gorgeous summer evening about fifteen years ago over dinner that Lucy Schafer told us all this story. In all these years I have never forgotten it.

Lucy grew up in Manhattan, New York City, in a Jewish family on the Upper East Side. They were religiously observant Jews but "culturally assimilated," as Lucy put it. Her father graduated from Columbia in the early forties and then attended Yale Law. Her mother attended Barnard. Lucy explained that education—specifically Ivy League education—was absolutely essential to her parents' plans for her, so much so that she said at age five she knew she would not only be attending an Ivy League school for college but that she would go to an Ivy League school for graduate work. Those were the expectations. As it happened, she did, ending up at Dartmouth as an undergraduate and then at Yale Law School in the mideighties.

During her last year of college and into her first year of law school, Lucy started to experience unusual fatigue and would get sick frequently. Then, in the summer after her first year at Yale she began to experience tremendous allergic reactions. Her allergies to typical things like pollen and dogs and cats had already begun to intensify during college, but suddenly now she became tremendously ill and reacted badly to a host of new things: the smell of perfume and shampoo, the smell of pesticides, and auto exhaust. Almost anything with chemicals in it. It got to where even the print on newspapers would make her face swell up. She got so sick that she had to take a medical leave of absence from law school. She had been experiencing extraordinary fatigue and bruising for no apparent reason and although she was already thin, she dropped ten pounds nearly overnight, although she was eating everything she could. Her search for help took her to Massachusetts General, where she saw the head of immunology, and then to Yale Medical School and to many other prestigious hospitals in the Northeast. But for all her persistence, she couldn't get a good diagnosis, much less any kind of help.

In her desperation, she began speaking to other people who suffered from similar things and eventually heard about an immunologist in San Francisco at UCSF, who was having some success with a few patients. So she booked a ticket to San Francisco and flew there to see him. There was nothing to keep her in the Northeast. She was much too weak to continue her studies and the man she had been dating for seven years and whom she was planning to marry had left her, unable to deal with what she was going through. "I love you," he said, "but you're allergic to my life." The doctor in San Francisco thought he could help Lucy and began treating her. Eventually he and an endocrinologist he was working with came up with a diagnosis. Lucy learned that she had two autoimmune diseases—one that affected her thyroid and the other, her ovaries. These seemed to account for the mysterious bruising and fatigue she had been experiencing. The doctors were able to control the thyroid disease with extremely high doses of thyroid medication. But there was nothing they could do about the autoimmune disease affecting her ovaries. And the allergies continued to get worse.

She found a place to live in San Francisco's Outer Richmond district, on the ocean, hoping that the clean air would help, but her sensitivities to everything only increased. It got to the point that she could tolerate only a handful of foods and could drink only bottled water. To clean herself she could use only a special soap made of kelp. But eventually even the old paint smell in her apartment began to affect her, so she lined the walls with foil. Lucy tried to get work by doing freelance writing, but it was insufficient to pay for her high medical bills, and she went through all of her savings. She was finally reduced to going on food stamps and welfare. She had come a long way from Yale Law School.

But as bad as things were, Lucy did not give up hope. She was absolutely determined to get well, so she kept searching and trying new things. This led her into all manner of "alternative" medical cures. Most were very expensive, and none of them helped. She says that some of them actually made her sicker than before. Lucy tried acupuncture and even alternative "electro" acupuncture. She tried "positive thinking," homeopathy, and "alternative" homeopathy. She took vitamins intravenously. At one point, she went to the dramatic length of having her blood taken out and treated, in case her problem was caused by a fungal infection. She was desperate to try anything.

But through it all she knew that she must get back to Yale Law School. She was determined to have a rcal life again, notwithstanding the fact that years had now gone by. But eventually the San Francisco doctor said he had done all he could do. He advised her to move to the desert.

So Lucy moved to the desert in Texas. During this period she actually lived in a tent on an abandoned cattle ranch. The people who owned the place gave her a machete to combat the rattlesnakes. (She never used it. The only time she saw a snake, she turned and ran.) During this time Lucy continued to try every doctor possible and every type of treatment, including a number of whom she now describes as genuine quacks, if there can be such a thing. It was during this time in Texas that Lucy met a woman who had had something similar and who said she had been completely healed of it by God—and not just God, but Jesus. Lucy realized at that point that she had not once in the four years she had been dealing with this met a single soul who had been healed of these things, not by a doctor or by any alternative treatments. The woman came out to visit Lucy and told her story.

As it happened, the woman was herself Jewish and just a few years before had been healed of something very similar to what Lucy had. She explained that at that time she could eat only a few foods. In her desperation for a cure, she had visited a tarot card reader, whom she saw for a time. But eventually even the fortune-teller told her there was nothing she could do for her, and she actually suggested that the woman should go to a church. So she did. The people at the church prayed over her numerous times, and in the course of about a year she was completely healed. When Lucy met her, the woman was completely healthy: in graduate school, working full-time, and engaged to be married.

Lucy says that despite hearing all of this, she was hostile to the woman. She absolutely didn't want to hear about Jesus. Lucy's family had been Jewish for many centuries. Her mother's family could trace its roots all the way back to Aaron. Furthermore, the very idea of Christianity repulsed her. The Jimmy Swaggart and Jim and Tammy Faye Bakker televangelism scandals were very much in the public eye at that time. The woman realized this and told Lucy that she understood it wasn't something Lucy was interested in, but if that ever changed, she gave her the phone number of a man who had studied at Fuller Seminary in Los Angeles, who had a degree in Old Testament studies, and who she thought would be able to help. Lucy didn't throw away the number, but neither was she expecting to call it. But her encounter with the woman made her willing at least to think more about God. In her desperation she began reading the Bible. In her own way, she had prayed a number of times over the years for healing and was somewhat angry at God for not doing so.

Over the course of the next few years, Lucy met six or seven other people who said they had been healed by Jesus of something similar to what she had. She said she got to a point where she couldn't ignore the evidence. It was startling. Almost no one she had met with this problem— and she had met a tremendous number—had been completely healed by a doctor or an alternative medicine practitioner of any kind. But six or seven people claimed to have been healed of it by Jesus. This thought haunted her, so at some point she called the man whose number she had. The number still reached him. After speaking with him she agreed to study the Bible with him over the phone, although getting to a phone from her remote location was itself a great difficulty. But over the course of the next two years she studied the Masoretic text of the Old Testament. She read little of the New Testament, but she surprised herself by eventually coming to believe that it was indeed quite possible—probable—that Jesus was the Messiah to the Jews. But she knew she wasn't going to do anything about it. She was adamantly opposed to "accepting him" or "receiving him," or whatever it was Christians would say she should do.

During these years Lucy's health continued to deteriorate. She was now living in a foil-lined trailer in the Arizona desert. Her illness and sensitivities had become so severe that even if someone who had been near pesticides or other things came onto her land she would have a reaction. By necessity she therefore lived in almost total isolation from other people. But when the motor in the well on her property broke, she had to have someone come out to fix it. So a man came, but when he did the job he resealed the stainless-steel pipes with "pipe dope," which contains trace amounts of fungicide. Lucy didn't know this, but when she showered, she got extremely sick, much sicker than she had been up to that time. "Could it get worse?" she wondered. Now that water itself was making her ill, she began to wonder whether she was going to survive. She simply couldn't imagine what might be next.

One day the effects of the water in the shower caused Lucy to feel so ill that she left the trailer with the shower running. The trailer flooded. It remained flooded long enough that it became ruined and uninhabitable, so she had to find another place to live. She had just recently met a woman who was selling a similar kind of trailer—in which she had herself recovered from a similar illness—so Lucy got in her foil-lined Toyota pickup and drove out to visit her.

It turned out that the trailer wasn't adequate for what Lucy needed, but in the course of conversation with the woman the woman told her that she had been healed of essentially the same disease as Lucy. She said Christ had healed her, through prayers for "healing and deliverance." She then asked Lucy whether Lucy realized that the illness was "demonic." Lucy says that any time in the six years previous she wouldn't have been able to hear this or take it at all seriously, but she had dealt with so many quack doctors and had considered so many bizarre alternative paths to healing that at this point it didn't sound so strange. It seemed less strange than having the irises of her eyes "read" to determine which vitamins she needed to take or having her blood removed and treated, as she had done. She was at this point utterly desperate and open to hearing anything. She was even open to having this woman pray for her.

After the day she heard this woman's story, Lucy relented and began to read the New Testament. It was then, she said, that the Bible became alive for her. It wasn't just a text to be dissected. And she began to believe that God really could heal. Then, with some trepidation, she couldn't remember precisely when, Lucy said, "Okay, God, if Jesus is the Messiah to the Jews, then I accept him. If not, please forgive me."

The woman and her husband and some others from a local church began to pray for Lucy, and there was over time undoubtedly a positive change, albeit a very slight one. Lucy said it was the first time in six and a half years that things had improved at all. But that little bit was enough to encourage them, and they continued to meet and pray for the next few months. Lucy's health improved, but she still had a long way to go.

The woman who had been healed recommended Lucy pray with a woman who was an expert in praying for healing and deliverance. Lucy was open to this too, so the woman came and prayed with Lucy. They prayed together the whole day. Whatever was happening in Lucy's heart during this time is impossible to say, but despite the fact that nothing happened that first day, they prayed another full day and then another. Finally, at the end of the five days of prayer, something happened. It was clear to both of them that something was different. "I felt lighter and there was enormous peace," Lucy said. "The woman I was praying with confirmed it. She said, 'It's over,' and I said, 'I know.'"

There was no question about it: Lucy was healed. The whole thing was, of course, amazing and dramatic. Lucy's life changed utterly. She found that she could do anything she liked. She could take showers. She could go to any restaurant she liked. She could wear makeup. For years she had worn only prewashed cotton clothing and used only kelp-based soap, and now she could go to any store to buy clothing, regular soap, and food. It was a complete turnaround from what she had experienced before.

During all of these years, Lucy was on massive amounts of thyroid medicinc and other drugs, including transfer factor and intravenous immunoglobulins, to try to stimulate her immune system. Now that she was better she decided she wanted to go off all these medications. She called one of her doctors in San Francisco who had been prescribing them and explained to him that she had been healed. When he asked how that had happened, she told him flatly that people had prayed for her. "Well, prayer works," he said, as though it were the most normal thing. Lucy was stunned to hear him say that.

Another of Lucy's doctors explained that going off these medicines, in particular the large doses of hormones that she was taking, would put her body through terrible withdrawals, so if she really was serious about going off them she would need to exercise. He also cautioned that he thought Lucy would fall ill again without the medication. Lucy decided she would swim while going off the medication. At first she was too weak to swim a single lap in a pool. But within three months she was swimming a mile a day. By then she was completely off the medication and as healthy as she had ever been in her life. In the meantime she had begun wondering what she would do next. Her credits at Yale had by now expired, so she would have had to reapply for admission there and start all over at the beginning. The man she had been planning to marry had himself gotten married and now had children, and because of the expenses from her medications she was now in deep debt. There was simply nothing for her to go back to.

So one day she asked God what she should do. She got a clear sense as she was praying that she should get her résumé together, move to Washington, DC, and get a job there. She had never heard from God in any way before, but the urging to do this that day was strong and clear. A friend asked her what kind of job she thought she would like to do. During this period Lucy had gotten into the habit of watching nightly news programs, and she liked them so much she had gotten practically addicted to them. She would have loved to work for a news program. And that's just what happened; it was the beginning of her career in network news. That was twenty-three years ago.

# GRANDFATHER IS HEALED

My friends Jeff and Christine live on Long Island, New York, where they run a technology consulting business. Both are Chinese, and Christine came to this country from Taiwan. She is a fifth-generation Christian, which is something extraordinarily rare for someone of Asian descent.

In the early part of the 1900s, her great-great-grandfather Gu Kim Fui traveled from China to Hawaii and became an extremely wealthy man, controlling a large part of the sugar trade. At one point he owned more than half of the island of Oahu. He became the first Christian in the family and started a church, which exists to this day. He returned to China and started churches there. Eventually Gu Kim Fui became the consul general from China to Hawaii.[15]

Christine's first encounter with the miraculous took place when she was fifteen years old and

---

15. Interestingly, the father of modern China, whom we know as Sun Yat-Sen, went to Hawaii to learn English and came to faith at the church that Christine's great-great-grandfather cofounded. (Sun Yat-Sen is revered by both the Nationalists of Taiwan and the Communists as the founding father of the Republic of China.)

living in Taiwan. She had been having a number of challenges at that time in school and elsewhere. She had no difficulty believing that God was real, which is to say that he existed, but she didn't know him in any personal way, although her parents both did. Perhaps because she was going through a challenging time she began to feel that she really ought to try and have a relationship with God in the way that her parents did, but she simply didn't know how. So one day she prayed a very simple prayer. "God," she prayed, "I know you are real. Everybody says you are real, but I've never personally experienced you myself. So if you are real, show me that you are real." That was all. But it was sincere and heartfelt.

During this period, Christine's grandfather was living with them. For about six months he had been experiencing some kind of illness, though they knew not what. He was unable to stand up straight or to walk at all. He was able to hobble from his bed to the bathroom, but only very slowly and with great difficulty. Beyond this, there were no symptoms.

That summer, one of Christine's aunts returned to Taiwan from New York. During her time in New York, she had experienced a healing during a church service, which affected her faith dramatically. So at some point, with Christine and her father present, the aunt came into the grandfather's room and, with great directness, asked him: "Do you believe God can heal you?" On hearing these words, the grandfather began to weep. He said, "I believe . . . I believe . . . I believe only God can heal me. I have seen doctors, but none of them can help me. I'm just too old."

Christine's aunt decided to pray for the grandfather right there. She put her hands on the grandfather's legs and prayed a very powerful prayer that he be healed. A moment after she had finished, the grandfather stood up and immediately started walking. They were all stunned to witness it. Christine said that even now, so many years after it happened, remembering it makes her very emotional. She remembers thinking that she couldn't believe it was possible for a miracle to happen right in front of her eyes, that in just a moment's time God could wipe away so many months of misery and pain.

Christine remembered that moments later her grandfather decided he must go outside. When the neighbors saw him walking around, they were all stunned. "What happened to you?" they asked. "We haven't seen you in such a long time! How could you be walking?" Her grandfather was beaming with joy and simply continued walking, talking to different neighbors. "After that moment," Christine said, "I decided that I would never doubt God again. I suddenly realized just how real he is and how powerful. Christine's whole family had their faith changed by witnessing the miracle. They had previously believed in God, but perhaps in a somewhat abstract, intellectual way; after this experience their faith in God and his power was tremendously deepened.

## A WATCH STOPS

It was early Friday morning, May 7, 2004. I was in the sanctuary of Saint Paul's Episcopal Church in Darien, Connecticut, for a weekly gathering of what we call the New Canaan Society, a group of men that gets together to hear a speaker, to pray, and to encourage each other to be better husbands and fathers. The group had grown like a weed, so we had to move out of my friend Jim Lane's house and into this church. This morning the speaker was our friend Paul Teske. He was then fifty-five years old and the pastor of a Lutheran church in nearby Westport, also called Saint Paul's.

It was my job to introduce the speakers every week, so I introduced Paul and then sat down in the front row to hear his talk. He told us that he had planned on giving a talk titled "Christian Ethics and Morality in Business." But at the last minute he had felt "led by God" to change his direction and instead talk about Saint John, the disciple closest to Jesus, who alone among the twelve lived to a ripe old age. He is believed to have been about ninety years old when he wrote what we now know as the Book of Revelation, the last book in the Bible. He was then imprisoned in a Greek penal colony on the Isle of Patmos.

What none of us knew as we listened to Paul that morning was that roughly two minutes into this forty-minute talk he found that he suddenly couldn't put any weight on his left leg. He said that when it happened, he was utterly baffled, but instead of stopping, he just clung to the podium, kept his weight on his right leg, and continued talking, as though nothing were the matter. I was in the front row and noticed nothing, nor did anyone else notice. But as he was giving his talk, Paul was wondering what in the world was happening. Perhaps it was sciatica? Or a pinched nerve? He felt otherwise fine, so he just kept talking and making his points, all the while continuing to puzzle over what had happened to his leg, which just hung there, as he later said, "like a sack of potatoes."

When Paul was finished with his talk, he calmly said, "Would somebody be able to help me into a chair? I seem to be having a problem with my leg." Those of us in the front row leapt up immediately. What did Paul mean? He was obviously putting all his weight on his right leg while holding on to the podium with both hands. As soon as a few of us grabbed his arms to move him to a chair it became clear that this wasn't going to be easy. In fact, Paul started to go down, and instead of bringing him to the chair, we found ourselves just easing him onto the carpeted floor of the sanctuary.

There was a doctor among us that morning. He came over, knelt down, and began taking Paul's vitals and asking him questions. Paul said he couldn't move his left leg or foot at all. Other than that, he felt absolutely fine. Not long after this an ambulance arrived and the EMTs took Paul to the hospital. We all stood around, wondering what had happened.

Paul was told by the doctor in the ER that he didn't seem to have the symptoms of a stroke. If he had had a stroke—which is a cerebral hemorrhage—he would likely have had a headache so painful that he would have passed out. Paul confirmed that he hadn't had any pain whatsoever. Paul began to wonder if perhaps it might be a brain tumor. But after a CAT scan, the doctor said that Paul had indeed had a cerebral hemorrhage—which is to say, a stroke. Why there hadn't been any pain was a mystery. But he was checked into CCU for the night and an MRI was promptly scheduled for the following morning.

Once Paul was settled in the CCU, a physician stopped by to let him know that the situation ahead was not at all certain. He said that if Paul's brain began to hemorrhage again, medical intervention was "not promising." He even told Paul that it would be best to get his affairs in order, "just in case." This was, of course, sobering.

Paul told his wife, Rivers, the news. Then he told her that he had two requests if he were to die. First, that the congregation of his church throw a huge "Easter celebration" because he would be home in Heaven. Paul said, "If there is no resurrection then I have been in the wrong business." Then he said that he didn't want anyone to wish him back from death: "Who would want to leave Heaven for any reason? I will be waiting for the rest of you to finally arrive." They wept and hugged each other and Rivers went home.

The night was happily uneventful and the next morning Paul woke up feeling fine. But he still couldn't move his leg a millimeter. He began to think about living the rest of his life in a wheelchair. He had never considered not being mobile. A bit later he had his MRI, and for the rest of the day he cheerfully dealt with a steady stream of visitors and phone calls. The next day the doctor came in to say that the MRI hadn't told them much, so they scheduled another test in the hospital's angioplasty unit. But that test also failed to clarify what had happened. This much was clear: A blood vessel had ruptured and had then clotted itself. But no one knew why. What they did know was that the blood that issued from that hemorrhage had flowed into that part of Paul's brain controlling the left side of his body, below his hip. The doctor made it clear he had no real idea whether Paul would be able to walk again. "We'll have to wait and see," he said.

Paul was then transferred to the neurological unit, where he would have therapy and try to regain movement in his foot and leg. It took a long time, but eventually he thought he was able to move his big toe ever so slightly. But the rest of his foot and his whole leg were utterly immobile. After a couple of days he could move his foot slightly and then his leg, but only slightly. They said he had regained about 15 percent of the use of his leg. So he was taught to use crutches and a wheelchair. The days passed.

Almost two weeks after being in the hospital, Paul had an experience with God. The first thing that happened, he said, was that God impressed a Bible passage on his mind very strongly, so strongly that he knew it was related to his situation. The Bible passage was Hosea 6:1–3. But Paul had no idea what Hosea 6:1–3 said. He just felt that God wanted him to look it up and know that it was God's promise to him. So he did. Paul read the following:

Come, let us return to the Lord;
For He has torn, but He will heal us;
He has stricken, but he will bind us up.
After two days He will revive us;
On the third day He will raise us up
That we may live in His sight . . .

Four years earlier, Paul had been prayed for by a pastor from Ghana named Kingsley Fletcher. That pastor had "prophesied" over Paul and said that God was going to do something over a span of twenty-one days. When that twenty-one-day period was supposed to be was unclear, but for some reason, when Paul was reading this passage from Hosea, he remembered that prophecy and strongly felt that God was telling him that he would be healed twenty-one days after he had had his stroke. According to Paul, since he had the stroke on May 7, he reckoned that the day of his healing would be May 28. Paul felt so strongly about this that he wrote it in his journal and told his wife, Rivers. In fact, he actually told just about anyone who would listen. For sure, some of them must have thought he was crazy. I confess that if he had told me this I would have struggled mightily to make sense of it or believe it. How did he arrive at that date? Nonetheless, Paul was supremely convinced that this was what God had told him and he had no doubt that God would heal him on that date.

Paul was released from the hospital on May 20, and the following morning, a Friday, the New Canaan Society would again meet at Saint Paul's in Darien. Paul wanted to be there, but of course he couldn't drive. So he asked Rivers to drive him. They would have to leave their house in Westport just after 7:00 A.M. Before they left, Paul asked Rivers if she knew where his watch was. She said that it was in his briefcase. It had been locked in there with his cuff links when they were taken from him that first day at the hospital. Rivers handed Paul the briefcase as they drove out of their driveway, and there in the passenger seat he opened it and took out the watch.

He immediately saw that the hands weren't moving. Then he noticed that the time on the stopped watch was 7:58. And the date was May 7—the day he had the stroke. Why would a self-winding watch have stopped on that day? Paul advanced the hands on the watch to see if the date would change over to May 8, when the hands passed twelve. But the date did not change. So he knew that the watch had stopped at 7:58 on the *morning* of the seventh, which was either exactly when he had his stroke or within a few minutes of that time. There was no doubt about that. Of course, he immediately told Rivers as she was driving and they tried to figure out what might have happened. Paul had worn the watch for perhaps an hour after the stroke. The New Canaan

Society speakers always ended around 8:20. The watch hadn't been taken from him till close to 9:00. It had obviously stopped around the time when he had had his stroke, while he was standing at the podium giving his talk.

And now as they drove toward Darien, he wondered: Was the watch broken forever? Paul gave it a little shake and the hands immediately started working again.

Paul's arrival at the New Canaan Society that morning, two weeks after his stroke in that same place, was moving. When asked to say a few words he hobbled to the podium with a four-legged aluminum walker, wearing a brace on his left leg. We gave him a standing ovation, of course. Paul said that his being there that morning was by God's grace. Then the famous evangelist Reinhard Bonnke spoke and afterward prayed for Paul, but Paul did not expect to be healed that morning. He simply "knew" that his appointment with God's healing power was May 28, seven days hence.

Paul was not supposed to be doing much traveling in his condition. The doctors forbade driving for six months since he was taking seizure medication as a precaution. But Paul felt that he must go to Baltimore, to the Benny Hinn crusade taking place on May 27 and 28. Benny Hinn is the world-famous, if sometimes controversial, preacher with a renowned healing ministry. Paul wanted to be in the audience at Hinn's event on the appointed date. But before he went to Baltimore to claim his own healing, another healing took place.

That Tuesday the twenty-fifth, Paul got a phone call from another Lutheran pastor who was his friend. Pastor Mark Zehnder, who pastored in Omaha, Nebraska, was calling to say that their mutual friend Pastor Greg Smith was ill. Greg had flown from Saint Louis to Connecticut to fill in for Paul when he was in the hospital, but on his return to Saint Louis he had experienced tightness in his chest. After what had happened to Paul, Greg wasn't taking any chances. He immediately saw his own physician, who gave him an EKG and a stress test. They revealed that he had major blockage around his heart and he must come in the following day, Wednesday the twenty-sixth, for an angiogram. If it confirmed what the physician knew it would—major blockage—Greg would need to have surgery so that a stent could be inserted, or perhaps he would even need bypass surgery.

On the phone with Mark, Paul confidently declared that God had Greg's heart "in his hand" and Paul said that God was healing his heart and he even boldly declared that the next day the doctors would be confounded by what they saw. Then Paul and Mark called Greg. Together Paul and Mark prayed that any damage to Greg's heart would be completely healed and that the doctors "would be confounded" the next day.

That following day, Rivers and Paul left for Baltimore. On the way, Paul left a voice mail message for Greg. Paul felt what some Christians call an "anointing" in his prayers and "faith" for what God was going to do in Greg. In his voice mail he said that he felt this "anointing"—or "unction" as it is also sometimes called—and he said that he saw Greg as "Greg the lion-hearted," and he said that Greg would "run with the lions."

Later that day Paul got a call from Greg, who was almost speechless as hc told Paul about what took place that morning. After the first angiogram test, the physician said he had made a mistake and decided to do another one. After the second angiogram, he said that what the first angiogram showed must be correct: Greg was absolutely fine. There was no blockage whatever and he could go home. Paul told Greg that God had healed him, and informed him that he must tell his congregation about it. Greg was rather less bold than Paul on this score, but he agreed in principle to share this story with his congregation.

Paul and Rivers checked into their hotel in Baltimore that Wednesday, and on Thursday morning they headed over to the huge arena for the Benny Hinn crusade. Paul was now using a cane, and the brace was still on his leg, albeit under his trousers. Paul knew someone in the organization who had arranged seats for them. Still, Paul was thrilled to see that they were seated in the fifth row. There were many thousands of people there that day, so to be right down front was something unexpected. Even more unexpected was when Benny Hinn himself came down off the stage to pray for a few people. Indeed, as if on cue, he walked over and prayed for Paul and Rivers. It was a gentle prayer—and again, Paul "knew" his healing was to happen on the twenty-eighth, the next day, not the twenty-seventh—but Paul and Rivers nonetheless "went down" under the power of the Holy Spirit. This is a phenomenon in some Christian healing services where the pastor who prays for healing often has the effect of causing the people for whom he is praying to be "slain in the Spirit": For no explainable reason they wilt and fall down, as though the power to stand has gone right out of their bodies. To be sure, some people do this because it seems to be expected of them, but I have spoken to many people who promise me that it had nothing at all to do with them, that it was real, that they fell down as soon as they were touched. There are usually "catchers" at these services too, to help the people go down gently. Still, Paul had not been healed in any discernible way, and he hobbled back to his hotel room with his brace and his cane.

The next morning, Paul awoke feeling extremely

fatigued. Although he felt that this was his day to be healed, he thought he should stay in bed and rest, skipping the 10:00 A.M. service. But Rivers wouldn't hear of it. She volunteered to go over to the arena early and save seats for them. Paul followed at nine thirty. They were seated in the seventh row when someone approached them. He was with the Benny Hinn ministry and thought they looked familiar. He left and then reappeared, telling them to please follow him to the center section, second row. After they were seated there for a while the man returned again and asked them to please leave their scats and sit in the front row.

The service that morning was wonderful, and at the end Benny Hinn told all pastors in the audience to please come forward so that he could pray a blessing over them. The pastors were escorted onto the large stage, but because of Paul's leg brace he didn't dare try to negotiate the stairs leading to the stage. Instead, he stood at the edge of the stage, on the ground level. That was plenty close anyway. But a woman approached him and insisted that he must come onto the stage to receive the blessing. Someone helped him up the stairs and while he was on the stage Benny Hinn prayed individually for those standing there. When it was Paul's turn, he prayed for Paul twice. And then prayed for him a third time. Paul wasn't sure why he was prayed for three times, but he certainly felt blessed. But he had not yet been healed.

That Friday evening, Paul again hobbled to the arena with Rivers—using his cane and wearing his leg brace. He expected to be healed that evening. It was May 28, 2004, the twenty-first day after his stroke. Paul realized that the pastor in Ghana had given him that prophecy the Friday evening before Memorial Day in 2000. That was precisely four years earlier, because May 28, 2004, was also the Friday before Memorial Day. Paul says that he absolutely knew that his hour had come, that this evening he would be healed. He and Rivers had prayed toward this end with great faith and intensity and were doing so at that moment.

That evening the person who had arranged their special seats in the front row told them that he was sorry, but those seats were reserved for the evening's service. Of course they told him they understood and were very grateful for his help that morning. But when they arrived at the arena that night a woman took them to those same seats. They asked her whether she was making some mistake, but she told them, "The Lord told me to seat you here."

Next to them was a young woman pastor who told Paul and Rivers she had been very sick a few minutes earlier in the restroom near the entrance. She didn't feel at all well and she thought it wise to return to her hotel room. But Paul insisted that she must stay, saying Satan wanted to rob her of her joy. He prayed for her on the spot and thirty minutes later she told Paul she felt terrific and was very glad she had stayed.

Paul said that he could feel the presence of the Holy Spirit as the worship music played and they sang along, worshiping the God Paul felt certain would heal him that very night, in that very place. Then it happened. Without any warning, Paul said that he began to involuntarily shake "in a way that I cannot duplicate to this day, like a jackhammer that is used to break up concrete." He said that this "jerking" lasted for about five minutes.[16]

Around this time Benny Hinn declared from the

---

16. Many thousands have experienced these strange physical phenomena during services like this over the decades. Even Jonathan Edwards in the early eighteenth century recorded similarly strange phenomena during his own preaching, as did George Whitfield. I have only witnessed anything like it once, with my own brother, John, in a chapel at Yale in 1991. As I was praying that he would "receive the Holy Spirit," he shook involuntarily and began weeping and praising God, lifting his hands up. It was a supernatural experience, but also a profoundly and palpably physical one. When I later asked him what was happening to him, he said that it felt as though "everything bad that was in me was flowing out of me and God was pouring into me."

stage that there had just then been several healings "including someone with a brace." Paul couldn't believe his ears. But had he indeed been healed? Benny Hinn immediately said that anyone with a brace who thought they were healed must immediately take off the brace and come onto the stage. But Paul's brace was under his pants. He didn't dare remove his trousers in public, with TV cameras rolling. Nonetheless, he felt guilty about it and prayed that God would see his heart. He was so gung ho with faith that he would have taken his pants off if he really felt God wanted him to do that, to show that he was healed. And yet he knew he had been healed. He shifted his weight onto his left leg, and for the first time in three weeks it could support his weight.

Benny Hinn then said that everyone who had been healed should come forward. Suddenly what must have been hundreds of people began walking toward the stage. How many of them had actually been healed we can never know. But Paul knew that he had been healed. Still, he had been on the stage that morning and didn't feel the need to move from his seat this time. Paul began wondering what would happen when he got back to the hotel room and took off his brace. He wanted to see his leg and be able to enjoy his healing. But for now he would just stay put. Still, if God really wanted him to leave his seat and be up on the stage, he was willing to go. But God would have to make it happen somehow. Otherwise Paul was determined to stay put.

Then, amid all the clamor and celebration going on in those moments, Benny Hinn suddenly walked straight to the pulpit, looked down directly at Paul and Rivers, and said, "Come up here!" He didn't know who they were, so Rivers couldn't believe he was talking specifically to them. But Paul knew that he was, that God had answered his prayer. He also knew that this short journey to the stage would be the ultimate arbiter of his healing. Climbing those stairs would normally have been a painfully awkward, slow-motion effort of several minutes, but this time Paul walked up the steps normally, as though both legs were fine. Paul was so thrilled by this that as soon as he reached the top of the stairs he told a man standing there that God had just healed him.

Paul and Rivers walked toward Pastor Hinn, who had summoned them. "Who are you people?" Hinn asked them. Paul explained that he was a Lutheran pastor from Westport, Connecticut, and mentioned that he was friends with Harald Bredesen,[17] the

_____

17. Harald Bredesen (1918–2006) was a legendary figure in the Christian Charismatic movement, which believes in "the baptism in the Holy Spirit" and "speaking in tongues."

famous pastor whom Benny Hinn knew well. "You are the Lutheran pastor he is always talking about!" Hinn said. "Do Lutherans believe in this?"

"This one does!" Paul said. With that, Benny Hinn touched them both on their heads, as he does—and down they both went. As they were being helped to their feet, someone mentioned to Benny Hinn that Paul had received a miracle that evening. Pastor Hinn told Paul to tell everyone about it, thrusting a microphone toward him. Paul then told the assembled thousands about his stroke three weeks earlier and how he felt that just moments earlier he had been healed. Then Pastor Hinn made it clear he knew nothing about this healing. He said to the crowd that the reason he had called Paul and Rivers up onto the stage was because God had told him that they were to have a healing ministry. This was certainly a surprise to Paul.

Benny Hinn then spoke aloud a prophecy over Paul and Rivers, with the thousands in the audience listening. A prophetic "word" is when someone has the supernatural gift of "hearing" what God is saying about someone or something and then "declaring" it with one's own mouth, so others can hear it. The Greek word "prophet" simply means "to speak forth." What Pastor Hinn spoke at that point was recorded. He said this:

Stretch your hands toward them that this Sunday miracles would happen in that church . . . We believe! As the gospel will be preached out of this man's lips and his wife's, that they'll see mighty signs and wonders as in the Book of Acts. That [their] church will experience such a flow and an overflow and an abundant flow of the Spirit. That Ezekiel 47[18] will be fulfilled in that congregation where now only their feet are touching the water, but soon that glorious water of life will flow so great and so deep that it will draw thousands into that congregation. Lord, I pray healing ministry would be granted to this couple who've served you for years. Give them that mantle. Touch!

This happened on May 28, just as Paul was sure it would. What should we make of that? Or of what Benny Hinn said from that stage to those thousands of people about Paul and Rivers having a ministry of healing? Of course there was a strange poetry to the idea that in the moments following his miraculous healing, Paul would learn that God had a healing ministry for him. But did God really have such a thing for Paul after

---

18. In Ezekiel, chapter 47, Ezekiel has a vision of a river that heals all it touches and brings life out of death.

all? It was easy for someone like Benny Hinn to declare such things, but who would follow up to let him know if what he had so boldly declared had never happened?

The next day Paul woke up and the healing he had felt the previous night had not diminished. He did feel a bit weak, but he didn't need the brace or cane at all. Rivers drove back to Westport and the following morning, a Sunday, Paul said that he wanted to go to their church to see if people would indeed begin coming there to be healed. After what had happened to him, he was not scheduled to preach for another two months, but he would go and just sit in the back as a parishioner. After the sermon, a lay minister asked for prayer requests and Paul stood up and said that he requested prayers for what God was doing through his people "and our church." Next, a woman stood. She had never been to the church before, and she had arrived late, sitting just in front of Paul. She said, "God told me that if I came into this church today, I would be healed." She had no idea that Paul was the pastor but said, "When I heard that man speak, I knew I had come to the right church." Evidently this woman had had such severe pain that she had been forced to leave her job six months earlier. She had driven thirty miles to be there that morning.

After the service, Paul offered to pray for her. The following morning she left a voice mail on the church phone, saying that her pain was gone and she would be returning to her job. Before Paul left the sanctuary a woman approached him with a picture of her eleven-month-old grandson. She said the doctors were concerned he might have leukemia. His blood cell count was two hundred; a normal count would be one thousand. Paul took the photo and prayed that the boy be healed and that the test results would "confound the doctors." Later that week the woman called to say the count was at 720 and that the doctors had ruled out leukemia. Four weeks later his count was normal and the doctors said the problem must have been an "unidentifiable virus."

Three weeks after the Benny Hinn crusade a staff person from his ministry called, saying she was curious about the prophetic word that Pastor Hinn had publicly spoken over Paul and Rivers. She had reviewed the tape and had copied it out. "I've never seen or heard him speak this way," she said. Paul told her that just what Pastor Hinn had said was already beginning to happen. There could be no denying Paul's healing happened ten years ago. Since then, Paul and Rivers Teske have traveled to six continents and sixty countries, preaching and teaching and healing in God's name. It happened and is still happening.[19]

---

19. Paul Teske's complete story can be found in his book, *Healing for Today.*

# NUTS

Since the extraordinary experience related in the previous story, my friend Paul Teske has indeed been active in "healing ministry." He travels the world telling people his story, telling them Jesus can heal them today, and then praying for the healing of anyone willing to come forward. I asked him to share some stories with me and from the many he had to share, I thought the following story from May 2012 was the best to include. It deals with a malady that is on the one hand rather pedestrian, and on the other tremendously debilitating, and even deadly, and that for some reason afflicts more people today than it used to. I'm talking about nut allergies.

Paul was invited to speak to a group of about three hundred business people at a conference in Daytona Beach, Florida, in May 2012. As he always does, he told the story of his own healing, and then launched into the subject of miraculous healing today, making it clear that this is not something that only happened during New Testament times, as many Christians have been taught in their churches, but that continues to be available to us now. When Paul finished talking and asked whether anyone in the audience needed prayer for healing, no hands went up. There was the standard awkward moment of waiting for someone to break the ice and then a middle-aged woman raised her hand and Paul called her forward. She did so rather reluctantly, because she was a member of a Baptist church where the concept of "healing in the church today" was actively frowned upon. Paul asked her what her name was and then asked her what she needed prayer for. She told him that her name was Juanita and that she had a "severe nut allergy," which had plagued her from birth. He asked her to explain the severity of her allergy. She said it was so severe that whenever she flew, she had to be in what is quite seriously termed a "nut-free zone." The woman explained that over the years she had been rushed to the emergency room numerous times due to inadvertent exposure to nuts. One of those visits had been nearly fatal.

As he usually did, Paul silently prayed, asking God to tell him anything else that this woman needed prayer for, since people were often too shy to reveal certain things. Paul said that as he prayed, the words "broken heart" immediately came to him. So he quietly asked her: "Who broke your heart?"

"My father," she replied, and burst into tears. Paul probed more deeply into the woman's relationship with her father and found that it was severely strained. He then walked her through a prayer to forgive her father and to "release him to

God." Then Paul prayed, asking God to heal her heart. As with all such prayers of forgiveness, it does not wipe away the enormity of the other person's sin—whatever that sin might be—but it enables the person affected by that sin to place the other person in God's hands, to free themselves of the burden of the deep resentment and unforgiveness they've been carrying. In essence, one is free to "love" the person who has done the harm because one actively trusts God to justly deal with that person.

Paul then asked God to allow the woman's nut allergy to be healed as evidence of the restoration of her healed relationship with her father. Juanita then informed Paul with a measured amount of concern that the only way she could be sure of being healed was to eat some nuts—which had, until that point in her life, obviously been very dangerous to do. After Paul spoke a few more words of affirmation, Juanita expressed her gratitude and left. Other people then came forward for prayer.

Paul said that that night, as he lay in his hotel room trying to fall asleep, he felt an urge to continue to pray for Juanita, asking God to protect her. He understood the seriousness surrounding her allergy and knew that the consequences of her going into anaphylactic shock from eating nuts could be fatal. Paul recalled that he woke up several times that night to pray for her.

The next morning, most of the conference attendees had departed by bus for a local restaurant, where they were to hear another speaker over breakfast. Paul had previously decided he wouldn't be going to that event, but before the buses departed he walked through the hotel lobby, trying to find Juanita, but he didn't see her anywhere. After the buses had gone, Paul decided to call the person hosting the conference to see whether she had spoken to Juanita. But her phone went straight to voice mail. Paul left a message and then tried the number again several times, to no avail. He then decided to walk the boardwalk, where he prayed silently as he walked up and down the beach.

About an hour later, Paul got a call from the conference host, who said that she had indeed met the woman at the breakfast and had spoken with her. The woman told her that after the prayer service the night before she had decided to test the supposed healing. So she had deliberately sought out a candy bar containing nuts. She found one, purchased it, and took it back to her room. On the desk near her bed she had placed the syringe she carried containing serum, in case she started going into anaphylactic shock. She then took off the wrapper and slowly placed the candy bar into her mouth, praying as she did so. She bit off a hunk, chewed, and swallowed. Then she waited. For several minutes there was no allergic reaction. She continued to wait. The allergic reaction never came. She said that's when she knew she had been healed. In her entire life, getting no serious reaction from eating nuts had simply never happened before. Indeed, nothing close to it had ever happened. The conference host told Paul that the woman had saved the candy bar wrapper and had pulled it out of her purse that morning as she excitedly shared her story with anyone who would listen.

That evening the conference ended with a banquet. The host invited Juanita to the mic, asking her to share what had happened with the audience, which she gladly did. She ended by saying she had learned two things: first, that there was no doubt that Jesus still heals today. That she was standing there after having eaten nuts was dramatic proof of that. And second, that she actually didn't like nuts.

By way of background, the severity of Juanita's allergy is dramatic. For years, Juanita has worked as a meeting planner and a convention sales manager, so she would always have to ask how every food item was prepared to determine if it was safe for her to be around, always needing to clarify that it was not just nuts themselves that were a concern, but any kind of nut oil or nut by-products. Needless to say, many people found these questions and concerns fussy and annoying. As her allergies intensified, she was eventually forced to ask that her entire workplace be a "nut-free zone." Predictably, this invited frequent jokes, but the less fun quotidian reality was that the front desk had to check out every food item that was brought in and if it was found to contain any kinds of nuts or nut oils, it had to be removed from the building posthaste. Coworkers rather often inadvertently brought in Thai food or something else prepared with nuts, and Juanita was forced to leave work for the remainder of the day.

Whenever she traveled, Juanita requested that the pilot or flight attendants make an announcement that someone aboard had a severe nut allergy and they requested that no nuts be consumed during the flight. She traveled with hand wipes and wiped down armrests, seat-back trays, and anything else she could reach. Entering a hotel room, she would wipe down the door handles and light switches, and then the TV remote, clocks, hangers, and anything else she might come in contact with. Wherever she went, she always used her own pens, never touching anyone else's.

She once attended a Christmas party at a local hotel and had to leave gasping for air because some of the desserts contained nuts. Even seemingly innocuous things like candy canes at Christmas were risky to be around because many times they were processed in facilities that processed nuts. Her life was consumed with dealing with the allergy, as was her husband's and the lives of all around her. Juanita was perpetually reading ingredient labels—every label on everything.

Her closest call with death came one day at work, when someone left an open container of pistachios out. Suddenly, Juanita couldn't breathe very well. Sometimes being unable to breathe made her unable to think clearly, so others would have to tell her to use her inhaler, but this time she remembered to use it and then left work immediately. But even after she got home ten or fifteen minutes later, her breathing had not improved. She asked her husband for help and injected herself with her EpiPen, but that too was, for some reason, completely ineffective. Her husband then drove her to a local clinic, where she was given additional meds, but they too had no effect. Juanita said that being unable to breathe on her own for such a long time was very frightening. Finally an ambulance was called and Juanita was taken to the local emergency room. The medical team there quickly understood the situation and gave her a number of other drugs, which finally helped her breathing. But they also gave her what she described as the "worst migraine I had ever experienced." (She had also suffered from migraines for many years.) The ER doctors then gave her more drugs to combat the painful migraine.

So when Juanita was healed of this allergy at the conference, it was almost incomprehensible. But the evidence was impossible to ignore. Five weeks and a day after the conference, Juanita wrote on her blog about what had happened. She said that her world had been "rocked" by the experience, restating the extreme severity of her allergy and how difficult it had been at times to deal with. But she said that since Tuesday, May 8, she had "consumed a variety of nuts, nut by-products, and nut oils" with absolutely no adverse effects.

She said that as a result of this miraculous healing she had told her story to many groups, large and small, and that the response had sometimes been overwhelming, with several people in tears.

But she said that the greatest part of it all was watching her husband as he heard her tell the story over and over. She said he still tears up and remarks on how wonderful and amazing it all is. They now enjoy going to ice-cream shops—something that was unthinkable before that May 8—and visiting new restaurants where she tries dishes she had never previously been allowed to touch.

She also said that the previous weekend she had visited her local supermarket and out of habit began reading the ingredients of a product when it suddenly hit her that she no longer had to do that. She remembered that she could eat anything she liked. The thought struck her with such force that she suddenly verbalized it right there in the aisle, saying, "I can eat everything in this store!" and got a strange look from the woman standing nearby, who obviously thought she was nuts. Ha. On the blog she said that her boss had told her she seemed like a new person. At the end of her blog post she thanked the people for putting on the conference and said there were "no words to describe what happened and how I feel. 'Thank you' is barely a beginning."

That November she also stopped having migraines, and in 2013 she removed the Medic-Alert bracelet she had worn for more than thirty years.

## A BEGGAR IN GHANA

Central Presbyterian Church in Manhattan, on Sixty-Fourth Street and Park Avenue is a gorgeous, historic church, from whose pulpit the controversial Harry Emerson Fosdick once preached, before fleeing northwest to the Chartres-inspired Riverside Cathedral, created for him by John Rockefeller. Fosdick didn't believe in miracles. In fact, in 1922, just before taking the pulpit of Central, he preached an infamous sermon titled "Shall the Fundamentalists Win?" in which he made clear that it was ridiculous for "modern" people to believe in any of the fundamental miracles of the Christian faith, including the virgin birth and the resurrection. Today, the theological climate at Central is markedly different. Although not typically focused on it, the pastors who preach there clearly believe that the miracles of the Bible are true, and also that miracles can happen today.

On the morning of October 6, 2013, pastor Doug Webster preached a sermon that touched on a miracle he had been close to. Doug teaches at Beeson Divinity School, which is part of Samford University in Birmingham, Alabama. He was also senior pastor at Central for a few years, and for many years, Doug has been involved with a ministry in Ghana, which he has visited regularly. That Sunday morning, in the course of talking about Jesus feeding the five thousand, Doug told the story of what had just happened among the people of this ministry that previous week in northern Ghana. It is headed up by an amazing man named David Mensah, whose own life story is filled with astounding miracles. They're recounted in his book, *Kwabena*.[20]

---

20. David came to Canada after a deeply troubled childhood, which is recounted in his book. He eventually got a PhD from the University of Toronto and has by now devoted over twenty-five years to a holistic ministry in Ghana. It is a very poverty-stricken area, but David and his ministry have built several hospitals and have brought agricultural development to the region. They have planted thirty-seven churches.

Part of the agricultural development they were doing recently involved getting heavy equipment and bulldozers into the country. In his sermon, Doug shared how that very week, those pieces of heavy equipment had finally cleared customs and could at last be put to work. It was the culmination of a very long process of prayer and fund-raising, so everyone in the ministry was thrilled. But something else happened that week that eclipsed even this event in terms of getting everyone's attention. It had just happened, and since he knew those involved, Doug was so excited about it that he couldn't help but tell us.

What took place involved a man named Simon, who is the chief driver for the ministry. Simon had suffered with diabetes for years and in August 2013 a sore had developed on his left foot. The foot was deteriorating badly. In fact, David was sure Simon would need to have the foot amputated. But he didn't have the heart to tell him that, knowing that for a driver to lose his left foot—his clutch foot—meant that he would also lose his livelihood. It would be a bitter blow.

As the foot got worse, Simon finally went to the teaching hospital in the city of Tamale to get a professional opinion. The doctors corroborated what David had feared: The foot would have to be amputated, and soon. Simon returned home and told his wife that his driving days were over. What would they do? But the next morning he decided to go to a prayer service in the gazebo in the village of Tamale, where the staff of the ministry gathered each morning. The people at the service prayed for Simon's foot, although he felt nothing in particular when they prayed.

Later that day Simon was filling his truck with gasoline at a fuel station. While he was pumping the gas, a man who looked to him like a beggar approached. Simon instinctively reached into his pocket to give the man some cedis, the currency in Ghana. But the man said he didn't want money, which of course surprised Simon. What beggar refuses money? The man then told Simon that he had seen that he was limping and asked if he could pray for him. Simon assented, and the man took out a small vial of oil, anointed Simon's leg, and prayed for him. When Simon finished fueling his truck a few moments later, he tried to find the man, but inexplicably, the man was nowhere to be found. Simon looked everywhere, but the man seemed to have vanished. It was all very strange. Simon was dying to know how the man could have vanished as he did, and he was also dying to know who the man was and why he had done what he had done.

But things that day got stranger still. When Simon got home, for no reason he could discern, his foot suddenly felt warm. It seemed that something was happening, and in the next few minutes he saw what. He said that in a matter of hours from that moment, his foot and leg were completely and miraculously healed. He said that he actually saw the coloration change with his own eyes.

When Simon went back to the doctors and showed them the foot, they said that from all they knew, what had happened to his foot—a reversal of the worsening deterioration—was impossible. They said that they felt it was miraculous.[21] Simon knows that it was miraculous. He believes that not only was the healing a miracle but also that the beggar who prayed for him that day was in fact an angel in disguise.

---

21. Just before this book went to press I bumped into Doug Webster at Central Presbyterian. He told me that he had just been to Ghana and had seen Simon, whose foot was still healthy and who was still the principal driver for the ministry.

# 11

## MIRACLES OF INNER HEALING

When someone is healed of a disease or injury in a way that seems miraculous, we cannot help but marvel. But there is still something to marvel about in all healing, even when it is slow and "conventional." The idea that our bodies can heal themselves is in its way amazing, and to watch a wound heal over time is itself extraordinary, just as recovering from an illness is. If all good comes from God, then we may acknowledge that he is behind all healing, whether it is of the "miraculous" variety or of the slower, more typical kind.

The same is true of what has been called "inner healing." Anyone who has suffered grief knows that time usually heals the awful wound we feel when we first lose someone. Similarly, in many cases, our bitterness or unforgiveness toward someone who has hurt us may soften over time; the wound they inflicted gets better and we are not as debilitated by it as we once were. Of course, just as with a physical wound, we may be affected in a way that improves over time, but that never goes away entirely. We may have the equivalent of a scar or a limp that never goes away.

Miracles of inner healing are instances when God seems to do in a few moments what would typically take years to heal—or which would perhaps never heal. Sometimes, inner healings can be linked to physical healings, as in the case of Juanita in our previous chapter, whose forgiveness of her father seems to have been a necessary precursor to physical healing.

## FORGIVENESS

April Hernandez and I became friends as cohosts of *100 Huntley Street*, a nationally syndicated Sunday-morning TV show. She and her husband, Jose, have been married eight years and have a young daughter. April and I both were born in New York City—and "in the boroughs" to boot, she in the Bronx and I in Queens—and we share a typically irreverent New York brand of humor. I soon realized she was a genuinely gifted actress, and then learned that she had starred with Hilary Swank in the acclaimed movie *Freedom Writers* and that she had had roles on major TV programs like *30 Rock*, *Dexter*, and *Person of Interest*. I also learned she had done stand-up comedy and was genuinely hilarious. I could also see that her faith was authentic and solid, but I had no idea about the tumultuous past that led her to that faith. In hearing about it, you certainly wouldn't get the idea that she was marked for showbiz success.

April grew up in a tough part of the Bronx. In her teens she was in and out of relationships that were physically and emotionally abusive. It was very disturbing to hear her talk about how bad it all was, to think that this beautiful, charming, sweet, and funny young woman had been physically abused by boyfriends. She now does a lot of public speaking about that time in her life.

One day I asked April if she had ever experienced any miracles in her life. She thought for a moment, as though she was trying to figure out whether she should share something with me. Then she said, "Yes, I have," and immediately told me the following story.

She explained that when she was nineteen, after spending the night with one of her various boyfriends, with whom she wasn't even in any kind of relationship at the time, she found that she had become pregnant. When she discovered this she felt as though her life had ended. Thinking about it tore her apart. She was filled with shame and disappointment. As far as she knew at the time, she had absolutely no choice in terms of how to deal with it. There was only one choice: She would have an abortion. She said it was the most difficult decision of her life, because she knew when she had the abortion the April her parents had raised her to be would no longer exist. A part of her would die. But she simply felt there was no other way.

The abortion clinic was in Manhattan, in a tall corporate-looking building on Park Avenue and Thirty-Second Street. So very early one Saturday morning she left her home in the Bronx and went there. Outside the building were people protesting abortion—monks, Catholics, and other pro-life people. There was actually a policeman there to escort her in "for her safety." She felt the whole thing to be surreal. How had she ended up here? As she walked into the clinic she was surprised to see about forty mostly very young women there, most of them urban minorities like herself, all waiting to have abortion procedures.

The receptionist was extremely cold, emotionally speaking. She handed April a paper to fill out, but at this point April was crying so much that she could barely comprehend what was going on. The woman finally acknowledged that April was having some difficulty and asked April if she would like some help. April said no. She took the clipboard into a corner and began filling it out. As she sat there, she was struck by the emotional coldness in the room. "There was no feeling in anyone's eyes," she said. When she had finished filling out the form, she went back to the reception desk and paid her $450.

She was now instructed to wait. The waiting seemed interminable. It was hours before her name was called. They took her weight and blood pressure. Then they took a sonogram. April was eight weeks pregnant. At that point, the baby's heart is beating and the brain and spine are developing, so as the nurse was printing the pictures of the sonogram, April fought hard not to look. But she couldn't help herself and suddenly saw the image of what was inside her. She began to sob. She continued sobbing, but the nurse didn't say a word or comfort her. There was complete silence, punctuated by the sound of her sobbing.

April now had to return to the waiting area and wait for a very long time. In fact, it was several more hours. As the time passed, her dread at what she was about to do increased. She didn't want to go through with it. She imagined fleeing the scene and running out of the building. She didn't have the strength to do this, but she desperately wished someone might stop her from doing what she was about to do. As she sat there thinking, she overheard depressing conversations. "This is my second abortion," one young girl said. "I just want to get this shit over with."

Finally April's name was called and she felt chills, realizing this was it. A nurse handed her paper slippers and a blue paper gown. Through the bottoms of the slippers she could feel the frigid tile floor. She remembers thinking that it all felt like a *Twilight Zone* episode. When she came to the room where the procedure was to be done, she stopped at the door and noticed spots of blood on the floor. There was a machine with a suction-like tube that looked something like a vacuum cleaner. "Please come in and sit on the seat," the nurse said. April asked her what was the highest number of abortions a girl here ever had. In a cold voice, the nurse said, "Thirteen." Then the nurse asked some questions: "Where is the father?" April said, "He is not in our lives."

"Okay, well, the doctor will be in shortly," she said, "and this will be over in a flash."

April doesn't remember anything about the doctor, neither his face nor his voice. She just remembers hearing that it would be over in "five minutes." She was injected with anesthesia and told to count backward and then she lost consciousness. When she awoke she was in a room with six other girls, all recovering from anesthesia. April's mind was hazy and her vision blurred. Suddenly she called out to the nurse: "I killed my baby!" Then she began crying. She could not stop crying. A nurse said to her, "You did what you had to do. Everything will be okay." But April knew she would never be the same again. She was devastated.

Once the anesthesia began to wear off she was given water and a cookie. It had been many, many hours since she had eaten anything. Finally she was able to leave the building. As she came out of the building she saw that it was a bright and sunny day. The contrast of this sunny day with what she had just experienced was painful. Park Avenue South was bustling with people. She wondered if any of them could guess at what she had just done. But one of them could. As she sat in front of the building waiting for her ride to arrive, an old woman came over to her with a pamphlet that said abortion was a sin. April didn't dare make eye contact with her, but the woman persisted in making her take the pamphlet. April made it clear she wasn't interested, and the woman said, "You're going to hell for what you have done."

In the days, weeks, and months that followed, April was unable to escape the guilt she felt over what she had done. She says she felt like "a dead woman walking." But she simply accepted her sentence. As far as she was concerned, she was a murderer. She knew she would carry this awful burden forever. She felt that she had now become part of that awful stereotype and statistic: another Latina from an urban community who would never amount to anything, who would live on welfare and have children out of wedlock and have no purpose in life but to exist. The years that followed the abortion were very difficult.

After a few years, April began going to church.

But she under no circumstances was buying into "the whole Jesus thing." She would go and sit in the back, where she felt comfortable and safe. She had somehow ended up in a predominantly Dominican church in the Bronx. Although she was a Latina who spoke some Spanish, her first language was still English. So she often didn't understand everything the pastor was preaching about. But one Sunday morning as she sat in her usual seat in the back, things felt different. She found herself understanding more of what the pastor was saying, and she noticed that a number of times he said the Spanish word for "forgiveness." The word "forgiveness" spoken over and over began to have an effect on her and she suddenly felt a desperate desire to want to be closer to God.

April remembers that suddenly she was stretching her hands in the air, almost as though she were falling and reaching out so that God could grab her hand. The feeling was overwhelming. April began to cry, and as she was crying she heard the pastor say that if anyone in the congregation needed forgiveness they should walk up to the front. He repeated this over and over and he said that God was right there in the room. April absolutely didn't want to go up because she knew people would be looking at her and she didn't want anyone to see her, but at the same time that she was resisting she felt another part of her pushing her to go, as though her life were at stake. Slowly she began walking toward the front, weeping as she went. She could feel her heart beating, and she longed to return to her seat, to run out of the church. But she kept walking.

"If you need to be forgiven," the pastor said, "God is here and he loves you." When she got to the altar she shut her eyes tightly and reached her hand out again desperately wanting to be touched by God and out of her mouth came the words, "Father, please forgive me for what I have done! Please forgive me, Father! I am so sorry!" April says that as she continued to sob she was practically screaming out these words: "Father, please forgive me!" Suddenly she lost all sense of everything around her and she felt an immense heat or energy traveling throughout her body. The power of it was so overwhelming that her knees became weak and she fell to the ground in the fetal position. As she lay there weeping and feeling this heat moving through her body, she heard a voice very clearly. It spoke with profound peace, in a kind of whisper: "I forgive you, my daughter. Cry no more." She knew it was the voice of God. Then it said: "But I need you to forgive yourself." April said that at the same time as this she could actually feel the energy healing her uterus, as if it had been damaged in some way. "I physically felt God move in my body," she said. "It was being put together again, being made whole." During this entire experience, she was lying on the floor. It seemed as if she had left the realm of time, as though it all were taking an eternity. But later she realized it had taken only a few moments.

April said that when it was over, some women in the church helped her up again, and when she rose, she said, "It felt like a huge weight had been lifted off my soul, spirit, body, and mind." Her nose was running, her mascara was smeared all over, and she could barely walk straight as she made her way back to her pew in the back of the church. But for the first time in her life she had experienced God's unconditional love and forgiveness and she would come to see that it wasn't a temporary fix: It had changed her forever. She realized that before this healing she had been walking around with a deep pain and wound in her heart and that it had affected her and all she did and thought. Now, at last, she felt free.

But the healing wasn't finished. When she left church that day, she was in a state of shock over what had happened. She didn't say a word of it to her boyfriend (now her husband), Jose, who was with her. Neither of them had really figured out "all of this God stuff." They were attending the church but hadn't really understood or bought into all of it yet. They were still on a journey, individually with God, and with each other as well. All April could say to Jose that day was, "Babe, he forgave me. He forgave me." After what happened in church that day, she knew she was no longer bound by what she had done, by her past. She no longer felt like a murderer. God had forgiven her, and she felt that forgiveness and that freedom in every part of her being. Part of that was God telling her that she needed to accept his forgiveness and forgive herself, to see that she was just a scared girl who had made the only decision she knew to make at the time. She knew what she had done was wrong, but God that morning had overwhelmed her with his love and complete forgiveness.

That evening as she lay in bed next to Jose, they were both trying to process what had happened. April remembers that Jose was speaking when suddenly it was as if she were being taken to another realm. She could hardly hear Jose's voice anymore. There was a kind of echo and she felt as though she were drifting. Her body became somehow numb and she stared at the ceiling and suddenly she had a vision. She said it began like the drawing from an Etch A Sketch. At first she saw a small figure and then as the vision became clearer and more detailed she could see that the figure was a little girl playing happily in a green field surrounded by daisies. April knew the girl's name was, in fact, Daisy. The girl turned around and April now saw that she was about five years old, the age her daughter would be if she had brought her to term. April saw that the little girl looked a lot like she did. It was obvious the girl was in Heaven, full of joy and life. Then the girl spoke: "It's okay. I'm okay. You need to let me go." April knew God was showing her that she could now move on and finally forgive herself.

And so she did.

## SEEING JESUS

I've been friends with Eva Meyer since 1990, when we met through friends at Saint Paul's Episcopal Church in Darien, Connecticut. Eva grew up in the rather tony suburb of Westport, Connecticut. Her father, the late Dr. C. J. Meyer (without a jot or tittle of doubt the smartest person I have ever met; just speaking with him required great powers of concentration), was a physicist whose interest in finding a unified field theory was as serious and fascinating as he was, though he was kind and gentle as well. Despite having such a wonderful father, however, Eva has faced some tremendous challenges, many of them having to do with a tumultuous family life.

At the heart of the tumult was Eva's older sister, who essentially gave over the care of her six children to Eva's parents and to Eva—which is to say mostly to Eva, since Eva was taking care of her mother and doing whatever her busy father could not do. It's no exaggeration to say that all who know her know Eva as the definition of someone with a big heart. So her love for these children has been extraordinary to anyone familiar with the complicated situation.

It began in the early 1990s. Eva had been given the care of her sister's first daughter, then five weeks old, and then she had been given the care of her sister's first son when he was a newborn. She raised them and loved them as her own, giving years to caring for them. A large part of her motivation in sacrificing for them was her desire to shield them from the chaos of their parents' substance-abuse addictions and all that entailed. She couldn't turn them away, knowing what their lives would be like if she had left them to their mother's care. But since they weren't legally her children, she was subject to the whims of their mother. So she had all the responsibility of caring for them and loving them, but none of the rights of a mother. Caring for these children whom she so loved was therefore a joy and an agony both. Saying good-bye to them when their mother capriciously decided she wanted them back was deeply painful, but Eva was powerless to do anything about it.

Then in January 2002, ten years later, it was all happening again. That was when Eva's sister again gave over the care of her children to Eva.

But by now there were six of them, ranging in age from eighteen months to ten years. The three youngest were all under five.

Eva's sister had arrived in Connecticut for Christmas with them, coming all the way from Seattle. This time Eva had really thought it would be different, that her sister had really finally gotten her life together. Eva had paid for all of their plane tickets. But over the next few days it began to dawn on Eva that she had been duped again. Her sister's soon-to-be-ex-husband had flown out west to be with his children, but her sister was already living with a new boyfriend. It was clear she had no intention of trying to make things work with her husband, of trying to raise these children with him. She had brought them all to Connecticut at Eva's expense with the plan to dump them on Eva and then disappear with her new boyfriend.

The youngest of the six was Jonathan, eighteen months old. Eva's heart was so scarred from the back and forth with these children that she was determined not to let herself open her heart up to Jonathan. She simply could not let her heart be torn in that way again, so she held him at arm's length emotionally. Eva saw that her sister had used Eva's love for the oldest two, whom Eva had taken care of from their birth to age four—to manipulate Eva into paying for nearly everything, doing nearly everything, sacrificing nearly everything. Then she had held them as ransom, away from Eva for the previous eight years. And now she was back, abandoning them all again, all six of them now.

After Eva's sister had left, the reality of it all sank in. She realized there was a baby in the next room with no one but her to care for him. There was simply nothing she could do now but deal with it. That night, Eva went to bed burning with anger at her sister. She had never experienced such anger and hate for anyone as she did that night for her sister. She fumed over how much pain her sister had caused these children—and her parents and her—because of her selfishness. She had stolen years from Eva's life by abandoning the children the first time, and now she had done it again.

Eva lay in bed, crying out to God at the injustice of it all. "Where are you?!!" she cried. She pled with him in her anguished prayers, telling him that she simply could not possibly go through this again. The injustice of it burned inside her. Her anger overwhelmed her and a real and hideous hate bloomed in her heart in a way that frightened her. She lay in bed weeping and weeping, and crying out to God over and over.

"I wanted my heart to petrify," Eva told me, "so I could be spared the pain of loving yet another child. I could not bear another decade of heartbreak, being jerked around by my sister's unpredictable whims of dysfunction. Another decade of emotional blackmail. I can honestly say, I have never in my life felt such loathing as I did that night. I felt like I was going to be swallowed whole by rage. I was drowning in it."

As Eva was rolling over in bed, trying to silence the screaming fury in her brain, she glanced out her bedroom window. It looked out over the driveway. The neighbors' bright garage light always cast the silhouette of the trees between the two lots onto her white curtain. But this time, the silhouette looked different. It looked for all the world like the Shroud of Turin. Eva found herself staring at it, trying to make sense of it, but she couldn't. And the more she stared at it, the more vivid the image became. She said it was like developing a print in a darkroom, watching the image grow stronger and clearer with each second. Eva said that the image grew in size and seemed to come closer to her. And then she realized that it was indeed Jesus she was looking at.

"At first, he looked like a giant negative," she said. "His eyes were burning like balls of fire and his right hand was raised. And he was clearly right outside the window. Or in the window." When it became clear to Eva that she was no longer merely looking at a shadow produced by the trees, she was filled with terror. She was awed and speechless.

As this image came yet closer, she pulled the covers over her eyes, hoping she was simply imagining it. But then she pulled down the covers and peeked out and there he was, even closer now, standing in the room between the window and her, at the bottom left corner of her bed. Eva saw that his eyes were still burning like fire, and she felt that she could hardly breathe. She was consumed with fear and now she began to become painfully aware of the rage and hatred inside of her. It was an unbearable feeling, and as it came to a head, she desperately found herself blurting out, "Have mercy on me, Jesus!" And then she spoke words that echoed what Isaiah famously spoke when he found himself in the presence of God: "I am a woman of unclean lips and I live among a people of unclean lips!"

She was surprised that it came out of her mouth, but it did. She was still seized with terror, and as those words came out of her mouth she expected to feel God's wrath visited upon her. She knew that for the bitter hatred she was feeling she deserved it. But the instant the words left her lips she saw that the image was beginning to become clearer. It was Jesus—his face, his beard, his linen robe, his hand raised up over her in silent benediction. She saw him clearly now, and Eva understood that he was praying over her.

Suddenly all the fear melted away and she found herself being bathed in his love and a warm, comforting presence. She said that "waves and waves of the safest, warmest love enveloped me. I felt like I did when I was a baby and my dad rocked me in his arms till I fell asleep. I kept whispering . . . oh, please, Jesus . . . stay with me . . . I love you . . . thank you, Jesus . . ."

Jesus stayed at the foot of her bed all night until after sunrise, and during this time she soaked up every drop of his presence. During the whole time his presence comforted her. But Eva says that no words can possibly do justice to what he imparted to her that night. But the words that come to mind for her are "courage" and "strength" and "peace" and "joy" and "overwhelming love." The rage and the hate she had felt a few hours before had vanished. They seemed a distant memory.

After dawn, Eva began finally to drift off to sleep but then woke herself up, just to make sure he was still there. He was. "He was as real as I was," she said. It was about seven when she last glanced at him, still silently praying for her. She felt that she didn't want it to end, ever. He had "somehow managed to untangle all the knots in my heart," she said, "all the strangling, choking hatred and hurt and fear inside of me."

Sometime shortly after seven she must have fallen asleep, because she was awakened just before eight by Jonathan crying in his crib in the next room. Immediately Eva jumped out of bed and ran to him. Seeing him standing in his crib, sobbing and confused, her heart broke like a dam. The love she now felt for him was surging, overwhelming. She swooped toward him and swept him up in her arms, and she hugged him to her, rocking him and comforting him, telling him that she would never, ever leave him. Eva says that the love she felt for Jonathan at this time was unlike anything she had ever felt before. Her anger toward her sister and toward the whole situation simply didn't exist anymore. The love she now felt for this little boy was all that seemed to be there, and in the midst of it she had a very keen sense that Jesus had given him to her, that she was free to love Jonathan with her whole heart as her own.

A decade later, Eva was married, and just before Christmas 2012, almost ten years exactly from when this happened, Eva and her husband, Paul, were officially declared to be Jonathan's sole legal parents.

# GOD AND MARRIAGE

Perhaps the first story I thought about when I considered writing this book was the story of my very dear friends Paul and Lisa. It's a genuinely amazing story. I couldn't remember some of the details of the story, so I met Paul and Lisa at a restaurant in New Canaan on July 30, 2013, to hear their story again—this time to take notes. Although I had no idea, that date just happened to be their nineteenth wedding anniversary.

I first met them in the spring of 2004 in New Canaan, Connecticut, about twenty feet away from the restaurant where we had our lunch in July 2013. That 2004 dinner was at an evening event of something called the New Canaan Society, a men's fellowship I've been very involved with since 1995, when we started it—in New Canaan, Connecticut, hence the name. I say "we" generously—generous to myself, because it was really my friend Jim Lane who started it. It began as a small men's group in Jim's house. Jim had just returned from a few years in London, where he had been working for Goldman Sachs.

When Jim returned to New Canaan he wanted to have some kind of men's group—not necessarily a Bible study, but something where men could encourage one another. He knew that it should be as much fun as possible and shouldn't feel like some overbearing "religious" group, but should simply be a group of men with the common goal of wanting to be real friends. Of course, any real friendship would mean that we would encourage one another in our commitments to our wives and children. It so happened that there were lots of men looking for something like this, and the New Canaan Society, as it came to be called, grew and grew. Within a few months our number had grown to twenty and soon leapt to forty. We quickly outgrew Jim's family room and moved to his living room, which, given his position as a former partner at Goldman Sachs, was appropriately vast. Before our burgeoning numbers—and Jim's long-suffering wife, Susie—forced us to leave Jim's house for other spaces, we actually had two hundred men there every Friday. Those who couldn't fit into the living room sat on folding chairs in his dining room and foyer, and some gathered in his family room, watching on closed-circuit TV. We still laugh about that, but it's all true. It was around this time that Paul came to visit.

Paul was typical of the sort of person attracted to the fun and general bonhomie of NCS. He was a Harvard grad who was now a partner at one of the so-called white-shoe Wall Street law firms that cannot be named here, as the case may be (hereinafter designated as "the Firm"). He was also typical in that he was discovering that the tremendous worldly success he had dreamt about was now his but was not delivering the happiness and satisfaction he thought it would when he started out after it so many years before. He had a spectacular home in Fairfield County and all of the professional plaudits one might have hoped for. His wife, Lisa, was beautiful and tremendously accomplished, and they had two wonderful children.

Then one day in the fall of 2003, all of these things were threatened. Paul had assumed everything was fine in his marriage before then. There had been a disconnect between him and Lisa for some time, but he rather cavalierly dismissed it as typical of marriages after a few years, where both partners are busy with life. It didn't seem to warrant serious concern. As he saw things, being a good provider made him a good husband and he was certainly being that. Paul usually left for work before his children had woken up and returned after they had gone to sleep, and he was so exhausted and distracted with thoughts of work at the end of each day that he had little capacity or desire to engage with Lisa. He remembered that his way of dealing with her periodic bouts of crying was to withdraw and simply hope it would go away. But this day Paul saw that something was a little more wrong than usual, and he at last felt obliged to ask Lisa about it. "Is something wrong?" he asked her. Her reply was a shock. In a cold and detached tone, she said, "I don't know where to start," and then proceeded to tell Paul that she was profoundly unhappy in their marriage. She said emphatically that she could "not go on like this."

Hearing these words from the woman at the center of the grand edifice of success he had been building all these years was a shattering blow. As he fully took it in, Paul came undone. He had been working so hard and so single-mindedly at building and maintaining this great edifice that he had no idea of his wife's feelings and the depth of their troubles. It was as if he were putting the finishing touches on the highest parts of that edifice and was suddenly being told that the base had begun to rot and it would all come down at any moment. Hearing Lisa's words and tone made him see this, that everything was collapsing. It was too much to bear, and Paul began to sob and did not stop for almost two hours. But Lisa, whose heart had been hardening over the last few years, said she was almost a distant observer. She could not feel any compassion or empathy. If there was any emotion, it was anger, as she wondered how this uncaring and unfeeling man in front of her could have been so incredibly and selfishly oblivious to her great pain.

But the devastating news that day led Paul to do something he had never done before. He viscerally understood that there was no human solution to this crisis, the crisis of his life. He was suddenly desperate and now, for the first time in his life he had no resources to draw on within himself. So he cried out to God, whom he had been ignoring since he could remember.

Paul and Lisa had no real relationship with God up till that time, but they were not atheists. They had both been raised in devout Catholic homes, but as life progressed, they had slipped into being nominal "Christmas and Easter" Catholics. When their first child was born they felt some inchoate urge to do something "spiritual" and decided to go to a church in their neighborhood in London, where they were living at that time. They first tried a Catholic church but quickly became frustrated with their inability to understand the African priest. A few days after making the decision to try something else, Lisa was hailed in the street by a neighbor, a fellow expatriate and American, who introduced herself and that night left an invitation to a garden party being thrown by Saint Michael's Church in Chester Square. Lisa went to the party and found that she liked the people, so that Sunday morning she and Paul went to the service. Lisa loved it, but Paul was so uncomfortable with it all that he never went back. The pastor at that time—and at the time of this writing—was a man named Charles Marnham. Unbeknownst to Lisa, he was no ordinary Anglican vicar. Charles and his wife, Tricia, had essentially invented the now wildly popular and successful "Alpha Program," which has by now brought faith to literally millions around the globe. So at Saint Michael's one found something far more powerful than the standard Church of England fare, and in a short time, Lisa was attending a women's Bible study with the rector's wife. She seemed on her way to a real faith.

Before this seed was able to germinate,

however, Paul's job called them back to New York. Just before they departed, Tricia Marnham told Lisa that in order to make sure her fledgling faith didn't dissipate, she should find a solid "Alpha" church in the United States and read the Bible daily, which Lisa said she would do. But by the time she and Paul found their home in Fairfield County and got properly settled, she had become distracted by other important things, not least the birth of their daughter, just two months after they returned. She found herself missing the excitement of what she had at Saint Michael's just before they had left. She and Paul were now living on a tony street in a very tony town, and there was a traditional church right across the street. Paul saw this as an opportunity to return to a style of service with which he was comfortable, and Lisa went along with his desire because it meant the whole family could be together in church. Since it was so convenient, it somehow seemed just the ticket, and Lisa soon forgot Tricia Marnham's advice and her own good intentions. So it was in this upscale suburban environment that their marriage continued to fall apart and Lisa's faith began to slip away.

During this period, Lisa spent more and more time at a local health club in an effort to medicate her unhappiness at home. It was there that she connected with a group of Fairfield County housewives who were either already divorced or wishing they were. As soon as they heard of Lisa's growing unhappiness, they strongly encouraged Lisa to leave her out-of-touch husband for greener pastures. The constant drumbeat of this took its toll, until Lisa ceased caring about keeping her marriage together or trying to communicate with her husband about their troubles. So, unbeknownst to Paul, by October 2003, when she delivered her devastating answer to Paul's question, it was all but over. Lisa hadn't quite thought through the next steps, but for her things were now moving decidedly in the direction of ending their marriage.

But something else was happening during this time too. The very week Paul and Lisa had their painful conversation, Lisa was volunteering at a book fair at their children's prestigious private school and was manning the sales table with a woman named Deborah, whom Lisa had never met before. But for some reason Lisa opened up to Deborah about what was happening at home. Deborah was a woman of faith, so she told Lisa that she would be praying for a miracle in Lisa's marriage, and she asked Lisa whether Paul would be interested in attending a Christian men's group called the New Canaan Society, which a friend named Rocky had been attending. The day after Lisa met Deborah, she and Paul bumped into Deborah again, this time in the middle of a crowd of hundreds at the school's homecoming football game. Deborah mentioned the New Canaan Society to Paul and even gave Paul the number of her friend Rocky. Paul was skeptical about attending a Christian men's group, but he nonetheless looked it up online. The only thing he found was the eulogy that Jim Lane had delivered at the funeral of David Bloom,[22] who had been an NCS member. One line jumped off the screen at Paul: ". . . it's about men supporting each other to be better husbands and fathers—men being better men." Paul knew he needed that. So he called the number Deborah had given him and learned that we all met at 7:00 A.M. on Fridays at Jim Lane's house in New Canaan, just fifteen minutes away from his own home. That Friday, Paul drove there, ostensibly to meet Rocky. He walked into a house filled with about two hundred men. Paul saw the four hundred or so shoes of those men on the front steps and learned that Jim's wife had only two rules regarding Friday mornings: No food in the living room and no shoes in the house. Paul never found Rocky that day.

---

22. David Bloom was the former NBC White House correspondent who in 2003 died of an embolism in Iraq while embedded with the troops to cover the war. My story about him and his involvement with NCS can be found at http://www.ericmetaxas.com/writing/essays /but-sweet-will-be-the-flower-the-life-and-death-of -nbcs-david-bloom.

The speaker that morning was Tim Keller, the pastor of Redeemer Presbyterian Church in Manhattan. Since my wife and I attended Redeemer at this time, I introduced Tim that morning. His message was titled "How to Pray," and like all his messages it was as impressive as anything one was likely to hear. After Tim's message, my friend B. J. Weber got up and invited new attendees to stay for a short introduction to NCS. In describing his own background, B.J. mentioned that he did marriage counseling. That was all Paul needed to hear. He grabbed B.J. and scheduled an appointment for the following week. Amazingly, for the next several months, B.J. met with Paul and Lisa every single Friday, right after the NCS meetings.

As is often the case with this type of counseling, progress is hard to measure. Lisa brought a boatload of anger to these sessions, but she didn't communicate this very much and somehow it was never really dealt with. On the surface it seemed they were making progress. In January of 2004 they all agreed that the marriage was over the proverbial hump and even hosted a dinner at their home to thank those who had helped them along the way, including Deborah, Rocky, and B.J. Soon thereafter, B.J. asked Paul to get up in front of the hundreds of men at the annual NCS retreat at the Mohonk Mountain House in upstate New York to tell the happy story of how NCS had saved his marriage.

But he had spoken too soon, because despite these outward appearances, Lisa's anger and resentment had continued. In the next weeks, they somehow got the better of her and undid any apparent progress they had made. So in April of 2004, after all that had transpired, she delivered a staggering bombshell. She told Paul she wanted a divorce. The news was, of course, unexpected and devastating. But Paul was prepared for it in a way he had not been the previous October. His faith had been growing steadily all these months, even if Lisa's had not. Five months earlier, on December 5, he had officially made a decision to hand control of his life over to Jesus and prayed to accept Jesus as Lord. So he now understood that he had a tremendous battle ahead, but he also knew that he had weapons with which to wage that battle, along with the faith and the will necessary. Paul also believed that deep down Lisa wanted their marriage to work but thought it an impossibility. Because she believed she had tried everything over the years to repair their relationship, Lisa saw only two choices: to remain in a hopelessly and desperately unhappy marriage, or to get out. Paul saw a third path: a restored and happy marriage. But he knew that it required nothing less than God's intervention.

Through NCS speakers like Tim Keller, Dudley Hall, and Jack Deere, Paul had learned about the verse in the Old Testament Book of Malachi where God declares that he "hates" divorce. He also learned that God would "never leave him nor forsake him," loved him "unconditionally," and would never give him more than he could handle, and that "nothing is impossible with God." Paul also believed that God's will was for his marriage to be saved, and he was determined to do everything in his power to stand for his marriage and to trust God to do the rest. He vowed to never take off his wedding ring and never stop telling Lisa that he loved her. Paul also vowed not to move out of their home, despite Lisa's strong requests that he do so. The first person Paul went to after October 5 was one of his law partners who had become something of a father figure to him. Paul knew the man had been divorced many years before. The man said that his wife had asked him to move out and he always regretted that he had done so, because it had made the process too easy. His one piece of advice to Paul was to stay at home. Though the man was not a Christian, Paul was sure God had sent him and others to guide Paul on his journey through this trial.

Paul had been developing close friendships at NCS—something he came to realize had been absent in his life. So the first thing Paul did was tell the news to some of these close friends. Although NCS typically took a break during the summer, this year Jim Lane had decided to organize the men into small groups that would meet weekly over the summer to talk and pray. This was the goal of NCS, to connect men with other men in friendships, and NCS itself was now far too large for that. Paul joined one of these first NCS "Energy" groups and shared his story. When he did so, one man in the group, named Preben, who was a big proponent of the idea that we are to take "God's promises" in the Bible seriously, said that because God was for marriage and "hated" divorce, we could stand with God against divorce. He would be with us as we did so. So the small group agreed to stand with Paul in prayer and stand on God's promise. All they had to do was believe and pray. Paul's small group continued to meet every Friday, to share their stories and troubles and to pray. So during their time together and in their private prayer times throughout those weeks, the group stood with Paul in faith against divorce.

Practically speaking, Paul had decided that one way he would live out his faith in that Scripture was by doing nothing to cooperate with the divorce Lisa wanted. He didn't fight her, but neither would he lift a finger to help it along. But in July Lisa filed for divorce and a state marshal came to their door to deliver the papers. As it happened, Paul and Lisa's five-year-old son answered the door that day, so it was from his son's hands that Paul received the divorce papers. He had no choice but to go along, but again, he would do all he could to work against it. Most important, in his eyes, was his and the group's continued prayers against it.[23]

Being able to "have faith" that what God says is true can sometimes be difficult, especially when circumstances and emotions work against what it says. In Paul's case, the outward reality of the divorce was overwhelming, but because of the encouragement of his friends in his small group he was able to stand firm in his mind against what was happening. In fact, it was in the small group

---

23. This idea of "standing on God's promise" or "standing on God's Word" stems from the idea that the Bible is the "Word of God." Although the New Testament Greek word "Logos" is translated in English as "Word," with a capital *W,* the real meaning is infinitely richer. In a standard dictionary, like Merriam-Webster, the first definition of "Logos" is "the divine wisdom manifest in the creation, government, and redemption of the world and often identified with the second person of the Trinity [Jesus]." The second definition of Logos is "reason, that in ancient Greek philosophy is the controlling principle in the universe." So the word means far more than just "word" as in "the words of the Bible." It means God's wisdom and God's "ordering principle" for the universe. Furthermore, in the New Testament, Jesus is referred to as the "*Logos tou Theou*"—the "Word of God." So if someone talks about "believing the Word of God," or "standing on God's Word," they typically mean believing what God has declared in the Bible.

that the seeds of the miracle that took place on Friday the thirteenth, August 2004 were planted.

On the morning of August 13, just two days after Paul's forty-third birthday, Preben, who had introduced Paul to the concept of "standing on God's promises," took the idea a bit further. Many Christians believe God will sometimes highlight a particular passage of Scripture for someone as he is praying or reading the Bible, such that it has a particular and personal application. That day, Preben told Paul that he felt in his own prayer time that God had highlighted something in Jeremiah 24 as a particular verse for Paul. People often enough get wild notions that in fact have nothing at all to do with God. So one must always be careful about taking someone else's word for such things. This is why Preben told Paul that when he got home that day, after the small group, Paul should himself pray over that Scripture, to see if he too felt that it was meant for him, from God. But Preben said that if he did feel that, the following week the group would "agree" with God on it and "stand on it," knowing that if this was indeed what God had spoken concerning Paul's situation, it couldn't fail—if only he believed it and "stood on that belief."

The verses in Jeremiah 24 that Preben strongly felt God meant for Paul and his situation referred to the exiled Israelites, whom God would restore to their land:

I will give them a heart to know me, that I am the Lord. They will be my people, and I will be their God, for they will return to me with all their heart.

Preben was saying to Paul that he felt that in his prayer time over this issue, God had told him that these verses were God's promise to Paul that he, God, would redeem the situation, would restore Paul's marriage, and would return Lisa to her relationship with God and to her marriage with Paul. So Paul should ask God if these verses really were for him and if he felt they were he must take this promise from God as a promise directly to him and must believe it and "stand on it."

Most serious Christians—much less nominal Christians or non-Christians—would think all of this a bit strange. But then Preben said something else that was stranger still. He asked Paul whether he'd ever invited Jesus into his home. Paul wasn't sure what Preben was saying. Did he mean this generally, or somehow more literally? Preben meant it literally. He told Paul that after he got home he should go to his front door and pray that Jesus come into his home and then open the door so that Jesus could in fact come in. Paul certainly thought this strange, but when one is desperate one often finds that one's faith is stronger than one's doubts and one can believe things one would scoff at when things are fine. Besides, what harm could there be in it? Even if it was nothing more than a symbolic gesture, it was a nice idea.

So after the men's group ended, Paul drove back to his capacious house. His children, five and three, were with their nanny[24] in the home, and Paul immediately went to his first-floor office to read the verses in Jeremiah that Preben had indicated. He found Jeremiah 24 and in praying about it he did indeed feel that this was God's promise to him, for Lisa and for their marriage. He decided then and there that he would remember this promise in his prayers, and he would remind God that he was in agreement with this—that he was believing God would indeed restore his marriage and Lisa's faith.

After he was finished praying in his office at about nine thirty that morning, Paul suddenly realized he had forgotten about the second thing Preben had said, about inviting Jesus into his home. He hadn't attached any special importance to it, but wanting to dot every *i* and cross every *t,* he walked to the side door of the house, which they used more often than the front door, and he

------

24. Long after this, Paul and Lisa learned that their Honduran nanny, a woman of strong Christian faith, had known something was wrong and was praying daily over their home and their children during this time.

stood in front of it. But when he now closed his eyes to pray, something truly strange happened. Paul told me that with his eyes closed, he could somehow "see"—and what he saw was a bright white figure standing *on the other side of the closed door.*

He said he couldn't make out features, but it was an extremely bright white figure whom he immediately believed to be Jesus, and it startled him, as it would anyone. So he opened his eyes. But with his eyes open he saw only the closed door. Then he shut his eyes again to pray and again immediately "saw" the white figure on the other side of the door. Paul knew he wasn't imagining this, and he knew it was a miracle. So with his eyes closed, and continuing to pray, he opened the door and "watched" the figure walk into his home. What happened next is hard to fathom, but Paul said that with his eyes closed, he walked with this white figure into every room in the house, seeing everything. He kept his eyes closed and simply followed. Paul watched as Jesus lifted his hands and prayed over every room. They walked upstairs—Paul's eyes were still closed—and did this in every room there as well. Then they went downstairs again, and the last room they entered was Paul's office. After Jesus had prayed over the office, Paul knew they were done, and he finally opened his eyes. He was alone. Paul assumed that since they had now prayed over every room, their mission was evidently accomplished. So he sat down at his desk, trying to fathom what had just happened. It was not easy to do. And so Paul closed his eyes to pray once more. In the very moment that he closed his eyes he again saw the figure standing in the middle of the room, and this time, his presence was different. It was overwhelming—so much that Paul got off his chair and fell to the floor, weeping, and embracing Jesus's ankles, undone with gratitude and joy and surrender.[25]

Paul never had anything like that happen again. But it encouraged him in his faith dramatically, as one would expect. From that moment forward he persisted more than ever in praying for his marriage and in expecting God to heal and restore it.

Paul found that after this amazing experience, God would routinely encourage him through others and through things he read. One day in the Friday prayer group a man named David Wagner showed up. David is known for being gifted in

---

25. While this event was occurring, Paul believed it was Jesus who had come into his home in response to his invitation. He has since come to understand that the white figure, which had no visible facial features, may possibly have been not Jesus but the Holy Spirit or an angel of the Lord, who are often associated with the color white and often appear as "faceless" figures in dreams and visions.

what some Christians call the "Prophetic," which means that he often hears things from God when he prays for people. David brought another friend, Len Ballinger, who had similar spiritual gifts. Len prayed and said that when he prayed over Paul a passage from the Book of Hosea kept coming to his mind. The verses he mentioned were Hosea 2:6–7.

> Therefore I will block her path with thorn bushes; I will wall her in so that she cannot find her way. She will chase after her lovers but not catch them; she will look for them but not find them. Then she will say, "I will go back to my husband as at first, for then I was better off than now."

Len said that Paul should pray this prayer when he was praying for his wife and their situation. Over the next weeks, Paul did this faithfully, and continued to pray and "agree with" and "stand on" the verses from Jeremiah too. When praying, he actually pictured in his mind a hedge of thorns growing up around her to protect her from anything that would harm their marriage or family. He imagined it growing so tall and thick that she could only look up toward God.

During this period, someone else in the group gave everyone a copy of a marriage book by our friend Emerson Eggerichs, titled *Love and*

*Respect.* Emerson had actually tested the material in the book at some NCS meetings a few years before. Paul devoured the book and was particularly struck by a chapter about what to do if only one partner in a marriage wants it to heal. It said he should look at his spouse as though Jesus were standing right behind her and love her out of obedience to Jesus, not because he felt like loving her.

That October Lisa had started seeing a therapist. It was not to help her with her marriage, which she had already consigned to the ash heap of her past, but rather to help her with the new self she was hoping to find to go along with her new life. One day the therapist, who was not a Christian, threw a monkey wrench into Lisa's future hopes and plans. As he listened to her talking about herself and what she had been feeling, he advised her to take responsibility for her own anger toward her husband. He said that it was not healthy to blame her husband and that she must own up to her own part in feeling that anger. Lisa says that for some reason this caused the beginning of a shift in her view of everything. She began to look at herself and her emotions more critically, and for the first time it enabled her to simply stop blaming Paul and focusing her anger on him.

Nonetheless, she was still firmly resolved to "move on," and although their marriage was not yet officially over, Lisa was living her life as though it was: She had not worn her wedding and engagement rings for months and had been sleeping in another room in the house. She had even begun looking for a place to move with the children. Although Paul had instructed his divorce lawyer to move as slowly as possible so that God had time to work, the legal process was moving forward and it would be only a matter of time before things were finalized and the marriage would be over officially and legally. But Paul was still standing on God's promises and praying the Scripture verses from Hosea and Jeremiah, believing that God would protect Lisa from any adulterous links to other men, and believing that God could and would restore her to the marriage and to God himself.

Then one Friday morning that November—it was the nineteenth of the month—Paul returned from an NCS meeting to deliver some startling news. He told Lisa that Jim Lane, who was the head of NCS, had just checked into a rehab for alcohol addiction. Jim Lane was the head of NCS, which Lisa at this time thought of as representing Christianity in their lives, even though she wasn't too excited about NCS or its particular brand of Christianity. So when Lisa heard that Jim had humbled himself in this way, had admitted his problem and had taken measures to deal with it head-on, she was deeply affected. The news hit her extremely hard. She remembered thinking that if this Christian leader had the courage to be that open and honest about his problems, and if he believed that God really could help him, then perhaps God really could help her too. But actually it wasn't just the idea that God could perhaps help Lisa. It was a much more startling idea that perhaps God could help the two of them, Lisa and Paul, heal their marriage. The news about Jim Lane seemed to suddenly cause her to shift from believing her marriage utterly dead and hopeless to being somehow within reach of God. Although she wasn't at all sure why—nor at all in touch with the feelings that were now unleashed—Lisa was completely and utterly undone by the news about Jim that morning, and about what she saw as its implications for her and Paul. Somehow she felt herself shift subtly toward God, toward yielding her will and her problems to his care. As a result of this slight but significant change in her heart and mind, the emotions that came out of her now were practically overwhelming.

But the famously buttoned-up Lisa could not at this time allow herself to be overwhelmed. She simply had too much happening that day especially to open herself up to her sudden emotions. What lay ahead required her undiluted attention. When Paul had returned from the NCS gathering, Lisa was getting dressed and preparing for an especially crucial meeting in Manhattan. In fact, she was about to drive to the Stamford train station when Paul returned. She was taking the train into the city to preside over an important presentation at a fund-raising luncheon for the Bowdoin Alumni Fund. So Lisa pulled herself together now, drove to the station, and got on her train. But as she sat on the train, headed to her important meeting, the feelings that had threatened to overwhelm her when Paul told her about Jim began to make good on their threat. She hardly knew what she was feeling or thinking, but her head was swimming and her emotions were beginning to get the better of her. There was so much riding on her presentation that she simply had to get ahold of herself. She couldn't. No matter how she tried, she couldn't get the upper hand on her disorienting emotions, neither as she rode into the city nor afterward. As a result, she failed to deliver the crackerjack presentation she had hoped to deliver. In fact, it was close to a disaster. Type-A personalities like Lisa weren't used to failing. But there was no getting around it: She was a complete emotional wreck.

After the terrible experience of the luncheon, Lisa thought she could recover herself by going shopping with a few friends, so she contacted some friends and did go shopping with them. But even this shiny weapon in her Fairfield County arsenal failed to deliver. But Lisa had one more idea. She contacted some friends in Stamford and made plans to have dinner with them. That should do it. She went to Grand Central, got on her train, and met her friends in Stamford at a favorite restaurant. But somehow Lisa's feelings continued to get worse. She was even beginning to feel physically sick. So right in the middle of dinner, she apologized to her friends and excused herself, saying she didn't feel at all well and simply had to go home.

But just now, when she got in her car to drive the fifteen minutes to her home, the dam burst completely. As she drove, Lisa began sobbing uncontrollably and screaming to God. "Save my life!" she screamed. "Save my marriage!" She screamed these phrases over and over in a way that she described as raw and guttural and completely unlike her. It was such an extraordinary unleashing of emotions that Lisa said she stopped the car six times and pulled over. She was actually afraid she wouldn't be able to make it home. She would pull over and then begin again, all the while crying hysterically, screaming, begging God to help her. She said it was as if she were praying from and with her whole body.

When she finally got home, Lisa went straight to bed, hoping that in the morning she would be able to get a handle on whatever it was that she was feeling. But she awoke feeling just as out of sorts as ever. But again reaching into her arsenal of type-A weapons, she decided she would go to the gym and take two spin classes, back-to-back. Intense exercise could always be counted on to blow away the cobwebs and make her feel great. But before she walked out the door, Paul saw her and let her know that he would be willing to see her therapist with her as she had asked. He had previously refused to do so.

Near the end of her second spin class, Lisa was about as physically spent as she had ever been. But the intense exercise had failed to deliver on what she had hoped. She knew that she was the same bona fide mess she had been when she began, and now the final burst of exercise proved too much. As soon as the last song was over she stopped, utterly spent, and leaned over the handlebars with her eyes closed. But just as she did so, Lisa had a sudden, vivid vision of Jesus hanging on the cross. "It was at dusk," she told me. "And there was light coming from behind him." Lisa had never had a vision before in her life, but there on the exercise bike, with her eyes closed, she clearly saw Jesus on the cross. She said that she then knew for the first time in her life that what he had suffered wasn't just a general thing for all of humanity. It was some-thing that Jesus had done just for her, and the realization undid her. All day long afterward, she remained an emotional wreck.

The following Sunday was her son's sixth

birthday, and Lisa promised that she'd spend the whole day with him, no matter what. For some reason, he declared that he wanted to go to church that morning and see the movie *The Polar Express*, an animated film featuring the voice of Tom Hanks, that afternoon. Paul had been regularly taking the children to church without Lisa for months. Lisa was terrified because she felt that the people in their church who knew what was going on in her life would judge her. She had good reason to worry, because it had been the "advice" of people in this same church that had driven her away months before. But to keep her promise, she went anyway, and was surprised that everyone that morning was especially kind and loving to her. Later that day, she and Paul took their son and daughter to see *The Polar Express*. The movie is not in any way Christian, but the message of the movie— *believe*—felt very personal to her. "I knew it was God," Lisa told me. "He pierced through that movie, with a one-word message to me: *Believe!* I didn't need to know how or when to believe. The message was just that I must believe and he would take care of the rest."

The next day, Paul came home from work and saw that Lisa had her wedding ring on for the first time in nearly eight months. When he asked her about it, she told him that it was a sign of her commitment to God "and to our marriage."

Needless to say, Paul was stunned and even confused by these words. Then the following day, after sleeping for the last eight months in another bedroom, Lisa moved all her belongings back into the master bedroom. That night Paul got home very late from work and when he went into the bedroom where he had been sleeping alone for the previous eight months, he saw his wife asleep in their bed.

# 12

---◆·◆·◆---

## ANGELIC MIRACLES

For He shall give His angels charge over
you.

—PSALM 91:11

The Bible is filled with stories about angels, but
many of us have had our view of angels confused
by popular misconceptions about them, the
principal of which is that angels do not actually
exist any more than fairies do, or wood nymphs
or water sprites. But they do exist and the Bible
attests to their existence innumerable times.[26]

The word "angel" is simply the New Testament
Greek word meaning "messenger," so angels are
powerful celestial beings created by God to carry

---

26. Another popular misconception is that angels are
"spirit guides," but there is nothing in the Bible to
support this view. In fact, if anything, the Bible soberly
instructs us to beware of contact with any spiritual
beings unless we are utterly clear that they are sent by
the God of the Bible and come in his name and for his
purposes. The Bible says that Satan comes "as an angel
of light," and warns us to be very careful and to "test
the spirits."

his messages and to otherwise do his bidding. In the Bible they are often said to be carrying swords—something my friend Peter Martin corroborates in the first story of this chapter. So in saying what angels are—according to what we know from the Bible—we must also say what angels are not. For one thing, they are not fey, effeminate creatures, languid as a Victorian heroine. They are also not chubby and unthreatening cherubs. Most angels we see in Scripture are exceedingly fierce and usually terrifying to humans, whether they have swords or not.

Many of us have heard the term "seraphs," which refers to the seraphim, the highest order of angelic beings, having six wings and being charged with guarding the throne of God. Many of us have also heard about the cherubim, who are the next order of angels, and who are pictured in Genesis as guarding the Tree of Life. But cherubim have become confused with the plump, toddler-like creatures commonly called cherubs, which we sometimes see depicted as Eros figures in Greek and Roman art, usually fluttering around Aphrodite or Pan. Those creatures, which we also see in the work of Raphael, are nowhere mentioned in the Bible.

There are various types of encounters with angels. A typical one is when they intervene to save a life.

My friend April Hernandez, whose story of

inner healing appears in a previous chapter, told me just such a story. It happened when she was thirteen years old. She had gone to the beach in the Bronx with some friends. But where they had decided to go into the water, far from other people, there was an immediate and very sharp drop-off. April couldn't swim, so she wasn't about to go in. Instead, she stood with her legs in the water, near the edge of this sharp drop-off, intending to go no farther. But as she stood there her friend—who herself wasn't much of a swimmer—began to tease April. "C'mon!" she said, goading her not to be such a chicken. Then, without warning, she grabbed April and pulled her into the deep water. April immediately went under and panicked. In a desperate desire to save her own life, she frantically grabbed at her friend and began pulling her down too. April knew she was drowning. Then, suddenly, she felt a powerful hand grab her by the arm and pull her the few feet to shore, saving her life. But when she opened her eyes and looked up to see who had saved her from drowning, she saw no one. It had to be an adult, because it had been a very strong grip and had pulled her right out. But there was no one there. On the sand around her there were no footprints. Nor were there many people on the beach at all, and certainly not near her. If it had been a person, surely he would have stayed there a moment to make sure that she was okay.

If he had pulled her out so quickly, he had obviously seen she was in trouble. But whoever had done this was not there, even seconds after it had happened. April knew without any doubt that she had experienced a miracle, that an angel had saved her life.

Another type of angelic encounter is when someone simply sees an angel or angels. In these instances the angels are not communicating with us, per se, or doing anything that involves us, but are just there doing what God has commanded them to do. Yet we are afforded the privilege of seeing into the heavenly realm. In the Book of Second Kings in the Bible, we read of how the King of Aram is at war with Israel. Elisha the prophet is traveling with Israel's army and when his servant awakes one morning, he sees the enemy army surrounding them, with horses and chariots. But when he tells Elisha this, Elisha is not concerned. He prays, "Open his eyes, Lord, so that he may see." The passage says that the Lord then opened the servant's eyes and he "saw the hills full of horses and chariots of fire all around Elisha." In other words, he saw what was there, but what had been invisible to him: God's army of angels with their "chariots of fire." Sometimes it seems that God allows us to see into the invisible realm simply to encourage us.

A third type of angelic experience occurs when we encounter an angel in the guise of a person. In the Book of Judges, both Gideon and Manoah converse with angels, but only realize after the angel has left. In the New Testament book of Hebrews, it says, "Don't forget to show hospitality to strangers, for some who have done this have entertained angels without realizing it." So the idea that angels sometimes are disguised as people is certainly a Biblical idea. Many people on the mission field tell stories along this line; the last story in this chapter is one such story, as is the last story in chapter 11.

## ANGELS IN CHURCH

My friend Peter Martin sometimes comes across like an upper-class caricature, complete with double-breasted navy blazer, bow tie, and lock-jawed pronunciation. He could be Frasier Crane's long-lost brother or a stock character from a Preston Sturges film. Peter knows more about British church choirs and private clubs than anyone you will ever meet. He's also the man who taught me how to fold my three-pointed pocket handkerchief.

Peter is therefore perhaps the last person one might expect to be able to see into the eternal realm and tell us about it. In fact, I hadn't even planned to ask him whether he had any miracle stories, but I happened to bump into him one

December Sunday at the annual Angel Tree party[27] our dear friends Richard and Pam Scurry annually throw in their Fifth Avenue duplex overlooking the Central Park Reservoir. I mentioned I was working on a book about miracles and before you could say "John Cheever," Peter was telling me that he had seen two magnificent angels at Saint Thomas's Church on Fifth Avenue within the past year—and he proceeded to tell the stories with all of the brocaded and filigreed asides one expects from Peter.

If Peter defies one's idea of the sort of person who would see angels, Saint Thomas's Fifth Avenue church doubly defies one's idea of the kind of place where someone might see them. It is as Anglo-Catholic Episcopal and Manhattanite upscale as any church could be. Peter told me he had adopted Saint Thomas's as his church in 1975 on his return from Oxford University. As a boy he discovered the glories of English cathedral choir at Saint Albans Abbey where his father lived. After reading Henry James during the day, he would end the day climbing the hill and listening to choral evensong while sitting in choir.

Peter said his first sighting took place on the fourth Sunday in Advent. The church was of

27. Sponsored by Prison Fellowship, these parties are held each December so that people can donate presents to the children of prisoners.

course crammed full of what Peter called "clubbable" types, hat-wearing ladies who lunch and so on. Peter said he was seated where he usually sits, in the fourth or fifth row on the aisle—on the Epistle side of the church, as he called it, because that's where the Epistle is read during the liturgy. They were singing a hymn when it happened. Peter said it was suddenly as if the optometrist had flipped the lenses during an examination, as when they say, *Is it better now? Or now?* Suddenly Peter was seeing differently. In fact, it seems that he was getting a look into another dimension.

"I saw an absolutely *huge* angel standing right by the memorial for the victims of the terrorist attack on 9/11," he told me. "The memorial has a quote from Queen Elizabeth that says, 'The price we pay for love is grief.' And the then Archbishop of Canterbury, John Carey, had sent along a stone from Canterbury Cathedral itself, and that's embedded there along with the queen's quote. A member of our parish had died during the attack on the Twin Towers."

Since it was the fourth Sunday in Advent, Peter told me, Saint Thomas's was of course doing the famous Milner-White "A Festival of Nine Lessons and Carols," where angels are spoken of in scripture and song. Like many things, it's famous once you're familiar with it, which we now all are. In any case, as the rector and other clergy processed, they would stop at an assigned spot and read a lesson and then everyone would sing a carol and then the procession would move on to the next assigned spot. Peter said he saw the angel right at that point where the procession was going by the pulpit. Peter had never seen an angel before. He said with typical exactness that it was thirty feet high and that it stood about that same distance—thirty feet—from where he was sitting—or standing, since they were singing a hymn. "It expanded my mind, because it looked like super HD. The colors and reality of it were illuminated and exceptional like the reality of Heaven in C. S. Lewis's *The Great Divorce*," he said. "It had huge wings and held a huge sword and wore a suit of armor, and the colors were just dazzling: golds and blues and reds. It sort of looked like fine needlepoint, but of course it wasn't. But it was incredible. It was just sort of looking over the whole congregation. This thing was huge." Peter said that he was utterly thrilled and "just completely bathed in its fearsome and awesome beauty."

And he said that he was awestruck, that he felt exactly as the shepherds in the field must have felt when they saw the angels in Bethlehem. He said he wasn't exactly afraid but simply awe-struck. It was a divine connection with the parallel world that was just awesome. He said he was just mesmerized as he saw it, and he felt incredibly grateful and worshipful, praising God as he took it in. He saw it for about twenty seconds, and then it was gone. Or, to be accurate, he couldn't see it anymore. Whether it was actually gone is another story.

That was the first time. The next time Peter saw an angel was also at Saint Thomas's, this time on Easter Sunday, prompting one to wonder if these angels show up only on special days in the church calendar. (Perhaps angels are more high-church than we've been led to believe.) This time, Peter was again sitting on the aisle in the fourth or fifth row on the right side of the central church aisle, and it again happened during a hymn and again it was just as if the optometrist had flipped to another lens. *Now? Or now?* This time, however, the angel was not thirty feet away but right next to him, slightly behind him, just over his left shoulder. And by his estimation it had to be fifty feet tall. It was certainly much larger than the thirty-foot angel he had seen. He said that "it really startled and rocked" him when he saw it. In fact, he said that he looked at it and then had to look away because it was so huge and awesome and frightening. So this time he only saw it for an instant. It was different but still very similar to the other angel. He said the colors were different but similarly brilliant. It had an absolutely huge body and huge wings and he saw the same kind of multicolored armor that gave him the idea of needlepoint. Was it hundreds of gems? He could not be sure, because it disappeared so quickly.

But that's what he saw at these two services at Saint Thomas's Episcopal Church on Fifth Avenue in Manhattan.

In early May 2014, just as I was completing this manuscript, I saw Peter at the New Canaan Society's annual retreat in Washington, DC. When I told him I would be including his two angel stories in the book, he smiled broadly, as he does, and then told me that it had happened again, just a few weeks before. Peter was again at Saint Thomas's on Fifth Avenue for the Great Vigil and First Eucharist of Easter, a service that begins in the last hour of Holy Saturday and extends past midnight into the first hour of Easter Sunday. Just a few minutes before midnight the church is darkened and then at midnight precisely the rector knocks loudly three times on the large closed doors of the church.

The celebrant gives the blessing of the new fire and then prepares the paschal candle (which will be lit during the Easter season and at all funerals during the year) with a knife, incising an outline cross and the letters of the Greek alphabet—alpha and omega—as he says the words of preparation. He then lights the paschal candle saying, "May the light of Christ gloriously rising scatter the darkness of heart and mind." At this point the doors are opened and the paschal candle enters, symbolizing the light of Christ entering the world. This candle is in turn used to light other candles in the congregation, which are used to light all of the remaining candles in the congregation, so that the whole sanctuary glows with the light of thousands of candles. Peter was in the third pew on the main aisle. When he heard the awaited knocking, he rose with everyone else and with everyone else turned in the darkness to face the great doors of the church. They were opened, and the paschal candle entered. Just then, Peter saw a "great warrior angel" by the front door, over the gallery organ. He said that its armor and color were tremendously clear and bright. "It was even clearer than 4K," he said, "which is brighter than 1080p." He said it filled him with awe to look at it: "It was ascending with the incense and the smoke from the new fire to the top of the nave."

Peter says that each time he saw the angels, he first felt tremendous exhilaration, followed by a great sense of awe. Something about the vividness of the colors especially made him feel privileged, because there was no question in his mind that he was seeing something outside this world.

But those of us who have never seen angels must wonder why Peter saw them. First of all, we may conclude that they weren't there just for Peter, because they didn't communicate with him.

Instead, we get the impression that they were simply there and that Peter was for some reason afforded the extraordinary privilege of seeing them. We hear stories of people who are allowed glimpses into the heavenly realm, who are allowed to see what is there, but what is invisible to the human eye, who are really seeing outside of time and space into the eternal realm. In the story of Jesus on the Mount of Transfiguration we have a picture of something exactly like that. Peter, James, and John see Jesus talking with Moses and Elijah. It's as if they are afforded a glimpse through a porthole into eternity. Moses and Elijah had left our world centuries before, but they are still alive in Heaven and Jesus was able to converse with them. Peter, James, and John were allowed to be witnesses.

Some people have a special gift of being able to see into this realm. I have had a few friends who have had the gift to be able to see into it very often, and I've had others, like Peter, who have seen into it now and again. In the course of our conversations about his angel sightings, Peter has also told me that he has twice in his life vividly seen Jesus as well. This happened at two churches in Connecticut, both of which are very different theologically and aesthetically from Saint Thomas's Fifth Avenue. One of them is extremely different, about as "low-church" and aesthetically bare, with folding chairs and painted cinder blocks, as Saint Thomas's is "high-church" and aesthetically sumptuous, with soaring Gothic arches and exquisite stained glass. So it does seem that some people are more inclined to be able to see such things. But we really cannot say. It is also possible that if we simply ask God to show us such things, he will.

## TOUCHED BY AN ANGEL

My friend Eva Meyer was thirteen and a freshman at Staples High School in Westport, Connecticut. In the first few days of school (this was in the 1980s) she made some new friends and one of them invited her to a sleepover one Friday night in early September. Eva soon realized that these girls were rather different from the ones she had been used to spending time with. For one thing, they were all interested in the occult. In fact, they decided they wanted to have a séance that night. One of the girls was heavily into the music of the Doors and said she wanted to invoke the spirit of Jim Morrison. But Eva did not wish to "break on through to the other side." She knew far too much about the dark side of the spirit realm to think this was a good way to spend the evening. She simply couldn't go through with it and she said so to her new friends. So the girls decided that they would all take a walk to the beach instead. The girl whose house it was lived within walking distance of Compo Beach. The quickest route there was straight down Hillspoint Road and over Hillspoint Road Bridge, which crosses 1-95, the heavily trafficked interstate highway that runs from Maine to Florida.

When the girls got to the bridge, Eva saw that there was a six-foot-tall stockade fence blocking the road. Evidently there was "roadwork" being done on the bridge, although they couldn't see past the tall fence to see exactly what was being done. But the girl whose house they were staying at told them she climbed the fence all the time and just walked across the bridge. She insisted that she had done it many times and explained that they just didn't want cars driving across it but it was absolutely fine to walk across it. Eva explains that for "some strange reason" they insisted that she go first. They would boost her up and help her get over the fence. To this day Eva cannot figure why she agreed to go first, but she did. She says that at the time she was "a five-foot-two, maybe one hundred forty pounds, somewhat chubby, very weak thirteen-year-old girl," who had never done a single pull-up in her life. Maybe this is why she agreed to the three of them helping her over first, or why they suggested it. So the three girls boosted her up with their hands and essentially heaved her up and over the six-foot fence.

It was in the next split second that Eva saw

the trouble. To put it in her own words, precisely as she typed them to me: "THERE WAS NO BRIDGE THERE!!! NOTHING!!!" It was an unspeakable horror, the sort of thing about which one has recurring nightmares. Eva remembers in that briefest of moments seeing a huge semitruck roaring right beneath her flailing legs, which were kicking in midair, and she remembers the feel of the rough top of the stockade fence, which she desperately tried to grasp as her body went over. Instinctively, she screamed: "Jesus!!!"

Then, just as she lost her grip and began to plummet to what she knew would be her death on the highway down below, with the endless speeding trucks and cars, she felt herself lifted up. She saw nothing, but in the blink of an eye she felt herself being scooped up in midair and carried back over the fence and placed onto solid ground—but a full ten feet away from where the three girls had tossed her over. She says that she remembers landing—"my arms were stretched out wide, as though a parachute had brought me to a soft landing." And then she remembers the unhinged looks on the faces of the other three girls. She remembers that they were "utterly horrified, scared witless." Eva says they were "white as sheets, with mouths agape, and eyes wide in terror." All three of them shrieked and instantly bolted the scene, running away as fast as they could.

Eva remembers the feeling of those moments. She felt strangely calm, but confused too. She knew without a doubt in that moment that Jesus had miraculously saved her life. She simply got up and walked home, not telling a soul what happened. But she remembers clearly that not one of those three girls ever spoke to her again. They wouldn't even glance in her direction or come near her.

Twentysomething years later, around the time of her high school reunion, Eva discovered that the girl whose house they had been staying in was a full-fledged Satanist. Eva saw that her Facebook page was filled with pentagrams and other dark, occult symbols. Needless to say, Eva "blocked" her.

## "YOU ARE *NOT* GOING TO DIE"

Elisa Leberis is my chief of staff, overseeing everything in our company. She is a Stanford graduate, brilliant and omnicompetent, and has accomplished extraordinary things in her varied career. But this story concerns a time that was a rare low point in her life. In fact, it was her first real experience of failure. Up until then she had been one of those achievement-oriented kids who was used to receiving praise and support from her family and teachers and friends. She graduated at the top of her high school class of six hundred students, got into every college she applied to, and talked about her experience of God in her graduation speech. Even teachers who disagreed with her beliefs praised her for having convic-tions. She entered Stanford with almost a year's worth of credits.

But when it came time to plan the summer following her freshman year, she felt aimless. She hadn't selected a major and didn't know what she wanted to do with that summer. In the end she cobbled together two part-time jobs in the northern suburbs of Chicago, not too far from where she would be living during these months. One was a teaching internship, and the other was working in her actual high school, the place where she had experienced so much praise and support. Her assignment involved cleaning out lab closets and sorting through specimens, most of the time by herself in a nearly empty building. To make matters even worse, Elisa had somehow decided that biking to work every day would be fun. On the map it didn't seem like such a long way, but after just a few days of biking through traffic in the high heat and humidity of a Midwest summer, Elisa knew she had made a terrible mistake and that there was nothing she could do about it. Every day as she made the long, dreary rides, Elisa spent much of the time wondering why she hadn't found one good job downtown, near a train station. She was bewildered things hadn't come together as they always had before, bewildered that, all at once, it seemed she had no idea what she was going to do with her life. She felt defeated.

Elisa remembers biking down Church Street in Skokie on a particularly hot and humid day, when it happened. In her impatience to get home, she was pedaling hard in a low gear and going extremely fast, as fast as she could go on her sister's yellow Schwinn Varsity ten-speed bike. She was approaching an intersection and in the oncoming traffic a truck was slowing down to make a left turn at that intersection. As she got closer to the intersection, she must have looked away for a moment, because when she looked ahead again, she realized that the truck had not stopped at all, but was already proceeding to turn. Elisa assumed the driver had seen her coming toward him, but she now realized to her horror that he obviously had not. He was steering the truck right across her path, and Elisa remembers that she was going so fast that before she could blink, the letters M-A-C-K on the front of the truck were right in front of her eyes.

At some point in all of this the driver obviously saw her. She heard the truck's brakes screeching loudly and a pedestrian shouting. Elisa says, "For a split second, it felt to me as if everything froze in space and time, and in that split second, I tried to figure out what to do but couldn't see a way out." She couldn't turn left, since the truck was to her front left. To her front right, just past the truck, was a concrete island and a stoplight post. It was too late for her to brake—she was going much too fast and the truck was just too close. "I know it sounds ridiculous," she says, "and I can't really explain why I responded this way, but my conclusion was, 'This is it for me. There's nowhere to go.' I don't know if I thought I was going to collide with the truck, or die, or what—but I sat up and released my hold on the handlebars."

Then something abrupt and shocking happened, which she says is hard to describe exactly. She says the best way to put it is that she heard a voice, but not an audible voice. The voice was clear, and forceful, and emphatic, and it rebuked her, saying, "You are not going to give up that easily! You are not going to die!" As she heard these words, she felt as though an invisible pair of hands grabbed the handlebars, and on the first "not" the handlebars jerked to the right to get her out of the way of the truck. But she was then heading straight into the concrete island, and on the second "not" the handlebars jerked hard to the left, directing her through the thinnest of gaps, perhaps two or three feet wide, between the truck and the concrete island. She whizzed by the panic-stricken truck driver, and then she was out—the truck and the island and the pedestrian were all behind her and she was continuing down Church Street without having ever braked or made contact. It all had taken place in a moment. Elisa looked back at the stunned truck driver and waved, and said, "I'm all right! I'm all right!" And then she turned down the first side street she could find, and started shaking, and said again, "I'm all right! I'm all right!" And she thanked God that she was all right.

"On the slow, shaky ride home, I didn't think about how poor my choices had been that summer," says Elisa. "I didn't think about any of my choices at all. Instead, I pondered how, in just a few split seconds, God not only miraculously spared me from terrible injury or worse, but also communicated to a confused and discouraged nineteen-year-old the powerful, life-changing truth that her life matters to him."

## CHANGSHA TRAIN STATION

John Bechtel is something of a legend in the world of international missions, but he is an outsize figure in general, someone who, had he not gone into missions, might have made millions in the business world. He is supersmart, funny, accomplished, capable, and resourceful, though his portly body and bald head somehow belie these things; it is a dissonance he shrewdly and often exploits to great comic effect.

I had the pleasure of meeting John five years ago at CAMP-of-the-WOODS, a Christian camp in the Adirondacks where he has been involved for nearly sixty years. His affiliation there began during college, when, working there as a summer lifeguard, he saved the life of a drowning man, and it has continued with his serving on the COTW board for more than forty years. Every year at CAMP-of-the-WOODS, John regales campers with his "missionary stories around the campfire." John is a gifted storyteller, and each one I've had the joy of hearing has been extraordinary, but the one I recount here concerns a four-hundred-mile train ride through China in the early 1980s.

By way of background, John was born in 1939 to veteran missionaries who served for fifty-one years in Hong Kong and China. As a toddler, he escaped with his mother on the last ship departing Hong Kong before the Japanese occupation of World War II. His father was interned by the Japanese in a concentration camp while John spent the war years with his mother in the United States, returning to Hong Kong at the age of seven. There he was educated in the British system at King George V School, where he was high school student body president and at eighteen represented Hong Kong on an international sports team.

After college graduation in 1962, John was

given a trip to Hong Kong, where the squalid and crowded conditions of the millions living there moved him to dedicate his life to working in missions. What he did over the next years includes creating a Hong Kong youth camp that has served hundreds of thousands of underprivileged youth, as well as spearheading a church planting project that eventually blossomed to more than 132 churches. John has built orphanages and has promoted missions in such places as New Zealand, Australia, England, Africa, Asia, the former Soviet Union and Europe as well as throughout the United States and Canada. In 1974, he was an official delegate to the Lausanne Conference. His many honors include four honorary doctorates.

But it was during the 1980s, when John held a position with the DeMoss Foundation, that the following story took place. John was working for the foundation as project director for Hong Kong, Taiwan, and China, and later worked as director of international ministries. In this capacity he found himself traveling with two people: Nancy DeMoss, the widow of Arthur DeMoss; and Scott Hall, who was also working for the foundation at that time. (He has since had a successful business career and is now retired.) Scott spoke Mandarin Chinese fluently, and John spoke Cantonese fluently and Mandarin quite well.

The three of them had traveled to the city of

Changsha, the capital of the Hunan province and the place where Mao Tse-Tung was famously converted to Communism. It was very difficult to travel there at that time. They had come to visit some missionaries who were running a computer training center there. One had to have a very good reason to be in China at that time, and this was what these people did to be able to live there as missionaries. When John and his companions had completed their visit, they went to the airport to board their plane back to Hong Kong. They were scheduled to go on a trip from Hong Kong to the Philippines in just a few days. But when they arrived at the Changsha airport, they discovered that their flight to Hong Kong was delayed.

So they waited in the airport. Nancy DeMoss was friends with the legendary football coach Joe Gibbs, who was that very day coaching his Washington Redskins in the Super Bowl (this was 1982 or 1983, since the Redskins played in the Super Bowl both years). Because they had time to kill, the three of them tried to figure out if they could somehow get the Super Bowl on TV at the airport. They couldn't. And the information they finally got about their flight was that it was not happening at all. Very few people traveled in China by plane at that time, and because of the Chinese New Year, there would be no flights at all that day. In fact, they were informed they would have to wait two or three days before a flight to Hong Kong would be possible.

Always resourceful, John now tried to book a private plane, but that too proved impossible. Finally, in their desperation to get back to Hong Kong they realized they would have to take a train. There was simply no other way. It would be far from ideal for the four-hundred-mile trip—but at least it was possible to get there and to catch their flight to the Philippines. So they left the airport and took a cab to the Changsha train station.

But as they approached the station they saw that train travel was rather popular. For a three-block perimeter around the station there were people camped out everywhere. The sheer numbers were staggering and intimidating. But John knew that at New Year's in China, everyone traveled back to their hometowns for the holiday—and every-one in China is a lot of people. The taxi could proceed no farther for the crowds, so the three of them got out and carrying their luggage struggled through the masses of people to the station. The inside of the station was equally crowded. John led Nancy and Scott along a serpentine path through the crowds until they were at the line for Canton, which is the city that borders Hong Kong. John figured that they might be able to scalp some tickets from people who were near the front of the line. The ticket for this trip was at that time only nine dollars, so in their desperation, John in his flawless Cantonese offered one hundred dollars to anyone in the line who would give them his ticket! No one was interested. But Nancy DeMoss was a wealthy woman, so John now offered two hundred dollars per ticket! Amazingly there were still no takers. These people wanted desperately to get home for this uniquely important holiday and had likely waited very long for their tickets.

But John always had another idea. He thought perhaps they could bluff their way into the VIP area at the train station and might have some success getting a ticket there. They were well-dressed and affluent Westerners. Who knew what they might be able to do? John told Scott and Nancy to follow him up the long marble staircase to the VIP entrance and not to make eye contact with the policemen who were stationed at the top of the steps in front of it. They should just keep walking like they knew exactly what they were doing. The policemen tried to stop them, but even as they did so, John led the charge, literally pushing the policemen to the side. But eventually it became clear that this approach was not working. Rather than defer to the wealthy Westerners, the policemen had become enraged. It was crystal clear that John and his companions were at an impasse, literally and figuratively. They would not be allowed into this VIP area under any circumstances. John now feigned ignorance and apologized profusely to the policemen, speaking in his sparklingly perfect Cantonese, but they remained angry nonetheless. John and Nancy and Scott retreated sheepishly down the marble stairs with their luggage.

Things were certainly now looking grim. After hours of great efforts, nothing had worked. Nancy and Scott at this point decided to go off to the restrooms, asking John to wait with their luggage. While he was standing there, surveying the endless hordes of people, a small, dignified Chinese woman approached him. In absolutely perfectly accented British English—the queen's English, John said—the woman said: "Good evening. How are you?" She was probably in her fifties, with a pleasant round face, and she wore the standard blue Chinese uniform beneath her opened overcoat. She also wore a blue hat.

"Good evening," John responded. "I'm fine. How are you?"

"I'm fine. Is there any way I can help you?"

John said, "As a matter of fact, yes. We're trying to go to Canton."

"Come with me," the woman said.

"There are two other people with me. They've gone to the restroom and will be right back."

The woman said, "That's all right. We will wait." That a woman should speak such perfect English anywhere in Red China was remarkable, but that she should exist in the city of Changsha seemed inconceivable. When Nancy and Scott returned, the woman said, "Good evening," to each of them—and then she said, "Follow me."

With great dignity, she walked immediately toward the marble steps leading up to the VIP area and began to ascend toward the entrance, which was still flanked by the same policemen with whom John and Scott had scuffled moments before. "This ought to be interesting," John said to Nancy and Scott. But as the woman drew nearer to the policemen, they saluted her, looking straight ahead, and let everyone in. The trio followed her through a room where another person saluted her and let them through a second door. Who was this woman? They now found themselves out on the train platform, where they continued to follow her the entire length of the train. Then she entered the train and led them not to seats but to their very own compartment. It was baffling. At that point the woman said, "Have a nice trip to Canton."

As John and his companions were putting their luggage away, Nancy said, "I hope you took care of her." In his confusion and amazement, John had not, so he immediately turned toward the woman to give her the largest tip he had ever given to anyone in his life. But already she was gone. Where had she gone to so quickly? John immediately got off the train to look for her, but he didn't see her anywhere. So he hurried all the way back to the place where they had come out onto the platform and asked the woman stationed there, "Can you tell me where the woman is with the hat who brought us through here?" But the woman said, "No one with a hat brought you through here."

John asked her, "Did I come through here?"

"Yes," the woman said.

"There were four of us," he said.

"No, there weren't," she said. "There were three of you."

"But where's the woman with the blue hat and the coat?"

"I didn't see her," the woman said. At this point, John was sure he must have been at the wrong door, so he went to the other door nearby.

There he asked another woman, "Did you see me come through this door a few minutes ago?"

"No," the woman there said, "you came through that door." She pointed at the other door.

"Did you see me come past here?" he asked.

"Yes."

"Did you see four of us?"

"No, I only saw three of you."

John was by now getting angry. "You mean to say you didn't see a little lady with a blue hat and a coat on?"

"No," the woman said.

At this point, John returned to the train

compartment to get Scott. Scott returned with him to the woman and asked her if she had seen the woman and she said, "No, this gentleman already asked that question."

"Didn't you see four of us?"

"No."

"Then why did you let us on the train?"

"Because I was supposed to."

"But who told you you were supposed to?"

"I just knew I was supposed to."

So John and Scott went back to their compartment on the train, baffled. The train left and in a little while food was brought to them. They asked, "Who told you to bring food here?" The men said that there was a note in the kitchen that they were supposed to bring food there, to that compartment. And they brought food again and again, the whole of the four-hundred-mile journey to Canton.

When they arrived in Canton, they prepared to get off the train. In China, one presents one's ticket at the end of the journey, not at the beginning. But of course they had no tickets. They walked to the place where the ticket man was and John said, "We don't have a ticket."

The man said, "I know you don't. Thank you very much. Carry on." And he waved them through.

In going over this extraordinary story in his mind scores and scores of times, and in talking it over with many people, including his two traveling companions, John came to the conclusion that the only explanation for what happened to them that day was that the woman was an angel in disguise.

# 13

---

## VARIETIES OF MIRACLES

In the course of collecting the stories for this book I saw that a number of them fit nicely into a category. There were some that would fall neatly into the category of "healing miracles" and others that I might put under the heading of "inner healing." Then there were some angelic encounters. There were of course conversion miracles. But what of the stories that didn't fit into any of these categories? What was I to make of them? In the course of thinking about this I marveled at the sheer variety of the stories I had heard and experienced myself.

As we have said earlier, miracles are always examples of God communicating with us in some fashion. The following miracles demonstrate this more than others. But they aren't just communications. There is a particular intimacy to them, as though God wants more than anything to let us know he is with us. He sees what we are going through and he cares. Furthermore, he is such a big God that he can afford to deal with us on an intimate level, to encourage us and to wink at us and to hold our hands when we need him to do that. He isn't a busy heavenly father who only has time for the big, important world-changing things. He has time for every one of us and he has time for the details of our lives. In showing us this, he shows us that our lives are important to him. He is not a God who is up in the clouds and who only begrudgingly descends into our world when he must. He wants to communicate with us that if something is important to us, it's important to him.

## THE DREAM THAT HELPED ME WRITE *BONHOEFFER*

I've never told this story publicly before, mainly because it's a little bit complicated and because it's so odd. One thing I know: I didn't make it up.

One night in 2006, I had a very powerful dream. For no reason that made sense logically at the time, it was deeply affecting. I've had many dreams over the years, but only one that was anything like this one, and that was my life-changing dream of the golden fish. I tell that story earlier in the book, but for several years before this 2006 dream I hadn't dreamt much at all. At least I couldn't remember any dreams, which made this dream that much more affecting.

I dreamt that I was in Germany, in the small village of Großstöbnitz, where my mother grew up, not far from Altenburg, in what was East Germany. It's where my relatives have lived for centuries. The house where my great-grandparents raised their twelve children is still there. One of those children, my grandmother, was born in that house in 1905, and my mother was born in it in 1934. Our relatives still live there. The tiny village church in Großstöbnitz was built in 1604. Generations of my family have worshiped there. Just up the road is the house where my mother's favorite aunt—Tante Walli—lived with her family and where my mother spent much of her childhood.

In the summer of 1971, around my eighth birthday, my grandmother and mother and brother and I, along with my aunt—whom we called Tante Eleonore—and two cousins, flew to Germany to visit our relatives. East Germany was tremendously economically depressed, so virtually nothing had changed since World War II. We arrived in Großstöbnitz on a train with a steam locomotive that seemed like something out of the 1920s or earlier. Tante Walli was then seventy-nine years old, and meeting her was like meeting a celebrity. I'd constantly heard about her growing up and now here she was. Her house had no indoor bathroom, just an outhouse, and there were chickens, rabbits, goats, and other animals. For someone of my age at that time it was all a dream come true, as if we had fallen into the pages of a fairy-tale book. My little brother and I became friends with the farmer who lived next door and we would visit him every morning to see his cows in their stalls and to jump from the hayloft down into the hay below. We also spent time playing with our cousin Jürgen, who was a year older than I. My brother and I remember one thing he said often: "*Nixon ist schlecht!*" Obviously it was something he had learned in his Communist grammar school. It's the only thing during that glorious summer that reminded us that we weren't really living in a world outside time.

Großstöbnitz was everything my mother and Tante Eleonore said it was, a magical place a million miles from the modern world of Queens, New York City, where we lived. One day during our time in Großstöbnitz, we went to the seventieth birthday celebration of another of my grandmother's older sisters, Tante Toni. It was a grand gathering of the whole German side of my family and a number of photographs were taken. I remember it was at that gathering that I formed my first German sentence: "*Bitte, gib mir ein Glas Milch.*" When we left to go home, we said that we would try to get back the following summer for Tante Walli's eightieth birthday, but traveling across the Atlantic was expensive and life marched on.

By the time I had my dream in 2006, the summer in Großstöbnitz was a distant memory from thirty-five years earlier. I almost never thought about my German relatives or my German roots. I simply hadn't stayed connected with that part of my life and background. I'd been to Greece many times to visit my father's side of the family, but the German side of me had atrophied to the point of near vanishing.

So what did I dream that night in 2006? I dreamt that I was in Großstöbnitz at a party that seemed to be just like the huge birthday party for Tante Toni. All the relatives were there and they were taking pictures. But in the dream I somehow realized it was all taking place at some point *before* I'd ever gotten to Großstöbnitz. It must have been 1968 or 1969 or 1970, because in the dream I knew I was five or six years old. So when all the relatives gathered for a photograph, I realized I wasn't really there yet. I stood on the edge of it all, wishing I could be in the photograph they were taking, wishing I could be a part of the whole family standing there, but in the dream I knew I just wasn't there yet. So I stood outside the photo, as it were. I powerfully longed to be in it, but I couldn't. Then I woke up.

But after I woke up, the longing to be in that photograph continued to stick with me, as did the whole dream. It was very powerful. It all had such a strange urgency to it that I felt I must call my mother and tell her about it. I don't normally do things like that, but the vividness of it all had somehow affected me and for some unknown reason I felt compelled to call my parents and speak to my mother about it. So I called. But there was no answer. Where in the world would my mother be at nine on a Saturday morning? She was always home then. The only explanation for her not picking up the phone was that she must have driven to my aunt's house on Long Island for the weekend. So, dying to speak with her as soon as possible, I dialed my aunt. When my aunt picked up the phone, she told me that my mother wasn't there either. But she did know where my mother was. My mother was driving to Madison, Connecticut, to visit my brother. I guess she'd spoken to my aunt just before she'd left Danbury and it sounded like she had left only a little while ago, so it would be over an hour before I could speak with her. But the burning desire to tell the story of my dream was such that an hour seemed like an eternity. So I decided to tell the dream to my aunt, whom I really hardly ever spoke with on the phone. But her affection for Großstöbnitz was equal to my mother's, and for whatever reason—I still cannot fathom the reason—I told my aunt the dream.

When I got to the part about being just outside the photograph and unable to be in the photograph, explaining that it was taking place a couple of years before I'd ever actually been in

Großstöbnitz—probably 1969 or so—my aunt said, "Gee, that's strange . . ."

"What's strange?" I asked.

"The photograph."

"What about it?"

"Just yesterday Kurt [her husband] got a photograph like that sent to us from our relatives in Großstöbnitz. They e-mailed it to us. And it's from around that time."

"What do you mean?"

"It's a photograph of all the relatives in Großstöbnitz and it's from around that time. They sent it to us yesterday and he printed it out last night."

Well, what was I supposed to say? I really couldn't believe my ears, so I asked a few more questions just to make sure I wasn't misunderstanding the wild facts of what my aunt was telling me. But I wasn't. She made it very clear that that's what the photograph was, and it was just as I had described the photograph in my dream, the dream that was so powerful and overwhelming that I had to tell my mother and when I couldn't tell her, told my aunt. Hearing her corroborate this was one of *those* moments. Just how is one supposed to react? Could this be true? But of course it was true. It was also too much to take in.

"That's unbelievable, Tante Eleonore!" I said. "That's amazing!!!" What else does one say?

Of course, it was just as amazing to my aunt. Neither of us could believe it, but there it was. We were nonplussed. "What do you think it means?" she asked.

"Well, Tante Eleonore," I said, "all I know is that it's a miracle. That much I have no doubt about. But why exactly God would do something like that I don't know. Sometimes he just does things like that to let us know he's real and he's with us, that he knows the intimate details of our lives and wants us to have a relationship with him. That's all I can say for sure. But I know that it's a miracle."

And so we left it at that. But before I hung up I asked my aunt to please send me a copy of the photograph, which I got a few days later and which is indeed precisely from that time, because Jürgen, who is in the photo among all the others, is a year or two younger than I remember him being. So what was I to make of this? Beyond the idea that it was amazing and miraculous, I simply had no idea. I had a sense that God might reveal more about it in his time, but I didn't know that for sure either. All I could do was shake my head and marvel.

But the more I thought of it, the more amazing it seemed. If I had reached my mother on the phone and had told her the story, my aunt would never have heard about it. I never had phone conversations with my aunt beyond maybe saying

*Happy Birthday* or something along those lines. So the idea that I couldn't reach my mother and then called my aunt to find her and then was told she wasn't there and then told my aunt the story of the dream was itself strange. But if not for that, I wouldn't be writing about this now. If I had reached my mother I would have never heard about the photograph from my aunt. There was nothing special about the dream or the photograph independent of each other. But because I told my aunt about the dream, it became an outrageous and amazing story. But how in the world could I have dreamt of a photograph that existed a hundred miles away in my aunt's house on Long Island? And what was the point of it all?

I've earlier said that a miracle necessarily seems to involve God communicating to people and I asked if a miracle happens in the woods, and there's no one around to see it, is it a miracle? As far as this miracle goes, the answer is emphatically no. The point of it seems to be that people have to be on the receiving end of it. God is trying to communicate to us in a specific way, to say, *I'm here,* in a way that's calculated to get our attention.

So I now told the story of this insane convergence to my mother and brother and wife, and all everyone could say was that it was amazing, but beyond that, what could one say? In one way, it was all almost as annoying as it was amazing.

In any case, time passed and I forgot all about the dream.

In early 2007 my Wilberforce biography, *Amazing Grace: William Wilberforce and the Heroic Campaign to End Slavery*, was published and I did a lot of traveling to speak about Wilberforce. Invariably people would ask me about whom I would write next. Most of them assumed that I had found my life's genre and would now write biographies of inspiring people. But I had never wanted to write a biography, and having written the story of Wilberforce, I assumed I was through with the genre. But the more I heard this question the more I thought that perhaps I might conceivably write one more, and if I were to write one more it would have to be about Dietrich Bonhoeffer.

I had heard Bonhoeffer's story the summer I came to faith in 1988 and was captivated by it. The idea that a devout German Christian had spoken up for the Jews—and had acted on their behalf by actually becoming involved in the plot to kill Hitler—amazed me. One never seemed to hear stories of people who did the right and heroic thing because of their faith, so I was stunned to hear about Bonhoeffer and doubly stunned I had never heard of him and his story. But I was also moved by his story because my mother had grown up in Germany during the horrible years of the Third Reich. She had lost my grandfather in the war when she was nine. He was thirty-one years old and a genuinely reluctant German soldier. My grandmother told me he would listen to the BBC with his ear literally pressed against the radio speaker, because if one was caught listening to the BBC in Germany at that time, one might be sent to a concentration camp. So the idea that Bonhoeffer was speaking out not just for the Jews of Germany, but also for Germans like my grandfather, moved me. But I had mostly forgotten about Bonhoeffer's story until people who had heard me talk about Wilberforce kept asking me whom I might write about next.

It was less the idea that Bonhoeffer was German that really captivated me than that he had, because of his Christian faith, stood up for the Jews—and had been killed by the Nazis as a result. As Wilberforce had given his whole political life over to speak out for the Africans who were being enslaved, Bonhoeffer had given up life itself to speak out for the Jews. It seemed natural that if I were to write another biography it should be about Bonhoeffer. In my mind, the two stories complemented each other.

So I leapt into the story of Bonhoeffer, reading all I could about him and his era. I had been so disconnected from my German roots for so many years that reading about Bonhoeffer and this time in history began to slowly reconnect me to this part of myself. But it wasn't until I was actually writing the book—some time in early 2008—that I was really thinking hard about that era and about my family, who had all lived through it. My mother and Tante Eleonore and my grandmother and grandfather and Tante Walli. All of them. They had all been there while it was unfolding. It had all been a part of their lives. So as I got into writing the book I thought about them and how they had actually lived through all of it. I felt more and more connected to them and to the fact that these were my people and they had lived through this painful time in history that I was now writing about.

One day during this time of immersion in this period it suddenly hit me. It was as if a loud bell had gone off in my head with a deep and resonant *bong*. I don't mean that I actually heard anything, but it was as if I suddenly had a clear understanding of something I had previously not understood at all. It happened in a moment. I wasn't thinking about it. One moment I wasn't thinking about it and the next moment I had a full understanding. That's because just now, for the first time in at least a year, I remembered the strange and powerful dream about Großstöbnitz, and now for the first time I understood what it had been all about. In the dream I had had a deep longing to be a part of my German family—but of my German family *before* I had actually been a part of that family when we visited in 1971. I had so wanted to be in that picture with all of them, before I was actually there, but I couldn't. And now I saw that that powerful longing to be in touch with my German roots and family before 1971 was being fulfilled in my writing this book. The longing in that dream was so powerful that I had to call up my mother and when I tried to track her down ended up telling my aunt.

In telling this I realize it's hard to communicate effectively what happened. It's tremendously subjective, for one thing. But the fact was that I simply hadn't thought about any of this before. It was a sudden knowing. I suddenly knew that that outrageous dream had been God's way of showing me that he had created me to write this book, to tell this story of what happened to Germany, and that in a way it was my story too. Through my mother and grandparents and all these other relatives I had been there too, and now in writing this book I was reconnecting to that part of myself, to that part of my own history as a German. And if there had been any doubt about any of this, God had performed the singularly outrageous miracle of having me find out hours after I woke up from that dream in 2006 that the photograph of which I had dreamt actually existed and had been printed out the night before. It seemed clear that he had done this to underscore it all in a very dramatic way so that

I would know it was a miracle even before I knew the point of the miracle.

But there's something more. Why would God want to communicate that to me? Why did he need to make me understand that he had created me to write this book, or had at least called me to write this book? It felt as though he had said to me, *This is my book. I have called you to write this book. I put that longing in you to connect with your German roots for a larger purpose.* But why did I need to know any of this? I was doing fine writing the book. Why did it have to be invested with such significance? Why did it all need to be so ponderous? Wasn't it just a book—the story of an inspiring man?

I thought so and really didn't understand why God felt it was necessary to underscore this in the undeniably dramatic way he had done until later.

The first part of that understanding came when I was in the awful throes of writing the book. Once the writing had begun I was on a tremendous deadline. I had never worked harder on anything, and that is not hyperbole. I knew that unless I finished the book in about five months, the publisher would not be able to get it out in time to coincide with the movie *Valkyrie*, which is a movie about the plot to kill Hitler. I felt that unless we had that little bit of extra help to promote it, it would sink—as any biography of a

German theologian would be expected to sink—like a stone.

So one day at lunch I got the publisher to agree that if I finished the manuscript by a certain date they would fulfill their part of the bargain and publish the book a bit earlier than usual, to coincide with the release of the movie. So I fairly raced home from the restaurant and began writing like a madman, typing twelve and more hours a day every day, seven days a week, week after week after week for more than five months. It was like sprinting a marathon and in the midst of it I felt an agony I had never felt before, as though I were being chased by a lion and couldn't stop, as though my heart might burst. I prayed a lot during the writing of the book, and when the agony of it all was too much, I remembered that God had communicated to me that this was his book, that he had his hand on it and all would be well. I needed to remember that. How I needed to remember that! Remembering that extraordinary miracle carried me through when I simply thought I couldn't continue.

But the difficulties would get worse. After finishing this endless sprint and turning in the manuscript I heard nothing from the publisher. After quite a while I contacted them via e-mail and was told via return e-mail shortly thereafter that they wouldn't be able to get the book out in time for the movie's release after all. It would have to be delayed by six months. I couldn't believe what I was reading. I felt like I'd been hit with a shovel. Had all that craziness really been for nothing? It was too much to take in. To what shall I compare it? I felt like someone with a bad heart who is told that his relay team has a chance at the gold medal and the world record in the mile. So, risking a coronary, he runs his quarter with all his might and main, nearly dying for the effort, but handing the baton to the next runner with a decent lead on the competition and a good shot at the world record—and then collapses onto the cinder track, praying his heart will hold out. Moments later he looks up and sees the man to whom he had handed the baton leaning against a railing with the baton in one hand and a cigarette in the other. He hadn't bothered to run his leg. So it was all for naught. That's just how I felt when I heard this news. The agony of the endless sprint had been for nothing. The deprivation of time with my family and all else. I was numb from disbelief.

It took me months to get my head around what felt like a tremendous betrayal by my publisher. But eventually I had no choice but to pick myself up and proceed with them. They also had insisted that I cut the book by more than a third. But I didn't see that there was much fat to cut. I felt that almost all that was there was bone and muscle and to cut into that would damage the book. I did my best and cut what I could, but it didn't amount to very much. I then handed in the manuscript, making it clear that if I needed to do anything at all to assure the book came out as soon as possible, they needed only to say the word.

But once again I heard nothing for weeks and months. Finally I sent an e-mail asking what had happened. I was again responded to fairly quickly and was told that for some reason the book actually would have to be delayed at least *another* six months. Perhaps another nine months. And that it still had to be cut by more than a third. There is no way I can adequately describe how this made me feel. I was now simply beside myself with confusion, anger, and depression. I had never been that broken with despair, and in all of it the only thing I could cling to was the memory that God had, through the miracle of the dream and the photograph, dramatically communicated to me that this was his book and that he had his hand on the book, that he had a plan for it, a larger purpose. I took what comfort I could in that and reminded myself of it and of the miracle with the photograph at least daily.

I knew that to cut the book would compromise it, so I eventually elected to change publishers, and changing publishers presented its own difficulties. But in all of it I continued to remember the miracle: that God had let me know that he had called me to write the book and that all would be well. I knew that I could trust him and must trust him. What that meant specifically I had no idea. I only knew that God was trustworthy and I would trust him with the details and the outcome of it all.

That the book would eventually become a bestseller was not something I ever imagined possible. It is the six-hundred-page biography of a German theologian. How many people would buy such a book? That the book would be voted Book of the Year by the prestigious ECPA[28] was also not something I imagined possible, nor that the book would be translated into sixteen languages (and counting) and would allow me the tremendous honor of meeting two US presidents. All I knew was that God had done something outrageously miraculous to get my attention and to send me a message of comfort that I would desperately need to get me through the hard times—that did get me through the hard times and that to this day encourages me still, every time I remember it.

---

28. The Evangelical Christian Publishing Association.

# THE LOST KEYS

Part of what makes the concept of miracles and God's intervention such a hot topic for so many people is that everyone wonders how a God who is presumably running the entire universe will not heal someone of cancer but will find someone else a parking space. How and when God intervenes—if he does—gives us a picture of who God is. And most people think that a God who wastes his time doing parlor tricks like finding people parking spaces, while allowing the Holocaust to happen, must be nothing more than an infinite-size superjerk. You cannot entirely blame them for thinking that. It's a question that needs to be answered, or at least discussed.

For example, I have a very dear friend named Kimberly Thornbury, who once lost her keys. Losing ones keys has to be a universal phenomenon, at least in that part of the civilized world where people have keys. But if we're not losing our keys we are losing our glasses, or a piece of paper with something on it that was important, or a shoe or a glove. People lose things. One study calculated that people spend 3,680 hours in their lifetime looking for lost items, which works out to 150 twenty-four-hour days. Can that be? Obviously a fraction of that is far too much.

Kimberly considers herself a fairly organized person, which is to say that those of us who aren't terribly organized consider her an enviably hyperorganized person. She is the wife of my dear friend Greg Thornbury, who is the president of the King's College in New York City, and her competence and attention to detail in what she does at the college and in general are practically legendary. But just like the rest of us, Kimberly once lost her keys.

This happened sometime around 2005. But it was no ordinary set of keys. Kimberly had a very important job at Union University in Jackson, Tennessee, at that time, so she had a tremendous number of keys on the key chain, most of them master keys to various buildings at the university. One might say that Kimberly had the type of job and responsibility given to people not prone to losing their keys. And not only were there a lot of keys on the chain; they were attached to a giant red plastic heart-shaped keychain that Kimberly had made during a mandatory shop class when she was in high school. So if they were anywhere nearby it would be exceedingly difficult to miss them.

Kimberly was during this time a full-time working mother, with two girls, then two and four years old. Her husband, Greg, traveled extensively during this period. In fact, he was away during the time Kimberly lost the keys, so she had no one to complain to about it, nor anyone to help her think through where she might have misplaced them. She was also so busy that there really wasn't much time to slow down and look for keys. She had groceries to buy, dry cleaning to pick up, and clothes to drop off at a consignment sale. So that Friday afternoon, without missing a beat, she grabbed the spare car key from the manila folder in her laundry room (have we mentioned that she was organized?) and continued with her multiple errands around town. She was similarly busy on Saturday, but in the course of her many activities in and out of the house, the keys simply never surfaced. It was a conundrum. On Sunday, she drove to church services—both morning services and evening services—all the while using her spare car key and hoping her other keys would turn up. They didn't.

On Monday morning, she drove her two girls to their nanny's, just up the street, before Kimberly went off to work at the university, where the missing keys would be far more missed than they had been over the weekend. The nanny had cared for Greg and Kimberly's daughters since they were born. They all considered her their Mary Poppins, wonderful in every way. As she usually did, the nanny stood near her garage waiting to greet Kimberly's two daughters and begin the day. Both girls burst out of the car, gave the nanny a big hug, and dashed inside her house. But the nanny stayed outside for a moment.

"How are you?" she asked Kimberly.

"I'm doing okay," she replied. "But—I know this is small and silly—but I lost my keys on Friday, and I can't find them anywhere. They contain the university master keys, and it's a big deal. Will you pray that I find them?"

There are many people who, when you ask them to pray, say that they will and a moment later simply forget all about it. Others remember, and do pray. Then there are others who, when you ask them to pray, knowing they are likely to forget all about it, do it immediately. Kimberly's nanny was one of these. She immediately grabbed Kimberly's hands, right there in the driveway, and said, "Why don't we pray now?" She then proceeded to take the problem to God in prayer, as she did all things, great and small. They said amen, Kimberly hugged her and then turned around to return to her car.

That's when she saw them. The nanny saw them at exactly the same time.

They were gingerly—indeed precariously—situated *in the middle* of the outside of the car's windshield. If Kimberly had been sitting in the driver's seat, they would have been immediately in her line of vision. They sat on the sloped glass, so perfectly in the middle of the windshield that Kimberly simply reached out her hand and grabbed them off the glass from where she was standing.

But what in the world had just happened?

It was mind-bending. But there had to be some explanation. God doesn't just make things appear out of thin air, does he? He made the universe simply appear, but that was an act of creation out of nothing. What was *this?* Where had the keys been before they were in the middle of the windshield? Had the keys perhaps been on the car's roof for these three days, and now for some reason they had just slipped down onto the windshield? But if that were the case, why now? And why would they have perched in the middle of the windshield? Wouldn't they have slid all the way down the windshield and been wedged into the slot where the windshield wiper arms nestle? Why were they right there, in the middle of the windshield, so absurdly prominent that it seemed like some sort of joke?

All Kimberly and her nanny knew was that for three days the keys were nowhere to be seen and then they prayed and Kimberly turned around and there they were, within arm's reach: the keys connected to the red heart keychain that she had made in high school shop class. They were right there, shining in the sun on an autumn morning. After Kimberly reached out and grabbed the keys she turned to look back at their nanny. Both of them had gaping mouths. It was an indescribable moment. They both knew that no matter how one sliced it, it seemed a miracle. And both of them had been there to witness it.

"There are far bigger problems in the world," Kimberly told me. "Yet in that moment, God showed up and cared for me. There is absolutely no explanation to how those keys could have appeared on the windshield. It was simply an example of God caring for me in that moment in an unexpected way."

# TWO HEMISPHERES, THREE SONGS

I first heard this story from my friend Larry Crabb at a New Canaan Society event in San Francisco. He is a well-known author and speaker with a PhD in clinical psychology and a veritable raft of professional credentials. The story is about his son, Ken, who fifteen years earlier had been through a very painful divorce.

Ken met his wife in college. In Larry's description, "She was a beauty queen and he was Mr. Popular. The marriage seemed made in Heaven. For about five years. Then it began to fall apart." Whatever was wrong, though, Ken was strongly committed to making the marriage work. But his wife was adamantly opposed to trying. She refused to go with him to counseling, saying that her mind was made up and she simply wanted a divorce.

Larry explained that at the time, Ken did all he could think of doing to keep his wife from going ahead with the divorce. He bought her gifts and at times simply begged her not to go through with it. But her behavior during this tumultuous and painful time indicated that in her own mind, things were already over and she was moving on.

Things did not improve. In the end, in December of 1998, the divorce went through and Ken was simply beside himself with grief: heartbroken and shattered. One day at his parents' home, he sat in front of the fireplace and wept, talking to his parents about his hopelessness and his feelings of anger at God, who had allowed this to take place. Ken believed that it was God's will that we do all we can to keep our marriages intact, and he had done that, with all his might, but with no happy results. It simply made no sense, as though it were all a cruel joke. Where was God in any of this? His father responded to Ken's outpouring by saying that what he was about to say wasn't meant to sound like a religious bandage, but that he simply knew with everything that was in him that God would not allow anyone to go through anything painful and heartbreaking without desiring to ultimately use that for his larger purposes. Somehow there was a larger purpose and all we could do was submit our pain and suffering to him and ask him to use it as he wished to use it and know that he would.

Of course Ken was not exactly in a place to hear these words or to act on them. His anger at God over this was very real. He wasn't at a place emotionally where he could cheerfully assume God had a purpose. The way he felt, it seemed to him that God was nowhere to be found in any of it.

Sometime during this terrible period Ken got hold of a gun. He loaded it and put it by his bed. One night, in a paroxysm of pain, sobbing, he took the loaded gun and stared into the wrong end of it, intending to end his awful suffering. He did this for about an hour before he finally decided not to follow through.

Still, the pain continued. Every night for four or five months, when he went to bed, Ken told God that he didn't want to be alive, that he wanted God to take his life. But he prayed that if he did wake up in the morning he would take it that God must have some plan. He had no idea what it was and he didn't especially care, but he would try to believe that his existence would ultimately mean something more than it did at that terribly low point.

A few months later he seemed to have passed beyond this suicidal period. But he was still very angry with God. Whatever relationship he had once had with God was long gone. There was a tremendous dryness at the heart of his soul. Whatever love and passion he had once had for God were mere memories. He knew that he was only going through the motions, trying to move forward dutifully, but really not feeling anything much at all. It felt empty and useless.

That fall had been a particularly busy time at his job and Ken felt that he needed to get away from it all, for his mental and emotional health. He wanted to take a short sabbatical from his whole life, to get as far away from everything as possible. He wanted to recharge his batteries and, more important, to try and find God again. Ken loved to surf and had saved enough money to be able to travel to Bali, in Indonesia, so he decided he would go there for a ten-day sabbatical. One friend of his quipped that what Ken called a sabbatical was really just a well-to-do Christian's term for taking a fancy vacation. To some extent that was true enough. In fact, Ken decided to stay at the exclusive Four Seasons Hotel on Jimbaran Bay, famous for its surfing. He knew this would take his mind off his difficulties, at least for a while. And it might even break the cycle of hopelessness, self-pity, and anger. That was his hope. And more than that, he hoped that during this time his feelings of anger toward God might change. He determined that during this ten-day period he would be very intentional about praying and reading the Bible. He might not feel like it, and probably wouldn't, but he would do it anyway. He felt that he needed to. He couldn't go on feeling the way he was feeling. Something had to change. Some days before leaving, he told his father, "If I don't find God in a way that I don't know him now, I'm not going to make it. . . ." He had really become desperate.

Before he left, his father told him that he could count on one thing while he was away: His mother and father would pray in a focused way for him every single day for at least fifteen minutes. It would probably be more on some days, but he could count on the fact that every day they would be praying hard for him for at least fifteen minutes.

Ken lived near Cleveland, so flying to Bali was not an easy trip. In the best scenario, the trip from Cleveland to Bali takes twenty-four hours of flying, with two stops. But when he finally got there, he was determined to do what he had come to do. He would do a lot of surfing, and every day, no matter how he felt, he would spend some time reading the Bible and praying.

During his first week, Ken found it very difficult. He continued to feel no desire to pray or to read the Bible, but out of a deep sense of duty, he did both every day. He found that praying was not quite as difficult as reading the Bible, because when he was praying he could at least express his anger to God. Reading the Bible was a huge effort. Nonetheless he did it dutifully. But mostly he spent his time surfing. The one book he brought with him to read during this time—besides the Bible—was Dietrich Bonhoeffer's classic devotional *The Cost of Discipleship*.

On the seventh day of the ten-day trip, Ken decided that enough was enough. He would get serious with God, which in his case meant that on that day he would not surf. He has surfed a lot in the days previous, but today he would not surf a single wave. He would walk the sands of Uluwatu Beach and just pray. So, wearing his swim trunks and carrying nothing, he walked the beach, determined to somehow get serious with God.

Sure enough, for the first time that day he felt a noticeable desire to communicate with God. But he wasn't sure what to communicate exactly. As he walked, he found himself not praying but singing. For some reason that was his deepest desire during this time, to sing to God. After so many months of feeling nothing like this, it was a great turning point, and for two hours or so he walked the beach, communicating with God in a gloriously joyful way, singing his heart out.

Meanwhile, back in Colorado, Ken's dad, Larry, had been praying for him every day, just as he had promised his son he would do. His prayer was that God would somehow get through to his son and let him know that he really did have a plan for his life, a plan that involved more than just hanging in there and surviving. He prayed that his son would know that God would bring him through this period and that he would get past the anger he felt at God and rediscover his joy in knowing God and loving him.

But Ken's dad had to admit to himself that his prayers hadn't always been as passionate as he would have liked them to be. One day in the middle of this ten-day period he found himself driving the ninety minutes from Denver to Colorado Springs for an afternoon business meeting. As he drove, he decided that he could spend the ninety minutes praying for his son—and so he would. But even now, his prayers weren't the most intense ones he had ever prayed. In fact, he had the radio on and was praying as he listened to the music, now and again changing the station. At some point during the drive, he realized that the seriousness of his son's situation merited more than these "token prayers," as he later described them. So he turned off the radio and passionately asked God to help him find the one thing inside himself that he could pray with power and deep conviction. He asked himself, "What's really inside of me and alive in me that I desperately want to pray, that I want to bring to God?"

As he continued to drive and now got serious

about what he wanted to pray, he suddenly found that he wanted to sing. It was a compulsion, really. And so he began to sing. Larry remembered that the first song he sang was the famous hymn "Great Is Thy Faithfulness." Larry knew all the verses and as he sang them he began to weep. He wept because as he meditated on God's faithfulness to him over the years, he now prayed desperately that his son, Ken, might sing this song and know God's faithfulness too, might know in his bones that despite everything that had happened, despite all the pain, God was faithful and would always be faithful:

> Great is Thy faithfulness, O God my
>   Father;
> There is no shadow of turning with Thee,
> Thou changest not, Thy compassions
>   they fail not,
> As Thou hast been, Thou forever wilt be.
> Great is Thy faithfulness!
> Great is Thy faithfulness!
> Morning by morning new mercies I see
> All I have needed Thy hand hath
>   provided
> Great is Thy faithfulness, Lord unto me!

After he had sung that song he began to sing "I Love You, Lord," a simpler song, written in 1980:

I love you, Lord, and I lift my voice
To worship you. O my soul rejoice!
Take joy, My King, in what You hear.
Let it be a sweet, sweet sound in Your ear.

Larry continued to weep as he sang this second song and he continued to passionately pray that his son would be able to feel what this song communicated: an overwhelming love for the God who loved him.

Finally Larry sang what he called the "Crabb Family Song." Without a doubt it was this third song that corresponded most directly to what Larry was praying for him. It was the famous hymn "It Is Well with My Soul," written by Horatio Spafford. Larry knew all four verses and as he sang them now his weeping turned to sobbing, so much so that he had to pull the car over. There, by the side of the road, he continued to sing the song over and over. The story behind this song is well-known to many who are familiar with it and is worth telling here.

Horatio Spafford was a prominent nineteenth-century Chicago lawyer, passionate about the Abolitionist cause and close friends with D. L. Moody, the famous evangelist. Spafford and his wife, Anna, married in 1861 and experienced numerous tragedies together, the first of which was the death from pneumonia of their four-year-old son in 1870. The following year he was ruined financially when the Great Chicago Fire wiped out most of his significant real estate holdings. But these things would pale in comparison to what befell them in 1873.

That year Spafford decided the family should take a vacation. They settled on a trip to England and planned to sail in November on the steamship *Ville du Havre*, but when business detained him at the last minute, Spafford sent his wife and their four daughters ahead, planning to join them as soon as possible. On November 22, in the middle of the night another ship struck their ship and the *Ville du Havre* sank in twelve minutes. Eighty-seven people survived the tragedy, but 226 did not. Among those who lost their lives were Spafford's four girls, aged eleven, nine, five, and two. Spafford's wife was found unconscious, floating on a wooden spar. Nine days later, she arrived in Cardiff, Wales, where she cabled her husband: "Saved alone. What shall I do?" Spafford immediately left Chicago to be with his wife. When his ship passed over the spot where his daughters had died, the captain summoned Spafford to his cabin, to tell him. As the story goes, it was shortly thereafter that he began composing the hymn for which he is now known. The first and most famous verse is:

When peace like a river, attendeth my way,
When sorrows like sea billows roll;

Whatever my lot, Thou hast taught me to
  say,
It is well, it is well, with my soul.

And the chorus is:

  It is well! With my soul!
  It is well, it is well, with my soul!

That this man would be able to think these
thoughts, much less write a hymn proclaiming
them, is almost unbelievable. It is simultaneously
convicting and profoundly inspiring to think
about it.

This was the third and last song Larry sang that
day, by the side of the road. He was there for
thirty or forty minutes, singing and singing and
praying and praying. He prayed that his son
might be able to sing this song and feel what
Spafford felt: that despite tremendous heartbreak,
God was in control and he could still trust him.

Finally, Larry pulled back on to the road and
continuing to weep and pray he drove the rest of
the way to his appointment in Colorado Springs.
He would pray every day his son was away, but
nothing would again approach what happened to
him in the car that day.

About two weeks after Ken returned from Bali
to Cleveland, he flew to Denver on business, and
while there, his father took him to lunch. Not

much time passed before he asked the question he'd been dying to ask: "How did your trip go in Bali?"

Ken told his father everything, but of course the whole story culminated with the walk he took on his seventh day in Bali, when he decided to forgo surfing and just walk along the beach and pray. He told his father that for no particular reason he could discern he suddenly felt the connection to God that he had been looking for.

"How so?" his father asked. Ken told him that as he was walking along the beach he had suddenly felt a real compulsion to sing, that his desire to connect with God had manifested itself in his singing as he walked along the beach.

Larry suddenly looked at his son in an intense way. "Do you remember what day that was?" he asked. His son told him. It was the seventh day that he was in Bali.

Larry did some calculations in his head and his eyes widened farther. How extraordinary! This had happened to both of them on the very same day. To Larry it seemed a miracle, but he didn't volunteer anything at that point. "Do you remember what songs you sang?" he asked.

As it happened, Ken did. He told his father that he sang "Great Is Thy Faithfulness."

"You did?" Larry said excitedly. "What else?"

Kenny told him that there were two other songs he had sung. One was "I Love You, Lord." The other was the Horatio Spafford hymn "It Is Well with My Soul."

Of course Larry could hardly believe his ears. In a moment he told his son about what he had experienced on that very same day and how he had experienced a compulsion to sing and had sung precisely those same three songs. Ken could hardly take in what his father was saying, but eventually the two of them had no choice but to recognize what had happened. On the very same day, nine thousand miles apart, they had both—unbeknownst to each other—been seeking to connect on a deeper level with God, and both of them had suddenly found themselves doing so by singing—and not just singing, but singing the very same three songs. Kenny then asked what time this had happened to his father and after a little calculation realized they had been singing it around the same time as well. Kenny was flabbergasted, as anyone would be. For seven days in Bali he didn't have the courage to really think about anything. He just read and watched TV and surfed. But on that seventh day he walked the beach and for nearly three hours sang those three songs, the same songs his father was singing on the edge of a highway in Colorado, half a world away.

Larry Crabb is quick to point out that this sort of experience was very far from typical for him. He joked that he "was raised on the Holy Duet.

The Father, the Son, and watch out for those crazy charismatics." But after this dramatic experience he realized he had been stiffing a third of the Trinity, and thereafter resolved to recommit himself to worshiping not just the Father and the Son, but the Holy Spirit as well.

As they sat there and took in what had happened, this father and son were simply blown away. The idea that God would do something this outrageous specifically to let them both know how much he loved them and how intimately he was involved in their lives and difficulties was obviously very moving. It was of course an answer to both their prayers. Before they parted, they wept and hugged. Ken finally knew deeply exactly what his father had prayed he might come to know, that God was there and is there, and he would not waste all of the trials Ken had been through. He would use them for his purposes, because Ken was willing to let him do that. It seems that already in telling this story to me so that I could put it in this book to encourage others, God is fulfilling that promise.

Today Ken is happily remarried with two beautiful children.

# ONE PHONE CALL

The first word that comes to mind when I think of my friend Larry Poland is "integrity." He's about as solid a citizen as you're likely to come across. Larry is the head of MasterMedia, a ministry that reaches out to Hollywood executives on behalf of the Christian community. We met him in 2000, when I began attending a Bible study they had started in Manhattan. I was at the time a writer for *VeggieTales*. Larry is tremendously gifted and was once the youngest college president in America, at age twenty-seven. Not long ago he wrote a book, titled *Miracle Walk*, about the many miracles he's experienced, and he has graciously let me include a couple of those stories in this book.

This first story is about a breakfast appointment with a director of photography (DP) in Hollywood. The man was going through a time of serious depression. In fact, it was so serious that Bryan, a friend of Larry's who was a film and TV producer, had called Larry about it, asking for help. Bryan had been working with the DP and said he feared the man might take his own life. He asked Larry if he could meet with the man, or at least try to meet with him. Bryan and his wife had tried to help him, but it was clear that whatever he was dealing with needed heavy artillery.

Larry's schedule was already packed with important meetings, so he hadn't been able to reach out to the man. Then one morning Larry's executive assistant, Ruthann, came out of her office to express her frustration with their appointment schedule. Larry regularly met with entertainment executives to encourage them in their faith in what is certainly a very secular business. He also met with executives who were not Christians to help explain to them what typical evangelical Christians are looking for in entertainment and why trying to create wholesome entertainment can help their bottom line, not to mention the broader culture.

But this morning, Ruthann said all the appointments were being scrambled. Several people had called to cancel at the last minute. It was all so out of the ordinary, that Ruthann had to tell Larry about it. It was unprecedented. "I don't even have an appointment for breakfast tomorrow morning!" she said.

Suddenly Larry thought of something. "Did you ever contact that depressed DP Bryan told us about?" he asked.

Ruthann said she hadn't. "Call him right now," Larry said, "and put me on the phone."

Ruthann dialed the number and, when it was ringing, Larry picked up. In Larry's description, the voice that answered was "rather subdued." Larry, whom I've never seen subdued in my life, has a booming, hearty, confident, and positive demeanor at all times, as far as I know. "Hi!" he said, "I'm Larry Poland. Our mutual friend Bryan said you were working together on a picture and that you seemed down. He thought I might be able to encourage you. I'm going to be in Hollywood tomorrow morning and wonder if I could treat you to breakfast."

There was a fairly long pause, and then Mark gave his halfhearted answer: "I guess so." It was clear to Larry that having breakfast with a cheerful stranger the next morning was not something the man had been planning to do. This is putting it mildly, as we shall see.

"Well, then," Larry continued, "where would you like to meet?" They settled on a Denny's on Sepulveda Boulevard, not far from where Mark lived.

When they met the next morning, Larry immediately saw that Mark was not doing well. He had a haggard, miserable look about him. Larry knew Mark's story from Bryan. He had been married but had left his wife for another woman, whom he described as the "love of his life." But Mark's wife wasn't impressed with this description of the woman with whom her husband was committing adultery, so she hit him with everything she had. The ugly divorce dragged on and on, costing

Mark $100,000 in attorney's fees. After five years with the "love of his life," she decided to leave him. That had happened recently. When Larry met Mark at Denny's that morning, the divorce was still far from settled. The recent departure of the "love of his life," after five years together, had broken Mark. He was clearly at his wit's end.

Mark was so distraught he could hardly eat. He said the only thing he thought his stomach might be able to handle was some hash browns. As they sat there, Mark told Larry his whole story, with a mixture of bitterness and pain, and when he was done, Larry said, "Sounds like you need God's help to deal with this."

Mark answered in the affirmative. "[Expletive deleted] right I do."

"Do you know how to get God's help?" Larry asked.

His negative response was similarly colorful.

"Let me tell you how," Larry said, and in the way that very few people can do as well as he, Larry took Mark through a step-by-step presentation of the basics. He explained that all we need to do is turn to God and ask his forgiveness, knowing that Jesus paid the price for all our sins and mistakes. Because he died for us and for our sins, we can turn our life—meaning our problems and everything—over to him and he can make us new again.

Mark had been raised a Catholic, so all that

Larry said was not entirely foreign to him. Larry then asked if there were any good reason why he would not like to pray with Larry to invite Christ into his life—to forgive him and give him new life. Mark said there wasn't. And there at the table at Denny's, Larry led Mark through a simple prayer surrendering his life to Jesus.

But when Larry spoke the "amen," Mark fell apart. Larry was taken aback to see it. He said that Mark began laughing and crying simultaneously, and it went on and on and on. Larry estimated that the emotional roller coaster went on for perhaps three full minutes, which is an eternity on an otherwise quiet morning at Denny's. It was so boisterous and strange that other diners looked up from their Grand Slams, wondering if perhaps they should call an ambulance. Was the man having some kind of seizure?

Finally, Mark calmed down. Fifty years of his life's burdens and guilt seemed to have been lifted from him. It was dramatic. Then he told Larry something he hadn't said before that helped to explain his emotions.

"Funny," he said, "yesterday when you called I was lying in bed with a razor in one hand and a bag of ice in the other, prepared to slash my wrists. I shouted, "God, if you're there, help me!" and the phone rang, and it was you . . . scheduling this breakfast."

Several weeks later, Mark showed up at a meeting. Larry was there, as was Bryan, the producer who had connected them. Bryan did the proverbial double take, because Mark looked so different that he almost didn't recognize him. The anguish and guilt that had distorted his life and features were gone. He looked peaceful. Mark went on to grow in his faith and he often tells people about the day he had a "really close call," when a phone call saved his life. He doesn't believe it was a coincidence.

## CALI TO BOGOTÁ

There have been seasons in Larry Poland's life when he was traveling almost nonstop. That was the case in 1977, when he was the head of the Agape Movement of Campus Crusade for Christ, a ministry begun by the great Bill Bright. Today it's called Cru. Agape was something like a Christian Peace Corps that would put young volunteers into developing nations. During this time, Larry spent several weeks traveling all over South America to work with nationals in various countries, in order to place volunteers in those nations.

He first flew from his home, California, to Miami, and from there caught a flight to Bogotá, Colombia, where he met a team of Cru staff. He then flew to Cali, Colombia, which was where the heart of the ministry was located. It was on the 250-mile flight from Cali back to Bogotá that this story began.

In the seat next to Larry on the plane was a Hispanic man—of medium height and somewhat stocky, with typically dark hair and eyes. But Larry soon learned he was actually an American who had grown up in New Mexico. He was obviously educated and seemed to be enjoying the opportunity to converse with a fellow American. Larry chatted with him for the whole flight, but despite what Larry calls a "prompting" to say something to this man about God, he didn't. He wasn't sure why, but for some reason, he simply didn't. When they landed in Bogotá, they said their good-byes and headed for the luggage carousel. The man—let's call him Ramon—got his bag first and left. That's when Larry heard God speak to him. It wasn't an audible voice, but the message was clear: "You didn't share your faith with him." Larry wasn't unused to hearing from God, but he was certainly unused to disregarding a prompting to share his faith. So he told God he was sorry and asked for God's forgiveness. Then he prayed: "If I ever get another chance to speak with him, I will obey your voice. If not, please get the message to him from someone else."

Life is full of regrets and for Larry, missing an

opportunity to share his faith—especially when he clearly felt a prompting from God to do so—was the sort of thing he would certainly regret. But he knew God forgives us if we really know we are wrong and are genuinely sorry about it. Of course, he was.

That week Larry flew from Bogotá to Lima, Peru, and then to La Paz, Bolivia—and then finally to Santa Cruz. There he met a team of Agape teachers whom he had placed a few years earlier. The lead couple was Dan and Nancy Pryor. They worked with disabled children and had actually started Bolivia's first school for special needs children. It's still in operation today.

About a week after that he was scheduled to leave Santa Cruz for São Paulo, Brazil. But when he arrived at the Santa Cruz airport, he learned that his flight had been canceled. This was Thursday, and the next flight was on Saturday! Larry knew this was not entirely atypical in a developing nation, so he did what he could to rearrange his plans for a departure in two days. What else could he do? Traveling 1,100 miles via ground transportation through dense rain forest was not an option. So he stayed with the Pryors for two more days. Happily, the flight to São Paulo on Saturday was not canceled, and Larry was glad to know that it was a nonstop. But when he got to the airport and went out to board the plane, he saw that the plane was rather old and not well maintained. The pilot himself was very scruffy-looking and disheveled, with a few days' beard growth and a necktie that was half-undone.

After they took off, Larry noticed that they were flying at a rather low altitude, so he found himself enjoying the view, which after some time included the lush grasslands of Brazil. They had traveled about five hundred miles when the pilot announced that they would be landing at Campo Grande. This was a very odd thing to hear, considering the flight had been advertised as a nonstop to São Paulo. But Larry took comfort in knowing that at least this wasn't an emergency landing. Besides, what options did he have? So he relaxed and watched as they slowly descended toward Campo Grande International Airport.

But as they descended, Larry didn't see any town or city that would have an airport nearby. There was nothing but farmland in every direction. Where was the airport? The plane had descended to about five hundred feet when Larry spotted a thin strip of grass amid the farmland. Evidently this was the landing strip, and the plane soon landed without incident.

Larry saw a building the size of a two-car garage with a tin roof—topped by a windsock. So he knew this was indeed some kind of airport and not just a place where planes could land if they needed to. The plane taxied to a stop. The door was opened and the stairway lowered. By now Larry saw two or three people, who seemed to be his future fellow passengers. They were standing together with some baggage handlers and began moving toward the plane. As they drew near, Larry saw that one of them looked familiar. Larry almost thought his eyes were playing tricks on him, but as the passenger drew nearer, he knew they were not. It was Ramon. To say that Larry was surprised can hardly do justice to what he felt.

The seat next to Larry's was free, so the moment Ramon entered the cabin, Larry leapt up and waved him over. He wasn't about to miss this second opportunity to do what he should have done the first time, over two weeks ago. His head was swimming that this was now happening, that he really would have this chance. Ramon put his luggage on the overhead rack, took his seat, and then gave Larry the strangest look. Larry wondered what he was thinking, and then Ramon told him. "This is weird," he said. "When I left you at the Bogotá airport, a voice said to me, 'You will see this man again. He has a message to which you must listen.'"

As much as Larry had been amazed to see Ramon approaching the plane, he was now even more amazed to hear what Ramon was saying. Larry had seen God do amazing things before, but it seems one never really gets used to it, nor should he. Larry saw that Ramon was seriously spooked by the whole thing, and he gave Larry his rapt attention, waiting for the message he was obviously supposed to hear. "I have only one message that is important to share," Larry said, and with that he told Ramon about the forgiveness and love of Jesus, and how God wanted each of us to turn our lives over to him. Larry had done this so many times in his life, but the way God had arranged this made it feel especially important. Larry then asked Ramon if he would like to pray to accept Jesus, but it seemed that the whole experience was so new and overwhelming to him that he couldn't quite take it in. But he didn't seem resistant to the idea either. So Larry suggested that he pray on his own, in private. From all that transpired to get them to that point, Larry had little doubt that he would. When they landed in São Paulo, they said their good-byes, and Larry entrusted his passenger into God's hands.

One often hears that God is a God of second chances, that he is rooting for us and wants us to succeed. Perhaps especially if we have screwed up, he is eager to give us another chance, if we are open to that. For my friend Larry, this was a rather dramatic illustration of that simple idea.

# A GIRL AND A SQUIRREL

My close friends Rick and Barbara Vlaha live in an area called the Woodlands, near Houston, Texas. Of course, there are a lot of trees in the Woodlands, so when in September 2008 Hurricane Ike swept up from the Gulf of Mexico and slammed into Galveston and up through Houston and the Woodlands, a large number of trees came down. Rick and Barbara were therefore especially glad that none came down in their yard. They were also surprised to see what did come down: It was an intact gray squirrel's nest, containing three baby squirrels. Their children, Grace and Christopher (at the time, ten and seven), were excited at the literal windfall, but saddened to discover that only two of the squirrels survived the drop. They tried to get the mother to take her children back, but for a reason unknown to them, she took only one back. So the Vlahas decided to care for the remaining squirrel themselves. They named him Isaac, after the storm that had delivered him into their life.

So many trees had fallen down during the storm that in the days following there were massive power outages in the area. It was so disruptive that they thought it would be smart to drive up to Tulsa to stay with some friends. Tulsa was eight hours north, but they had no choice but to take Isaac with them. Grace was thrilled and cared for him in the car all the way there. But when they arrived in Tulsa, it became clear to Rick and Barbara that Isaac wasn't doing too well. Was that why his mother had rejected him? Could she sense he wasn't going to make it, as animals sometimes can? Isaac was refusing to eat, so Rick and Barbara decided to try to find someone who would better know how to take care of him.

But by now Grace had grown so attached to Isaac that she wouldn't hear of it. Rick and Barbara knew it would break her heart, but what could they do? How do you explain to a child with an overwhelming emotional attachment to an incredibly precious furry creature—one that seemed to have fallen out of Heaven itself and into her life—that she needs to give it up for its own good? That they didn't know how to get him to eat and that he would soon die? They tried hard to explain that to Grace, but she remained unmoved. The plan was to take Isaac to a vet in Tulsa and leave him there. They continued to try to convince Grace that this was the only right thing to do for him, but she could not believe it. So Rick and Barbara prayed. They knew that the God of the Bible loves each of us as a father loves a child, so if their parental love made them want to assuage Grace's feelings over the squirrel, wouldn't her heavenly father want to do the same? So they weren't shy in asking God to help Grace want to do the right thing and "have peace" about that decision.

They all drove to the Tulsa vet with Isaac and asked him what to do. He told them that there was a woman who lived nearby whose specialty was in caring for orphaned squirrels and they should take Isaac to her. Had they just heard right? The woman's name was Stephanie, but everyone in the area knew her as "the Squirrel Lady." Rick and Barbara realized she didn't mind being called that when they pulled into her driveway and saw her license plate: "SQRLADY." When they entered her home, they could hardly believe what they saw. There were more than twenty squirrels living there, all in various stages of rehabilitation. Stephanie's gentle manner was a great comfort to Grace, who was nonetheless still upset they were following this course of action.

When Stephanie examined Isaac, she quickly realized that Isaac was not a he but a she. Rick, Barbara, and Grace immediately renamed her "Izzy." Stephanie said to them that she had another squirrel that was about the same age as Izzy. But it was not a gray squirrel; it was a red squirrel. Rick and Barbara also now learned that Stephanie was a Christian, because she told them that she had been praying for a playmate for the red squirrel for some time. It wasn't thriving, and she knew from experience that it needed another squirrel around its own age to help it along. She had even told all the other squirrel "rehabbers" in the area—yes, there were others—to let her know if they came across a squirrel around this red squirrel's age. But so far there had been no success. Until the Vlaha family showed up with Izzy.

After treating Izzy for dehydration, Stephanie placed her in the cage with the young red squirrel. What happened next, right before Grace's eyes, seemed downright magical. The squirrels immediately faced each other—almost touching, eyeball to eyeball—and then actually curled their tails around each other. It was almost unbelievable. To all watching, they seemed made for each other.

Grace was so taken with what she saw happening that the idea of leaving with Izzy suddenly seemed wrong. It was clear to her that Izzy was meant to be right here with her new friend, the lonely red squirrel. When they realized Grace felt this way, Rick and Barbara were overwhelmed with gratitude to God.

But there was more. Although Rick and Barbara had no idea how it happened, the story made it onto the local Tulsa news station. It seemed that perhaps Hurricane Ike had done one tiny positive thing after all, and people wanted to hear about it. Soon news outlets from California to Boston were picking up the story too, and before its media run was over, it was picked up by CNN, which aired it on Anderson Cooper's *AC 360°*.

The whole experience was a message for Rick and Barbara and their children: God doesn't always make things go the way we would like, and he doesn't answer every prayer the way we want him to, but in this case he seems to have answered the prayers of a woman dedicated to serving helpless squirrels. And he seems to have answered the prayers of two parents concerned for the tender heart of their ten-year-old girl.

# 14

## TOUCHING ETERNITY

All miracle stories are stories of eternity touching time—of Heaven touching Earth, of the creator touching his creation, of the supernatural touching the natural. But there are times when a miracle is more overtly an example of this than at other times. In the context of this book, the miracles in this chapter fall into that category. They also underscore the mystery of how our world of time and space intersects with the world outside our world, the world beyond time and space. Such intersections are truly beyond our full comprehension, as are our glimpses of eternity itself, but the stories here at least give us some ideas with which to begin thinking about the subjects.

## A SOBBING JUDGE

Alice von Hildebrand is an astounding woman. Now ninety-one, she has twice been my guest at the Socrates in the City events we put on in Manhattan. She emigrated to the United States from Belgium in 1940, just ahead of Hitler's armies, and met her future husband, Dietrich von Hildebrand, shortly thereafter. He is today considered one of the most celebrated Catholic thinkers of the twentieth century. His story, beginning with his birth in 1889, is well worth reading, as are all his books. After the death of his first wife, he married Lily, as her friends call her, many years his junior, but to those who know anything of it, the harmony of their union is deeply moving. She was a professor of philosophy at Hunter College in Manhattan for three decades—and has dedicated her years of "retirement" to writing and to the legacy of her late husband, who died in 1977. Lily herself retired from teaching in 1984 so she could accept most of the speaking engagements she had been putting off for so many years. So after 1984, she was on the road nearly constantly.

This story begins in the summer of 1991, when Lily was invited to speak in Ohio. She wrote those who invited her to accept the invitation and give them details of her flight, but shortly thereafter, she went to New Hampshire, where she still spends some time every summer. Because she left for New Hampshire so soon after accepting the invitation, she never got details on what to do once she arrived in Ohio. Whatever mail was forwarded did not seem to contain them. So she had no idea who would pick her up from the airport and where she was staying in Ohio, nor what was the exact location of the place she was to give her talk. As the date of the engage-ment approached, Lily found herself thinking about this and feeling stress over it. She then received an invitation to travel to Portugal and give a talk there, not long before the date she was to be in Ohio. That engagement would be in Fatima, where the famous visions of the Virgin Mary took place in 1917. So Lily flew to Lisbon, traveled to Fatima, gave her talk, and returned home. It was now just a few days before she was to fly to Ohio. But on returning to her apartment in New Rochelle there was still no letter of confirmation from the people in Ohio who had invited her. She had a phone number, which she called all day long for several days, with no answer. She began to get frantic. Would someone be at the airport in Columbus to pick her up? Had they never received the letter she sent them in June?

The end-of-summer travel to and from Europe had fatigued the then sixty-eight-year-old widow. Jet lag was the main culprit. She normally took mass transit from her home to LaGuardia Airport to save money, but this time she thought that given how she was feeling, it would be more prudent to hire a taxi. Lily didn't own a car, so she sometimes took very short cab rides from her home into downtown New Rochelle. The man who always drove her was Mr. Smith, a Jamaican man. He drove a cab for a local taxi company. He was extremely helpful to her. When he drove her to the airport, Mr. Smith would carry her luggage from her apartment to the taxi. Frail and small as she was, she required this kind of help. So on the morning of her trip to Ohio, she called Mr. Smith about a ride to the airport.

But Mr. Smith told her he was not working on the day she needed her ride. He knew how much Lily depended on him to do things other drivers would not do, especially carrying her luggage, so Mr. Smith said that although he could not pick her up in a taxi, he would gladly pick her up in his own car and take her to the airport. He always called her "Lady." "Lady," he said, "today's my day off, but I can do you a favor and take you in my own car." And on the day of her trip, he did.

But in her anxiety that day, Lily forgot her credit card at home. On the trip to the airport she was terribly worried about what would happen when she landed in Ohio. She didn't have much cash and now had to pay for the taxi ride. Would she have enough cash when she landed in Ohio? What if no one was at the airport to pick her up?

When they arrived at LaGuardia, Lily told Mr. Smith that she would of course pay him the same amount she would pay if he were driving his taxicab, but she said that in order to be reimbursed when she arrived in Ohio she would need a receipt, so she asked Mr. Smith to write on a piece of paper the details of the trip, how much she had paid, and so on, which he did. And off she went to catch her plane.

But when Lily was waiting in line at the airport, a large policeman approached her and rudely demanded to see her taxi receipt. She was of course blindsided by this request, wondering where he had come from and why he would need to see her receipt. She asked him. But he made plain that he was not to be trifled with and again forcefully demanded to see the receipt. Being a law-abiding citizen, Lily reached into her purse and took out the receipt and gave it to him, still wondering what on earth this was all about. Once the policeman was satisfied, he returned the receipt to her and marched off.

But all the way to Ohio, Lily could not stop thinking of what had happened. She was deeply troubled by it. "What have I done?" she kept asking herself. She was also unsure whether she would be met at the airport when she arrived. This contributed to the trip's unpleasantness. But when she landed she was met by the people who had invited her. They had gotten her letter after all. So she gave her speech and returned home. But no sooner had she gotten in the door of her apartment than she called Mr. Smith. She still had her coat on from the trip when she dialed. Mr. Smith picked up the phone and was clearly still very upset by what had happened. He told her that the policeman had detained him at the curb for one hour at the airport and had issued a summons for him to appear in court that October. He said that he would be fined $350 for illegally taking money in an unauthorized vehicle as he had done, and he would probably lose his driver's license for six months. Driving the taxi was his only source of income.

The blow to Lily on hearing this can hardly be overstated. Though none of this was actually her fault, she reproached herself terribly. This gentle soul's great kindness to her had led to this sorry pass, which might well ruin him financially. To lose his sole source of income for half a year was a draconian penalty for someone in such humble financial circumstances already. Mr. Smith told her that he must appear in court on October 15, a month hence. It was plain from his voice that he was terrified. Lily asked him to come to her apartment so that they could discuss it in person. Once there, it was obvious that the man was indeed deeply shaken. He showed her the document summoning him to appear in court. The policeman who had demanded her receipt that day in the airport had filled it all out. But Mr. Smith was required to underline "Guilty" or "Not Guilty" and had not done so. The man seemed terrified by the whole thing. Lily took the document and underscored "Not Guilty" very prominently and handed it back to him. She was shocked by the injustice and told Mr. Smith in no uncertain terms that she would accompany him to court on October 15.

The moment Mr. Smith left her apartment, she leapt into action. For her that meant prayer, first and foremost. There were two groups to which she now wrote letters, asking for their prayers for October 15. One was the group of nuns known as the "Poor Clares"—who corresponded to the Franciscan Order. The other was to the monks at a monastery in Vermont, which had been founded by a Jewish man who had come to the faith through her late husband, Dietrich von Hildebrand. So many had come to the faith directly through her late husband that at the time of his death he had nearly one hundred godchildren. The Jewish man who had come to the faith had not only come to faith but had founded a Carthusian monastery in Vermont. The Carthusians practiced the vow of silence and lived atop Mount Equinox in Arlington, Vermont. Lily wrote letters to the sisters and to the brothers, explaining that prayers were desperately needed for this situation.

On her own too, Lily prayed constantly. Her propensity for anguish was now in full fan and she lost sleep over the weeks as this date approached. Two days before, on October 13, she received a phone call from Mr. Smith. He said that the court appearance had been postponed.

They must now appear on January 2. Lily quickly wrote again to the two monasteries, telling them of the new situation and asking for their renewed prayers. Then in late December, Mr. Smith called again. The date had again been postponed. It was not to be January 2 but March 13. So again Lily wrote two letters, again asking for the prayers not to cease, but to continue for two more months.

On January 20, Lily received a phone call from a stranger. The man said that he was a great devotee of her late husband's work and of hers too. He had seen her on TV a number of times and hoped she might accept his invitation to lunch. Shortly thereafter she met him at a restaurant in downtown New Rochelle. After they had greeted one another, Lily was thrilled to learn that this man was the head of police for the entire surrounding area beyond New Rochelle. She immediately poured out her tale of woe, hoping he might be able to help. Instead, the man drew a grim picture of the situation. He said that there had been great problems with these so-called "gypsy cabs" taking people to the airport without licenses, and they must be punished. There was nothing he could do. He said not only would this man be fined $350, but he would very likely lose his license for the six-month period. Whatever hopes of divine intervention through this stranger inviting her to lunch were dashed. By the time she said good-bye, her prospects for March 13 were far gloomier than they had been before she sat down.

A few days before the dreaded date, Mr. Smith called again. He told Lily that the court had once again postponed the date. The new date was to be May 16. Lily could hardly believe her ears, but again she contacted the two holy orders and let them know they should continue their prayers, informing them of the new date. This was her fourth letter on the subject to both of them. She had all these months continued to lose sleep over this and had herself said innumerable prayers over it. In the week before the sixteenth, however, Lily got sick. Her speaking schedule had been exhausting. She had been scheduled to give a talk at Notre Dame and then would fly straight to Dallas to give another talk. But first she had to fly to California to give a talk there. When she came back to New Rochelle from California, however, she was so exhausted that she fell ill and had to cancel both the Notre Dame and Dallas talks. Her youngest sister had been planning to visit from Europe, but Lily asked her to come earlier, to take care of her, which she did. Right up to the sixteenth, she continued to be ill, and when the morning of the May 16 arrived, Lily's sister saw that she was simply too sick to go to the courthouse, and told her so. But Lily would not be dissuaded. "Living or dead," she said to her sister, "I must go! I must defend this man!"

So she prepared herself for the trip. Just before she left her apartment to go downstairs and meet Mr. Smith, who would drive with her to the court, she did something she'd never done before. She went into her bedroom and spoke sternly and quite loudly to the portrait of her late husband, fourteen years departed from this world. Like all Christians, she believed that those who are accepted into God's bosom at death never die. Catholics of course believe it is permissible—and advisable—to speak to those who have gone before, especially to those who are deemed saints—and to ask for their help. Lily did this all the time, but she had never addressed the soul of her husband in this way. "You have loved me and helped me and defended me my whole life," she said "But now—*today!*—you must prove to me that you are in Heaven. You must help me. But today!" He had been her great protector during his life, so she continued pleading with him, emphatically: "If you are still my husband, I ask you to help me today as you did so many times in your life. But I must see that you do this today—*today!*"

Then she turned on her heels and went downstairs to meet Mr. Smith in his old battered car. The ride took over an hour. All the way Lily continued to pray desperately. One of her prayers on this trip was that God would show them favor by sending them to a black judge.

When they at last got to the courthouse they

saw a huge chalkboard listing the five different judges presiding that day, with the numbers of their courtrooms. Lily saw that Mr. Smith was listed under courtroom number three. As they walked there, Lily continued to pray that the judge would be a black man.

But as soon as they walked in, Lily saw that the judge was white. "This was the first blow," she said. They took a seat in the back and saw that they were last on the list of about twelve cases that afternoon. Lily observed that the judge's demeanor was markedly unpleasant. After he had heard each case brought before him, without so much as looking up, as stiff as can be, he gruffly pronounced, "Guilty." "Guilty, guilty, guilty!" Watching him in action was something chilling to behold.

As the cases proceeded and their time drew near, Lily drilled Mr. Smith again and again on exactly what he must say. She told him that it was a very simple case and all he needed to do was tell the truth. He should explain that he did not ask to be paid, that he was simply doing a favor to this older woman because he knew that she needed help carrying her luggage and another taxi driver wouldn't do that. He must make clear that he had not expected to be paid, but that she had insisted on it, which was the truth. As she told him these things over and over, Mr. Smith said, "Yes, Lady. Yes, Lady," indicating that he understood. She reviewed these facts with him for about forty minutes.

At last their time came. The last case of the day. "Mr. Smith!" They approached the bench and Lily saw that Mr. Smith was literally shaking with fear as he stood there. The injustice of it all outraged her. The idea that a simple, uneducated man like this should have to be subjected to this unspeakably humiliating situation made her blood boil. The policeman who had rudely demanded the receipt from her in the airport nine months earlier was there and he first gave his version of the story. Then the judge asked Mr. Smith to speak. "Mr. Smith," he said, "what do you have to say in your favor?" But Mr. Smith was trembling and tongue-tied with fear. "Your Honor," he said, "she is a terribly nice lady . . ."

The judge quickly grew impatient with Mr. Smith. "That's all very good, Mr. Smith," he said dismissively, "but you haven't answered! *What do you have to say in your favor?*"

Still, Mr. Smith was almost unable to speak for fear. "She's just one of the nicest ladies I've met in my life," he said.

The judge made it clear he didn't have time for this nonsense. "Mr. Smith," he said sternly. "This is your last chance. What do you have to say in your favor?"

But by this time, Mr. Smith was unable to say much at all. "Nothing," he replied meekly, almost in tears. "Nothing . . ."

In his great fear, he had obviously forgotten everything he had heard.

Now Lily said a short prayer and then asked the judge if she could say something. Again, the judge sternly asked for her name, address, telephone number, and occupation. And then asked her: "Do you swear to tell the truth, the whole truth, and nothing but the truth, so help you God?" She did.

After this preamble, Lily told the judge the simple facts. She made it clear that Mr. Smith hadn't asked her for money, that he was doing her a favor because he knew that she needed help with her luggage and he knew that other cabbies couldn't be counted on to go to that trouble. She also made it clear that she had only paid him because she wanted to pay him for his time, not because he had been expected to be paid, and she said that she had only asked for the receipt since she would need to be reimbursed when she got to Ohio, since she had forgotten her credit card at home. That was all.

After she was finished, the judge spoke. "Case dismissed," he said. It was a stunning moment.

The policeman was obviously very displeased with this verdict and left the room in disgust. As for Mr. Smith, he was moved almost to tears. He looked at Lily with tremendous adoration, incredulous that after eight agonizing months he had finally come through this fire unscathed. In a moment, he too left the room quietly. Lily knew that he was headed to the garage to get the car.

Suddenly Lily was alone with the judge, and the judge spoke. "Von Hildebrand," he said, "von Hildebrand . . . Are you in any way related to Dietrich von Hildebrand?"

That this was tremendously surprising to hear in that context is obvious. "Yes, Your Honor," Lily replied, amazed. "I am his widow."

The judge now stood up and came down from his bench to stand near her. "You are his widow," he said, seeming to marvel at the coincidence. "You know, years ago—years and years ago—I used to attend his talks in his apartment in Manhattan, on Central Park West." Lily would later realize this must have been way back in the early 1940s. For years, her husband gave political talks against Nazism and Communism, and he also gave religious talks about God and the Church, but he had stopped giving the religious talks in 1945. Lily took the judge to be Jewish, which he indeed was, so she assumed that he had attended her late husband's political talks and not the religious ones, and she said so.

"No," the judge said, "it was his liturgical talks. In fact, I met my wife at his apartment." And then, quite suddenly and inexplicably, the judge began sobbing.

Lily said he was not weeping but sobbing— sobbing uncontrollably. He then put his arm over his face and continued to sob, standing there. Lily had no idea what to make of it. So she put her arm on his shoulder to comfort him, and said: "Your Honor, do you have any sad memories of my husband?"

"No, no," he said through the sobs, seemingly unable to speak another word.

Lily knew that God was somehow at work in all of this. "Your Honor," she continued, "for the last eight months I have been agonizing over this case. Because of my stupidity in not properly explaining things to the policeman I put this entirely innocent and good man in this terrible situation, endangering his livelihood. But now I see clearly that God's providence has permitted this so that I would have the joy of meeting you. I would very much like to remain in touch. Would it be possible to have your name and address?"

The judge, still sobbing, somehow assented and then quietly left the courtroom. Lily waited alone for about five minutes, after which the judge returned from his chambers no longer wearing his judge's robes. He handed Lily his business card. And then he put his arm up against the wall and continued sobbing, his face buried in his arm.

Mr. Smith's was the last case of the day, so no one came into the courtroom as all of this was happening. But as the judge continued to sob into his arm, Lily thought she should perhaps take her leave, so she said good-bye and left.

Downstairs she found Mr. Smith waiting in his

battered car. The relief he felt over this long-awaited verdict was visible. As she got into the car, he said: "Lady, I pray for you every single day, but you know, you know . . . you *should* have become a lawyer!"

When Lily arrived home that afternoon she got her mail and saw a letter from the nuns. Their letter said that on the day of the appearance before the judge they would all be on their knees praying. Lily then went into the bedroom and spoke to the photograph of her late husband. "Now I know," she said, passionately and emphatically, "I know, that you still love me and protect me!" She knew that her husband's immortal soul had somehow acted on her behalf. She knew that he was alive, and not just alive in some vague sense, but alive and able to hear her, *as himself*. He was not "one with the cosmos," as some religions maintain, but rather he was Dietrich von Hildebrand himself, alive in glory, and now part of that "great cloud of witnesses" of which Paul speaks, who cheer us on from their heavenly station. It was an extremely moving experience for her. Lily said that "something amazing happened. I had been a widow for fourteen years. But now in some mysterious way that I cannot explain, I no longer felt like one."

When she shared this story with different people immediately afterward, some refused to believe that a judge would sob like that in his own chambers. It was so out of order as to be completely unthinkable. But most who heard the story believed it and urged Lily to get in touch with the judge. They felt, as she did, that there must be some higher purpose to all that had happened. So about a week after the court date, Lily called the phone number on the card. A woman answered. "Who are you?" she asked, in a voice that was not very friendly. Lily explained and in a few moments the judge came to the phone. But he was quite reserved and ill at ease. He made it clear from his curt responses that he wasn't interested in continuing the conversation. After some weeks, Lily called again. She would soon be giving a talk in NYC and thought that this might be another chance for her and the judge to meet. But again he was cold, simply saying that he was not available. Lily remembered calling a third and final time, with no results.

But then a friend of hers suggested how she might get the judge to talk with her and perhaps reveal what was at the root of the tremendous sorrow he had expressed as he had sobbed and sobbed that afternoon in his empty courtroom. Lily was writing a book about her husband, and would be soliciting thoughts and reminiscences from people who had known him over the years. So she wrote a letter to the judge, explaining this. But she never heard back.

# USS WASHINGTON, JUNE 1940

The last time Dame Alice von Hildebrand was my guest at Socrates in the City was in November 2013, at the Union League Club. Afterward we had our usual Patrons' Dinner in the gorgeous wood-paneled Lincoln Library of the club. There Lily shared an extraordinary story. It happened to her in 1940, when she was seventeen, on board the ocean liner *Washington*, which was crossing the Atlantic for America.

Lily grew up in Belgium, to devoutly Catholic parents. In 1940, Hitler's armies were approaching from the east, so knowing that their two daughters' lives were in danger, Lily's parents arranged for their passage to America, where a relative had agreed to take them in. It was June 8 when Lily and her sister, Marie-Helene, boarded the *Washington* at Le Verdon. The ship first crossed the tempestuous Gulf of Gascogne and Lily became terribly seasick. On the tenth they arrived in Lisbon and all that day were anchored off Lisbon's coast as scores of people were ferried aboard, all escaping the war.

Lily told me that the ship typically held a thousand people, but because of the dire emergency of getting so many out of war-torn Europe, they took on two thousand. She recalled

472

that the ship's ballrooms were converted to dormitories.

One night, Lily was awakened from sleep by loud noises and cries. It was 4:45 A.M. She got out of bed and opened her door to the corridor to see what was going on and saw people chaotically running about, wearing life preservers. She quickly woke Marie-Helene and the two others in their cabin. (It was a first-class, two-person cabin, but because of the need for space, it now held four passengers.) They dressed in a mad haste. Lily remembered that she wore a cotton dress covered with polka dots. She grabbed only her purse and then out into the chaos and din of the corridor they went. They were making their way to the deck, where the lifeboats were, but Lily was terrified she might lose her sister in the endlessly jostling crowds, so she linked arms with her tightly and did not let go. With her pronounced ability for recall, Alice told Marie-Helene that the lifeboat assigned to them was lifeboat number 10. She even remembered where it was. But as they arrived there amid the tremendous chaos, they saw that it was already filled to capacity. No one else was allowed aboard.

As they stood there on the deck near the full lifeboat, they could hear the captain speaking, but neither of them knew enough English to understand. A nearby man who knew French helpfully translated what the captain had just said. It seemed that the ship had been stopped by a German submarine. The Germans had informed the captain that the passengers had precisely one hour to get into the lifeboats and abandon ship, after which the Germans would torpedo it. Huge passenger ships like this one could eventually be used by the Allies for the war effort, so the Germans planned to destroy as many as possible. Everyone must immediately get off the ship or go down with it. But lifeboat number 10 was already full.

It stood to reason that an ocean liner built for one thousand passengers had lifeboats for roughly that number. So there was no way all two thousand could be accommodated now, at least not without endangering the lives of the people already on the lifeboats. Lily and her sister were simply too late. In that moment, Lily said, she realized there was no escape for them; they were doomed. She was quite convinced that she was now facing death. As this grimmest reality settled into her mind, Lily remembers that she turned to face the sea. And as she looked out over the vast Atlantic Ocean, she experienced something transcendent and miraculous. "In one-hundredth of a second," she told me, emphatically and precisely, "I saw my whole life pass before me!" What evidently has happened to innumerable souls—and what one so often hears spoken as a cliché—was literally happening to Lily in that moment. It was a proverbial eternal moment. Time was suddenly utterly transcended and for an infinitesimally thin sliver of time she stepped into the timeless eternity outside time. Somehow in that moment she saw her entire life pass before her in the smallest detail. She said she somehow saw every single thing she had done and everything she had failed to do; she saw what she should not have done, and she saw all that she had wished for. Then it was over. But when it was over, she says, she knew that in passing over that moment she had been transported from youth to maturity. A moment ago she was a girl and now she was a woman—and it had all taken place in that tiniest fraction of a second. Lily stood there on the ship overwhelmed and speechless. The experience was so extraordinary and so absolutely sacred that she stood there and said nothing. Indeed, she was not to share it with a soul for many years. It was a profound and holy secret, she said to me, one that she must ponder in her heart.[29]

---

29. She told those of us around the table at the dinner that she has had three such experiences in her life, and each of them was so holy and so sacred she simply felt she couldn't share it. It was too intimate to share. In fact, she said that it was years after she had been married and more than twenty-five years after it happened, that she finally was able to share it with her beloved husband, Dietrich.

But as she stood on that ship's deck for that most anguishing of hours, prepared to step forever into eternity, Lily relived the extraordinary vision in her mind, over and over. God himself had revealed something to her and had changed her forever. But at the end of that terrible hour, Lily and all the others learned that somehow the Germans had changed their mind. The *Washington* would not take them to the bottom of the Atlantic, and Lily would live beyond her seventeenth year after all. After this unspeakably good news it took the ship a very long time to begin moving again, but eventually it did resume its journey, taking her to New York, where she has lived these last seventy-four years. She said that the experience convinced her that at the end of people's lives there might be hope for those who had not yet made their peace with God—and that just as he had given her that vision of her life, he might in his mercy give others this final opportunity to see the totality of their lives and to repent, to turn at last to him and to say: "Forgive me."

One final thought: Lily's story reminded me of the apostle Paul's words in his second letter to the church in Corinth. He says that he will now discuss some "visions and revelations of the Lord" and then refers to someone he knows who fourteen years earlier had actually visited Heaven, where he "heard things that are not to be told, that no mortal is permitted to repeat." It's often thought Paul was modestly referring to an experience he himself had. Whether that is the case matters not. What matters is the idea that some things are so sacred, that they cannot bear unveiling. Because we live in a culture where mystery has lost its value, where to hide something is often thought of as merely repressive, we don't understand this idea of "the sacred." We seem to have accepted the fashionable idea that all things once thought sacred and mysterious—sexuality most notably—must be freed from their mystery and "sanctity." But in most cultures throughout history the opposite has been true. Most cultures have a pronounced reverence for the sacred, which they veil out of deepest reverence and respect.

## BEYOND DEATH

There have recently been a spate of books about people going to Heaven, people who have seemingly slipped the bonds of Earth and flown to that other world—and then returned to tell us about it. It's an astounding claim, but these accounts don't come across as fanciful fictions. What are we to make of them? One of these accounts, in the book *Heaven is for Real*, was even produced as a major motion picture, about a four-year-old boy who seems to have visited Heaven. In the months following he tells his parents many extraordinary things they know to be true and that he couldn't possibly have made up. Oddly enough, the three accounts besides this one that leap to mind on this subject are all stories told by medical doctors. One, titled *To Heaven and Back*, tells the story of an orthopedic surgeon who dies in a terrible kayaking accident. Another, titled *Proof of Heaven*, tells the story of a brain surgeon who dies and returns. And finally, *Raising the Dead: A Doctor Encounters the Miraculous* tells of a Palm Beach heart surgeon whose prayer over a corpse raised the man back to life.

Actually visiting Heaven is the sort of miracle that makes things like healings seem almost pedestrian. As I thought about writing this book, I recalled the miracle stories I had heard from so many friends, but I knew of no one who claimed to have visited Heaven. But while I was writing this book I took a trip to Grand Rapids, and there, at a gathering in my friend Sharon's home, I met a man who had indeed visited Heaven. His name is Andrew DeVries, and he is a regional gift officer at Calvin College, though at the time of his story he was a professor there. In talking to him I realized that I already knew his wife, Kay. She and I first connected on a Bonhoeffer tour I led in Berlin two years ago, when she and Sharon and some other friends went around Berlin with me, to all of the Bonhoeffer sites. Of course Kay had mentioned her husband to me, but she had not mentioned his amazing story. But now here I was hearing it from the man himself.

I should say that like nearly everyone in Grand Rapids—or so it seems to me—Andy is Dutch, and like all Dutch men, he is tall and fair-haired. But unlike all others I've ever met, he has visited Heaven and returned to tell us about it. I don't remember how it came up in our conversation, but as soon as he started telling me the story I knew it had to be in this book.

The story begins with a horrific motorcycle accident. In 2002, Andy was taking a motorcycle trip with a friend of his, Jene Vredevoogd, who is, of course, Dutch. They were traveling through Holland, Michigan—which is even more Dutch than Grand Rapids—driving east on Thirty-Second Street, when an eighty-four-year-old woman ran a red light on Highway 31. Her bumper crushed Andy's leg against the motorcycle's engine, almost pulverizing the leg. It was broken in more than forty places and the car struck with such force that almost all the flesh was separated from the bone. It was ghastly. If Andy survived—and this was indeed a big *if*—he would probably lose the leg.

Before the accident, Andy had been an accomplished athlete. He played many sports well, but he played volleyball so especially well that he was part of a team that won the USA Open Volleyball Championship in 2000. This led him to try out for a team representing the states of Michigan and Indiana in the Masters Olympics of 2002. In fact, the tryout for that took place just two weeks before this accident.

Andy recalled the moments following the horrific crash. He said that he was flying through the air, seemingly suspended in time. Time seemed to stop and he felt peaceful—and then everything sped up as his right shoulder smashed through the car's windshield. He then bounced off the hood and onto the highway, where the car then ran over his other leg. His friend Jene, thinking quickly, immediately positioned his motorcycle to block traffic and called 911. The ambulance arrived fairly soon, but as the emergency workers prepared to carry Andy into the ambulance, Jene objected. Fearing his friend had suffered a head injury, he insisted they use a backboard to transport him. They did, and Andy now believes this may have saved his life.

When they got to the Holland hospital, the doctors were simply unprepared to deal with Andy's extensive and life-threatening injuries, so he was immediately airlifted to Spectrum Hospital in Grand Rapids. There, one of the finest orthopedic surgeons was waiting. It would take a superb surgeon to deal with the situation. Most of the ligaments around Andy's knee had been severed, so his kneecap was literally up near his hip. In the emergency room that evening they reconstructed his knee and pulled ligaments down from his groin to reattach it. A titanium rod was then inserted to keep everything in place.

Four days after the accident, the doctors were astounded that the leg was still "alive," without any vein to provide blood flow. Some capillaries were the only source of blood. But this became increasingly inadequate and an amputation had to be scheduled. But when the time came for the amputation, something odd happened. The orthopedic surgeon took Andy into surgery and had him on the operating table. The doctor marked where he must cut and then placed the saw on Andy's leg to begin. But somehow he could not begin cutting Andy's leg. He wasn't sure exactly why he could not, but even after having come this far, he stopped. He could not continue. In his mind, he reasoned that he could certainly take the leg off the next day if it was necessary, or the day after that, but once it was amputated he surely could never reattach it. So the doctor canceled the surgery and for the time being the leg remained attached to Andy's body.

But following this near amputation there were weeks and weeks of surgeries, most of them aimed at saving the leg. For Andy, it was a time of never-ending pain. He said that his thumb was almost glued to the button that worked the morphine pump. Every night was filled with pain, so he never really slept properly, and when he did doze off, there were awful flashbacks to the accident. The pain and the surgeries never seemed to end, so it was nearly impossible to be hopeful. Some friends brought headphones and some CDs, containing a combination of Southern Gospel hymns that Andy had learned from his grandparents and others he had sung in choir. He had never in his life felt his own helplessness so keenly. Andy was a man of strong faith and during this period, he found himself thinking over and over of Jesus and of what Jesus had endured for him in his suffering on the cross. Many times Andy sobbed uncontrollably as he thought of it. A number of visitors thought the weeping was from his pain and anxiety, but mostly during this time, Andy recalled, it was out of gratitude for what God had done for him, and for God's nearness to him during this long trial.

Over time, small improvements occurred, but additional surgeries were always needed. The gastroenterologist said that Andy's liver was not strong enough to sustain the pressure from anesthesia, so Andy's leg should come off as soon as possible. He knew that there was little hope Andy could keep it anyway, so to put off the amputation was compromising his ability to survive at all. But for now the gastroenterologist's advice was not heeded; they would try other things and still hope that the leg could somehow be saved.

One procedure involved grafting skin from Andy's healthy leg. But shortly after this procedure his body began to retain fluid such that his weight shot up to over 280 pounds. Then his skin turned black, an especially bad sign. At this point the doctors decided on a course of treatment called "debridement," in which dead and damaged tissue is continually removed in order to increase the potential for healing.

Despite all these heroic efforts, however, the situation was undeniably bleak. His overall health was still poor and not improving. The official hospital report over this time was that he was in "serious condition," but a number of times things took a turn for the worse, although Andy always seemed to pull back from the brink. Then one day, the doctors saw things take an especially bad turn, one from which they were convinced he would not recover. They now strongly suggested that the family should gather. Andy's son was at that time in the Grand Canyon, as part of a course he was taking through Calvin College. The college arranged to fly him home. Andy's daughter was teaching in Florida and she flew home to Michigan as well.

When they were all finally gathered at the hospital, standing around his bed, Andy was unconscious and unaware of their presence. But as Kay and their children stood there, and as his condition worsened, Andy had what he soon understood to be a vivid glimpse of Heaven.

He found himself suddenly in a different place. He remembers looking at a vast panoramic field. He says it was the most beautiful, calm, serene, and vivid place he had ever experienced. There were trees, flowers, and fauna, but everything he saw was in pale colors. The sky itself was a pale color. Then the colors began to deepen and deepen until they became the most vibrant colors he could ever imagine. It was all so visually stunning that he could even see the details in the tree bark. The wildflowers were every imaginable color, yellows and oranges and violets, and the sky was bluebird blue. Then a wind made the wildflowers in the meadow move the way a rolling sea moves. It was all breathtakingly beautiful.

Then Andy noticed a figure at the edge of the field. It looked like a scarecrow or a skeleton, and it began moving from the far corner toward the middle of the field. As it drew closer, the bones started to take on flesh and the musculature became pronounced. And it was skipping. Andy said that in all his years in teaching he had come to know that skipping is the one form of move-ment that almost always expresses happiness. It's very rare that someone skips without having a smile on their face. The man—and Andy now saw it was a man—was actually skipping as he moved across the landscape. As the figure drew closer,

Andy saw that it was clothed in the type of clothing he had worn himself, years before. The figure wore Levi's, a Henley-collared shirt with blue and white stripes, and docksider shoes. The face was beaming with joy. As it drew even closer, Andy could see the man's features. The face seemed familiar. Then he realized he was looking at himself. He was seeing himself in Heaven. For the brief period during which all of this happened, Andy recalled that he felt no pain at all, just joy. He had not been painless for so many weeks. Then suddenly the heavenly moment broke as Andy felt a sharp tug on his ankle.

"Dad! Dad!" the voice called. It was the voice of Andy's son, Drew. But Andy couldn't imagine having to leave that glorious, peaceful, joyful place. In his mind, Andy shouted, "No!" But then the colors faded back to pale. A white tunnel now appeared and Andy was "whooshed" through it to return to his hospital bed and his pain. Andy was extremely upset to have left what he knew was Heaven, but for some reason he had come back, and needless to say, he did not die.

But the experience so affected him that ever since it happened, he has absolutely no fear of death. In fact, just the contrary. He says that he looks forward to it with great anticipation, knowing that God has something beautiful and wonderful planned for him. He says that the experience dramatically changed his life.

A few months after all of this, Andy had finally gotten out of the hospital and was making a heroic effort to return to his teaching career at Calvin College. He was in a wheelchair, trying to maneuver through a door and having a difficult time, when an assistant chaplain saw his plight. He hustled over to help Andy get through the doorway and said that he couldn't believe Andy was back at school. He asked if Andy could remember when the surgeon decided against taking his leg. Andy certainly did, and he told the man the time and place of the surgery. The chaplain looked at Andy. "Do you know what was happening on campus at that time?" he asked. Andy had no idea what he was referring to. The chaplain said that at that very time a prayer vigil for his life and his leg was going on in the chapel. Hundreds who knew his situation were praying for him at that time.

The doctor who had brought Andy into surgery—who had the saw on Andy's leg—later told Andy that it was as though he "didn't have the strength to pull the saw." He said that something kept him from starting the sawing motion. Of course neither he nor Andy knew anything about the hundreds of people that very moment praying that Andy could keep his leg. That night in Sharon's apartment in Grand Rapids, I saw the leg with my own eyes. It's still his, all these years later.

# THE POWER OF GOD

My friend Brad Stine is a professional comedian. In a profile on him in *The New Yorker*, he was described as having a comic style that is "frantic, aggressive, and caustic, with echoes of Robin Williams, Sam Kinison, and George Carlin, who is his comedy hero."

Brad grew up as a Christian, but like so many Christians he never understood why God didn't seem to behave the same way today that he behaved during the times that the Bible was written. He believed the events of the Bible, such as the parting of the Red Sea and the miracles of the loaves and fishes and the healings Jesus did and Jesus rising from the dead and everything else. But why weren't these things happening in his lifetime, where he could witness them? Where was the God who had done those things and whom he knew existed?

Brad had often heard people refer to things as miracles, such as when someone survived what might have been a deadly car crash, but he wondered how we could know those things weren't just coincidences. What made something a miracle? Brad remembered the amazing stories from the Book of Acts, such as when the apostle Paul and his companion Silas are freed from their chains by angels while the guards nearby are sleeping. Now, that was a miracle. It couldn't just "happen." If it happened, there was no doubt it wasn't a coincidence. But Brad wondered if all of Paul's and Silas's friends believed them when they told that story and other amazing stories. Perhaps some of their friends would have been just as skeptical as we would if we heard amazing stories like that from our own friends.

Part of the reason Brad wondered how some of the people in the Bible wcrc viewed by people around them when they told of miraculous happenings is because something happened to him that no one else could ever corroborate. It is his word against the world's, so to speak. Why should someone believe his story? And yet he knows it's true.

By way of background, Brad grew up in the 1970s in a church that was very theologically conservative. Brad thoroughly adhered to their teachings and could himself be quite legalistic and rigid. His own beliefs and his church environment were not at all conducive to people sharing about supernatural miracle stories. But there were many other churches blooming in California in the 1970s where such things were more accepted. When Brad was in his early twenties he first experienced something of these "other" churches through the ministry of John Wimber. Wimber had been a musical arranger for the Righteous Brothers, but by the time Brad encountered him, he was the leader of the incredibly fast-growing Vineyard church movement, which was known for its openness to "the miraculous."

Brad liked what he saw there and slowly drifted in that direction, eventually attending a "charismatic" church every Sunday. Brad took the zeal and intensity he carried with him everywhere right into this church, so he would arrive at the services forty-five minutes early every Sunday to pray for the service, asking God to move powerfully through the pastor and in the congregation.

One Sunday his pastor spoke to the congregation before the service started about their own role during the service. He made it clear that they were themselves "the church," and they should feel as free to "minister" as he did. It wasn't supposed to be a one-man show. They were part of what God was doing every Sunday, so they must feel free to act upon anything they felt was God "nudging" them to do something or say something. He made it clear that this was a church where people should never be afraid of "stepping out in faith" and doing something like openly praying for someone if they thought that's what God wanted them to do. Even if they got it wrong, it was better that they should try than that they should just sit there for fear of making a mistake. He said that unless they all were willing to take some chances and make some mistakes, they would never learn anything, and it was his desire as their pastor to teach them to do what he did and, more important, to do what God wanted them to do. They must learn to "hear" from God and to be able to tell the difference between when God was really speaking to them and when it was just something that was in their own heads. It was an easy mistake to make, so they must be willing to step out "in faith" and learn. God would be with them in the process, and he wanted to reassure them that in this church they should feel free to make mistakes. If their hearts were in the right place, that was all that mattered, because as the Bible says, "God looks on the heart." He said that after each service, if we believe what you said or did was not from God, we will evaluate what happened and will try to help guide you. But he made it clear that "God would rather you have the faith to act on his direction, *even if you're wrong,* than to not practice hearing from the Lord and stepping out in faith."

So everyone took their seats for the service, ready to act. Brad remembered that the congregation was rather small that day, and things began with what they called a "special" song. To Brad's horror, it was an elderly woman playing "What a Friend We Have in Jesus" on the harmonica. Brad remembered feeling that it was tremendously cheesy and awkward, but he knew that her heart was in the right place and he tried to focus on that.

We should dilate for a moment to say that during this time in his life, Brad was a professional magician, making his living performing sleight-of-hand tricks at tables in restaurants throughout Orange County. He also had a very good friend who was a professional hypnotist. So Brad knew quite a bit about hypnosis and deceiving people through trickery. He generally thought of himself as someone who was especially adept at understanding our ability to deceive others—or be deceived ourselves. So he felt himself part of that "fraternity" of magicians going back to Houdini, who delighted in exposing fake psychics and other kinds of charlatans. He and his friend had even once attended a "spiritualist" church simply to expose the tricks that happened there. So he wasn't one to be fooled by what many Christians called being "slain in the spirit," when it was really just a kind of mass hysteria. He was adamant that if he ever would be "slain in the spirit"[30] it would have

---

30. This is a term some churches use to describe the phenomenon of someone being overwhelmed by a feeling that God has "touched" them. They typically lose their power to stand up and fall onto the floor of the sanctuary, sometimes for a few seconds and sometimes for quite a long time.

to be God himself doing the "slaying." He wasn't about to go along with it just because that's what others expected. Either God was going to knock him down or he wasn't budging. He had seen much of what seemed like "group-think" in some of the kookier "charismatic" churches and he vowed that he would never be taken in by anything like that.

Brad was in the second row of the service that Sunday, listening to the woman's awful harmonica interpretation of that wonderful old hymn whcn his pastor—the one who had just told everyone that they had a key role in the service—sat down right in front of him. Sure enough, no sooner had the pastor sat down than Brad felt a strong sensation that he should put his hands on the pastor's shoulders and pray. Brad felt that however strong this sensation was—and it was strong—it didn't make much sense, because just before the pastor had spoken a few minutes ago a whole group of people, Brad included, had "laid hands" on the pastor and prayed for him and the service. Furthermore, they were now in the middle of the service itself, so it would be awkward to do such a thing. It simply didn't seem the right time. But just as he was thinking this, he recalled the words the pastor had just spoken about learning to trust God. He had said that God wants to teach us to hear his voice and to do things that seemingly make no sense. Part of what

God is doing too is trying to get us to respond, *especially* if what he is saying makes little sense, so we will learn to tell the difference between his voice and our own thoughts.

So Brad worked up the nerve to do what he thought God was telling him to do. He laid his hand on the pastor's shoulder and began to pray. Just as he did this, closing his eyes and bowing his head, he saw the pastor glance back at him. Brad thought the pastor was probably just thinking Brad was trying to get his attention, but then realized Brad was going into prayer mode. But Brad remembered that it made him feel even more self-conscious about what he was doing, because not only had the pastor turned around, but many of those in the congregation could see Brad doing what he was doing and were probably themselves wondering what was going on. Brad thought that the pastor himself was probably thinking, "Oh, brother. Look at Stine getting all hyperspiritual on me to show his incredible holiness to me and the whole congregation. . . ."

In telling this story, Brad emphasizes that he didn't want to pray for the pastor, that he felt he was making a spectacle of himself and was extremely uncomfortable in doing what he did, but he felt he had to be obedient to what he thought God was telling him to do, especially after what the pastor had just said. But Brad had never done anything like this before and he wanted it to be over as soon as possible. He expected nothing to come of it. He just knew one thing: that he had a powerful sense that he should put his hand on his pastor and pray for him. So out of sheer obedience, he did it. But a moment after he "stepped out in faith" and did it, with his thoughts in this blur of contradictions and self-consciousness, something really did happen.

By further way of background, Brad explains that he had many times over the years begged God "in anguished prayer" to reveal himself in some palpable way. He had prayed God would give him a vision or any kind of manifestation that would make him real in a way Brad had never experienced. That had never happened. But now, not praying for anything like that at all, he suddenly began to feel what he very distinctly describes as "a warm sphere" emanating from the center of his stomach. Brad says that he uses the word "sphere" specifically and deliberately, because it wasn't a vague, "gooey" feeling. "No," he says, "this was an actual sphere, a ball, an *orb* that I could tangibly feel." He describes it as "warm, round, and pulsating." Then, while this was happening, he became aware of his prayer for the pastor "taking on a life of its own."

"I was speaking," he says, "but it seemed out of my control, like an out-of-body experience where I was doing it and being aware it was occurring *without my volition.* Suddenly the orb began to expand and pulsate while growing throughout my entire body. I literally felt like I couldn't stop it or control it and I sensed lightning bolts or shafts of light emanating from my body!" Brad says that "it was as though light was bursting out of my being like the grand climax when the Nazi gets exploded by God in the *Indiana Jones and the Ark of the Covenant* scene."

Brad says that the whole thing was tremendously startling, to say the least, because it was sudden and he never saw any of it coming. He is emphatic in saying that it was not a sweet, soft experience; it was so overwhelming that he says the only word that can be used to describe it accurately is "fear." A sheer sense of fear came over him, he says, because "I began to feel as though something was controlling me," he says. "And I felt that if it didn't stop, I was going to literally be obliterated, to explode. I even had to find my thoughts in the midst of this and pray 'God help me!' At this point I felt a voice inside me remind me that fear was never from God and that I was safe and could experience this as long as I chose, that I had the power to stop when I chose and that is exactly what I did. I reached a point where I felt spent."

Brad says as this continued he grew increasingly self-conscious and uncomfortable because of what the rest of the congregation would make of what was happening. He could only imagine what all of them were witnessing from their own points of view. It was so utterly mind-blowing and outrageous that he knew it must have been frightening and awesome to them as well.

"And so," he said, "as quickly and unexpectedly as it had started, I stopped. I slowly raised my head, opened my eyes and prepared to try to explain to everyone what I just went through and to tell them to not be afraid. But when I looked around, still being serenaded by the end of the horrible harmonica solo, I realized something even more amazing. No one—*and I mean no one*—had the slightest idea anything had taken place. No one was staring; no one was in awe; no one had even moved from his or her original place."

This itself was almost as amazing to Brad as what had just happened—the idea that the God of the universe had just reached down in a display of frightening and awesome power and majesty, and had palpably and physically touched one of his children in this overwhelming way in the midst of a crowd. And none of them knew it but Brad himself.

After he opened his eyes, he wasn't sure what to do. He was actually flushed from the experience and he heaved a huge sigh, but he really wanted desperately to scream out to everyone who was there about what had just happened. It was so huge and so overwhelming and beyond anything he had ever hoped God might do in all those prayers he had prayed over the years. God almighty, the creator of the universe, just now had come down and revealed himself in such power! But Brad didn't say anything. He just stayed there in his seat, in complete awe, thinking about what had just happened. The service continued as though nothing had just happened—and that was that.

But throughout the service, Brad could think of nothing else. The moment the service was over he buttonholed his pastor and tried to describe what had taken place, assuming that if anyone could appreciate it and understand it, the pastor could. "But he just kind of smiled," Brad says, and "told me that was nice, and went on his merry way. That's when I realized that for the rest of my life, I will have experienced something without explanation that had never happened to me before and will likely never happen again."

He reiterates that what happened to him is just like what happened to a number of the characters in the Bible, who experienced something all alone, just between them and God. People could believe them or not believe them, but there was nothing they could do but try and explain it and know that they were the only ones who had experienced it.

More than twenty-five years later, Brad still puzzles over what happened that morning. It was the most extraordinary physical and spiritual experience of his life, but sometimes even he almost wonders if it really happened. He knows it did, but it is hard not to wonder about what it was and what it meant.

"Why would God choose me," he asks, "to do this unique event, on that day, without warning?" And Brad wondered why God would then disappear back to that familiar but frustrating place where we cannot see or feel him, though we now know he is there. If Brad ever doubted God was there, though, he didn't anymore.

"It seems that on that one special Sunday," Brad says, "God almighty wanted me to experience just how much he loves me, that he was in fact real, and that one day I will 'know [him] as I am known [by him].' I will see clearly and not through a clouded lens—and all because this skeptical, pessimistic magician did the one thing God asked me to do. Obey."

# SEPTEMBER 11, 2001, NEW YORK CITY

Though only in her forties, my friend Lolita Jackson has already lived an extraordinary and dramatic life. I met her in 2007, when she had a high-level post in New York City Mayor Bloomberg's administration. She was also then thriving as a leader at Redeemer Presbyterian Church in Manhattan, founded by Tim Keller. In 2009, I accompanied Lolita and the small group she was leading on an Easter missions trip to Germany, where we sang in a gospel group at church services in Berlin and Hamburg. Over time I learned the dramatic backstory of this amazingly successful African-American woman.

When Lolita was six months old, she lost her mother, who was mentally ill, and was in and out of institutions for years afterward. Lolita was therefore raised by her grandmother in what were trying circumstances, including tremendous strife and poverty.

At the age of eight, Lolita had a supernatural experience. She saw a vision of her future in which she was living in New York City, speaking to large crowds, and somehow involved in ministry. But this was all far away from her present difficulties. In the meantime, she was bussed to an integrated school in the Central New Jersey suburbs, where she was the target of bullying and teasing by some white students, while her extreme intelligence and inclusion in honors classes made her the target of some fellow African-Americans, who mocked her for behaving "white." It was only in college—she was accepted to Yale and other Ivy League schools, but finally chose Penn—that Lolita began to leave behind the pain of her childhood. But for some reason,

God's call on her life—as shown to her in that childhood vision—seemed oppressive to her at that time, so she deliberately adopted a lifestyle designed to escape it, or at least to keep it at arm's length. Her successes at Penn led to an auspicious career in the world of finance and she moved to New York City, as the vision had indicated she would. The other parts of that vision, especially the idea of somehow being involved in ministry, remained far from her.

Lolita was working in the Twin Towers in Manhattan when the first World Trade Center bombing took place in 1993. This incident has been so eclipsed by the horrors of what happened eight years later, that it's hardly remembered. Six people were killed, but for most of the thousands in the building, it was eventually remembered mostly as a large inconvenience, something that became a bonding experience for those who went through it. At the time, however, it was frightening enough. Lolita would never forget the experience of walking down seventy-two flights of stairs in darkness and smoke, not knowing whether they would make it all the way down, nor what would await them at the bottom. But once the experience was over it seemed to evaporate. Everyone assumed they would never go through anything like it again.

Eight years later, when the horrors of the event now known as 9/11 unfolded, Lolita was still working in the Twin Towers. This time, she nearly died. She was working on the seventieth floor of the South Tower in the building known as 2 World Trade when the first plane hit. What followed would change her life.

At this time, Lolita still believed in God and attended church. She had never quite turned her back on God, but neither was she in any way eager to live out the vision she had seen so many years before. She was consumed with work and in her great professional successes was running further and further from the painful memories of her childhood. She felt these successes and the accolades that came with them had become her identity.

On the morning of that September 11, Lolita's department was in a meeting in a conference room on the southwest corner of the seventieth floor. The view was spectacular, and included the southern portion of the North Tower. Work started early for most of the people in finance in lower Manhattan. Lolita was waiting for her turn to speak when the first plane hit the North Tower at 8:46 A.M. She was staring out the window when the screaming mass of the commercial jetliner hit the building at six hundred miles per hour.

Lolita saw the tremendous fireball explode, and moments later an infinity of papers began to flutter down from the openings in the building made by the plane and explosion. Those who saw it from the ground immediately appreciated the tragedy and horror of what they had just seen, but no one knew what had really happened. News reports said that it had likely been a small plane that hit the building. But due to the side of the building they were on, Lolita and her colleagues never saw the plane, only the explosion.

But they didn't have time to think about it. Everyone in Lolita's meeting was there in 1993 when the two explosions rocked the buildings from below, so the moment they saw what happened they knew they must get out of the building without delay. Walking those seventy-two flights of stairs eight years earlier had seemed to take forever. There was no time to lose.

"From that moment on," Lolita said, "God was a very real presence to me, as though he were holding my hand throughout my entire escape."

A man named Robert was a close colleague of Lolita's at work and she began walking down the stairs with him. As they were walking down the stairs, Robert kept trying to call his wife on his cell, but because the stairwells themselves were concrete, it was impossible to get a signal. Lolita remembered saying this to him. They had walked down eleven flights and were on the fifty-ninth floor when everyone was instructed to exit the stairwell and take an elevator to the forty-fourth floor "skylobby." But Robert very much wanted to reach his wife, so as he and Lolita exited the stairwell, he told her that he was going to find an empty office on that floor and quickly call his wife to let her know he was all right. Lolita was planning to go with him and was on the verge of doing so when a voice spoke to her clearly, saying, "Don't go with him!" The moment she heard it, Lolita knew it was God's voice. So instead of continuing on with Robert, she told him she would meet him on the forty-fourth floor and walked toward the elevators while Robert went off to find an office for his phone call.

Lolita took the elevator and as she came out onto the forty-fourth-floor skylobby, she saw that there were hundreds of people standing and awaiting further instructions. She was standing amid this crowd when—at 9:03—the second plane hit. This one struck their building—the South Tower—thirty-three floors above them. Lolita remembered that the building didn't move back and forth from the impact. Instead, it simply moved several feet *in one direction*. To the hundreds of people standing there in the forty-fourth-floor skylobby, it felt for all the world as though the whole building was coming down. Lolita said that was the only moment she thought she was going to die. "But I was suddenly overcome with a sense of peace," she said. "I knew that if I were to die at that moment, I would be okay and would go to Heaven. I had never viscerally felt that before. Then the building righted itself and I absolutely knew I was going to get out. I was perfectly calm."

But Lolita saw that immediately after the building had righted itself, everyone began streaming toward one stairwell. Lolita in that moment had a sense that God was telling her to go to another stairwell, closest to where the building had been hit. Because of her experience in descending the stairs eight years before, she knew it would slow things down if everyone took the same stairwell. So she opened the door to the other stairwell and saw that it was well lit, with no debris to block their path. "These are clear!" she screamed, so everyone else could hear her, and immediately about fifty people followed. "I led people down that stairwell and tried to encourage them not to think about the trek," she said. "When we reached the fifteenth floor, I suggested we call out the floors as though it were New Year's Eve: 'Fifteen!' 'Fourteen!' 'Thirteen!' . . ."

When Lolita finally exited the stairwell she was on the mezzanine floor, which overlooked the plaza level, where the debris from both planes had landed. There were also mangled bodies of those who had already jumped from the buildings, and here and there were fires. "[But] God trained my eyes on something else," Lolita remembered. There were daily concerts in the plaza area, so there were always several hundred chairs set up. "Somehow, in the midst of the chaos, all the chairs were still standing," she recalled, "and I kept looking at them wondering how that was the case. I never saw anything else while looking out onto the plaza, even though it was a scene of horrors and devastation."

Lolita finally exited the building at precisely 9:26. She was told not to look up and not to use her cell phone, just to keep walking. She had walked two blocks before she turned around to see the unfathomable destruction. For her it was as though the end of the world had come at last. People were praying in the streets, calling out to God, while far up in each of the towers the flames were raging out of control. There was a level of chaos utterly unprecedented in most people's lives. Lolita now stood there alone, trying to take it all in, wondering what had happened and what was happening now. She remembered just standing there in the middle of the street, staring up at the fires as black smoke poured from the gashes in the two buildings. It was an incomprehensible sight, something simply inconceivable. Suddenly, as she stood there, Lolita heard the voice of someone she knew. It was a man who had done some consulting work for her company. He explained to her what had happened and then emphatically urged her to go home immediately. "Most of these people can't get home," he said, "but you live in

Manhattan and the subways are still running."

Lolita had never considered leaving the area, but somehow in response to the man's forceful tone, she began walking toward the nearest subway entrance, about one hundred feet away. It was 9:50 as she walked down the subway stairs. About one minute later a train arrived and Lolita got on. Later she learned that this was the last subway train to go through that station. A few minutes later all the trains were stopped, and at 9:59 the first building collapsed.

Lolita realized that if her friend had not implored her to leave the area, she would have been caught with so many others running from that dark gray cloud of dust and perhaps dodging the debris that shot out at three hundred miles per hour. She would later learn of many people who in those few minutes experienced profound, life-altering trauma: debilitating physical effects from breathing the choking dust, having to run for their lives and duck under cars when the buildings collapsed, and being almost eye-to-eye with the broken bodies of people who had jumped from the North Tower.

Lolita later learned that Robert—who on the fifty-ninth floor had gone off to call his wife—had been killed. He entered an elevator just three minutes after Lolita did, but while he was on that elevator the second plane hit the building and the elevator cable snapped. Lolita knew that if she had gone with him and had gotten onto that elevator with him three minutes later, she would have died too. Lolita said that the "realization of that—of God clearly keeping me out of harm's way—changed me forever."

It was two years before she was able to incorporate that change fully in her life. Following 9/11 and hearing God's voice as she did, and because of this having her life spared, Lolita increasingly came to see her work as an "idol," something that was keeping her from what God had for her. Over the next two years, she felt that she was "finally free to be fully used in ways God wanted for me all along."

Lolita had attended Redeemer Church in New York City, but her extreme dedication to her job kept her from being much involved there. Now she decided to join a fellowship group, "to help her through the great transition of leaving Wall Street." As often happens with Lolita, she soon became a leader of the group, and through that became a leader at Redeemer itself, joining their "diaconate" and leading a number of missions trips, including the one that I went on with her. She became involved in a number of ministries and began speaking all over the country at Christian conferences and events, just as she had seen in the vision when she was eight. Her previous goal of becoming a managing director at her old job now seems to her like a very small thing when compared with the life she now has, serving God with her tremendous energy and talents.

"In the darkest moment I knew he was right there," she says, "and that is something I always know, every day."

# 15

---

## HOW MIRACLES CAN CHANGE YOUR LIFE

We human beings live in the natural world, the world of nature and matter and time. To fathom what it might mean for something to come into our world of space and time from beyond that world of space and time is not easy. But if we believe there is a God who created this world of space and time, we have already accepted the idea of the miraculous.

The major miracles in the Bible are clear examples of this concept. Jesus's birth in the stable in Bethlehem—what we call the Incarnation— is the typical example of eternity entering time. God, who is by definition outside time and space, who is separate from his creation of time and space, suddenly enters time and space in the form of a human newborn. But actually this is a poetic statement and not at all accurate. Eternity entered time not at Christmas in the stable in Bethlehem, when Jesus came out of her womb, but rather in that moment when God touched Mary's womb and a human zygote formed therein. It was actually in that second that God came into this world and not nine months later.

Similarly at the resurrection, the life of God breaks through and cracks death in twain, like a powerful tree growing up through a sidewalk and splitting the cement. There too eternity enters time. Christians believe in that moment all of reality was changed, was redeemed. Through that act of God, resurrecting Jesus in the tomb, a pathway was opened between Heaven and Earth, between this realm—the realm of time and space—and the realm of eternity. Suddenly there was a way between them, and that way was Jesus himself, crucified and now resurrected. And because of this breaking of the boundary between these two realms, every human being who ever lived could now make that journey too. Heaven had suddenly been opened to us. Jesus had opened it and we could take that path.

There had once been no barrier between us and God and eternity. In the Garden of Eden, God walked with Adam and Eve. There was no separation between him and his creation. But in the Fall, however one interprets that story, the liberty we once had came to an abrupt end. It is the infinitely tragic story of our leaving eternity and God's presence, of our being exiled from our true home. So the story of Jesus is the story of Jesus rescuing us and bringing us back where we belong, where we were created to be in the first place. There's a grand poetry at work there. It's as if Jesus snuck from Heaven to Earth in that tiniest of life-forms, the single-celled human being, and then he grew and grew, but to get out of this world and to get back to eternity he would have to die. But he was willing to do it for us. And after he died, God resurrected him and the path between Heaven and Earth was again opened. Jesus could return to Heaven, and now he could take us there with him.

If we accept what he did by faith, we have already returned to Heaven and are able to live without that barrier between Heaven and Earth. We are by faith able to experience the miraculous as a natural part of our existence. And our new life becomes a foreshadowing and a promise of what we will do fully when we die, when we return once and for all to the place for which we were created, beyond time and space.

The idea that there is a God who loves us and who desires to help us be what we were always meant to be, who wants us to grow into the full measure of what he originally created us to be, is a staggering concept. That this God is not far from us, but is at all times right next to us, wanting to communicate with us and wanting to intervene in our lives for our benefit, is about as "empowering" an idea as anyone could imagine. So the question one must ask is why we would ignore this idea or even actively resist it. What could keep us from tapping into the benefit of the greatest resource imaginable?

The first answer has to be simple ignorance. Our culture is so deeply materialistic that it makes thinking about God along these lines seem "unscientific." Or it portrays God as our enemy and not as our friend and advocate. It portrays God as someone to be avoided, as someone who wishes to constrict us rather than as someone who offers us greater liberty. But there is a grain of truth in every lic, and the grain of truth in this lie is that the God of the Bible is indeed very much like a parent. In fact the Bible says that he is our heavenly parent. So the question is, in what relationship are we with this parent? Are we the rebellious adolescent who doesn't trust that the parent actually has our best interests in view and is therefore someone to be resisted or avoided? Or can we believe that this parent is someone who has resources we do not have, who has wisdom we can never have, who knows us better than we will ever know ourselves, and who loves us and wants to bless us beyond our wildest imaginings? Are we perhaps confusing God with our own parents or with authority figures in our lives whom it was not wise to trust? Ultimately we have to shake free of our preconceived notions and make an informed choice on this most important of all issues. We cannot let the people who ruined our lives as children continue to ruin our lives today by eclipsing our view of the God who loves us, by keeping us from the source of all we are actually looking for. Is it too much to say that actually making this choice in a way that is informed by the facts would be life-changing? As ever, we have to ask that cliché of a question: Do we really want to change? Aren't we at least a little bit afraid of the implications? What if we are wrong?

In the face of these questions we can look to Dietrich Bonhoeffer for an answer. He is reported to have once said, "Silence in the face of evil is itself evil." He went on to say, "Not to speak is to speak. Not to act is to act." The principle at work is that we think we can avoid making a decision, but we cannot. We may fool ourselves into thinking we are avoiding the question, but to avoid the question, to avoid answering the question, is to answer the question. Whether we acknowledge it or don't. We fool ourselves into thinking that to table the question or to wait longer before we answer it and make our decision is wisdom, when in reality it is self-delusion and folly. But the great river of culture in which we live is flowing in this wrong direction. It tells us that "agnosticism" is the wisest course, that not deciding is the smartest decision. It says that behaving as though the universe is all there is is the safer course. It is easy to float along the wide river of agnostic, materialistic, naturalistic culture. But into our lazy reverie Jesus makes the statement: "Enter through the narrow gate. For wide is the gate and broad is the road that leads to destruction, and many enter through it." Can we pretend we didn't read those words? Can we pretend we actually believe Jesus didn't say them or if he did say them that he is some sort of religious maniac who should be ignored?

This is the difficult situation in which we find ourselves. Everything says that to open ourselves to this God is to take a great risk, and it is a risk. But what if the facts say that taking this risk is a far safer bet than not taking the risk? What if swimming to shore to stop floating down the great river along which we have been traveling is a lifesaving action, because the river is getting stronger and faster with every second, and eventually we won't be able to get to shore because the current will be far too powerful and swift, and only then will we hear the roaring waterfall that will destroy us?

That is the question.

# ACKNOWLEDGMENTS

This book was not my idea, so if someone finds fault with it, you may evermore direct them to the short, first clause of this sentence. In truth, the idea for the book arose in a conversation with my editor, Brian Tart, with whom I matter-of-factly shared the story of a miracle I had experienced. We were having lunch in SoHo (for which cliché one must apologize), when no sooner had I finished telling my story than he brightly and strongly suggested that I must write a book on miracles, even helpfully promising to send me an outline for such a book. Flattered at his insistence that I must write the book, I nonetheless firmly rejected the idea, not just initially, but every time he put it forward in the months that followed. But Mr. Tart was very persistent, finally saying that if I absolutely couldn't see my way to writing it, he must and would find someone else to do so, because he thought a book on this topic that important. Inasmuch as anything can be said to have done so, it may have been this idea that began to prize me from the rock to which I had been affixed.

I also wish to thank my wife, Susanne, for her role in helping me decide to write this book. Without her encouragement to write it, it wouldn't exist.

Finally, I wish to acknowledge the spiritual guidance over the years of the pastors and people of Saint Paul's Church in Darien, Connecticut, and Times Square Church in Manhattan, New York. The openness of these communities and their leaders to the miraculous, and their willingness to breathe—boldly and cautiously both—the rarified air of that other world, has for me and countless others, been life-changing.

# ABOUT THE AUTHOR

**Eric Metaxas** is the *New York Times* #1 best-selling author of *Bonhoeffer: Pastor, Martyr, Prophet, Spy* and the acclaimed *Amazing Grace: William Wilberforce and the Heroic Campaign to End Slavery* ("spectacular* . . . a crackling bonfire of truth and clarity"**). His books have been translated into more than twenty languages. After graduating from Yale with an English degree, Metaxas published humor in *The New York Times* and *The Atlantic* and was a writer for Rabbit Ears Productions and *VeggieTales*. He has written more than thirty children's books, including the bestsellers *Squanto and the Miracle of Thanksgiving* and *It's Time to Sleep, My Love*, illustrated by Nancy Tillman. Metaxas speaks to tens of thousands around the United States and internationally each year. He was the keynote speaker at the 2012 National Prayer Breakfast and at the 2013 Canadian National Prayer Breakfast, and he has testified before Congress on anti-Semitism in Europe. Metaxas is the

---

\* *The Christian Century*
\*\* *Books & Culture*

founder and host of Socrates in the City, the acclaimed series of conversations on "Life, God, and other small topics," featuring Malcolm Gladwell, Dr. Francis Collins, N. T. Wright, Rabbi Lord Jonathan Sacks, Dick Cavett, and Sir John Polkinghorne, among many others. He is a senior fellow and lecturer at large at the King's College in New York City, where he lives with his wife and daughter. You can visit his website at www.ericmetaxas.com.

**Center Point Large Print**
600 Brooks Road / PO Box 1
Thorndike, ME 04986-0001 USA

**(207) 568-3717**

**US & Canada:**
**1 800 929-9108**
www.centerpointlargeprint.com